ERIN'S HEIRS

ERIN'S HEIRS
Irish Bonds
of Community

DENNIS CLARK

THE UNIVERSITY PRESS OF KENTUCKY

Library of Congress Cataloging-in-Publication Data

Clark, Dennis, 1927–
    Erin's heirs : Irish bonds of community / Dennis Clark.
        p.   cm.
    Includes bibliographical references and index.
    ISBN 0–8131–1752–6 :
    1. Irish Americans—Pennsylvania—Philadelphia—Ethnic identity.
2. Irish Americans—Pennsylvania—Philadelphia—Families.
3. Philadelphia (Pa.)—Social conditions. I. Title.
F158.9.I6C545   1991
305.91'62074811—dc20   90–25249

In memory of my sister,
Geraldine Clark Mulligan,
who could laugh at misfortune
and was courage itself.

Contents

Acknowledgments

It is the most pleasant of obligations to thank those who have helped me with this study. Foremost would be Dr. Randall Miller of St. Joseph's University, whose comments on the text were of great assistance. Others whose research was richly suggestive of interpretations were Dr. Michael Durkan, Dr. Harry Silcox, Dr. John Alviti of the Atwater Kent Museum, Dr. Mari Fielder Green, and Dr. Stephanie Morris. Dr. Mark Stolarik, director of the Balch Institute for Ethnic Studies, and Joseph Anderson, director of the Library of the Balch Institute, were consistently helpful. The staffs of the excellent archives in Philadelphia provided admirable professional services at the Philadelphia Maritime Museum, the Historical Society of Pennsylvania, the Van Pelt Library of the University of Pennsylvania, and the Urban Archives at Temple University. I am grateful to the many local sources of information, especially the *Irish Edition* newspaper, the Society of the Friendly Sons of St. Patrick, and the Donegal Association of Philadelphia. To my wife, who has encouraged my preoccupations with research over the years, I can only testify to the depth of a gratitude that has grown apace with those years.

Philadelphia's Irish Neighborhoods

Brickyard

Fenian Hill

Manayunk

East Falls

Swampoodle

BROAD STREET

SCHUYLKILL

North Phila.

Port Richmond

DELAWARE RIVER

Kensington

Corktown

RIVER

Northern Liberties

Schuylkill (Ramcat)

MARKET STREET

Angorra

South Phila.

Southwark

Moyamensing

N

SCALE

Figure 1. Since the Irish were a large population in Philadelphia, they were both widely distributed and concentrated. The heavily Irish neighborhoods shown formed, expanded, and declined between 1830 and 1930 as social mobility and transportation patterns altered.

Introduction

This study tells how the Irish tradition thrived in a setting three thousand miles from Ireland. It is about how an ethnic group maintained its identity through periods of repeated community change. The preservation of that identity was achieved by sustaining family memory and by fostering communication, association, and leadership. The process fashioned and enhanced the bonds of community and helped the Irish continually adapt to the conditions of a complex urban center. This book traces this development in Philadelphia but relates it to Irish communities in other cities.

The Irish are a people whose troubled history has provided them with a deep sense of life's tragedies, ironies, and contradictions. In this century, as in earlier times their experiences as a people have been marked by repression, emigration, and cultural dislocation. Their dispersion outside of Ireland required them to overcome the effects of emigration and discordant modern influences, and in response to these conditions, they have been able to find within themselves resources for social invention and adaptation. This has been amply demonstrated in the United States over a period of two hundred years. In urban centers such as Philadelphia, the image and prominence of the group has ascended and declined over the long course of their presence in the city depending upon immigration trends, the flexibility of local codes of acceptance, and the group's own capacity to assert itself. Through their consciousness of the broader Irish tradition, and through the cultivation of localized versions of that tradition, the Irish have been able to sustain their own history, morale, and cultural affinity. Study of this long record of adaptability should show us something about how various groups in modern society respond to change and opportunity.

The study of Irish-American social development has significance far beyond the interest that the Irish themselves might have in it. This significance arises out of the length of Irish immigration, the extent of the group's interaction with American life at various levels and in various periods, and the insights that this history affords about American life. Analysis of the Irish-American record has been slow to emerge, not only because of its considerable extent over time, but also because Americans have not been prepared to deal competently with the social history of ethnic groups in the United States until the last few decades. For most of the nation's existence, historians remained focused in their work on elite groups, major national events, and studies of prestigious political figures and institutions.

To fill the vacuum left by mainstream historians, the Irish-Americans developed a history of their group that was acceptable to them for their own purposes. This was especially true in the 1890s when their organizations became intent upon presenting a more positive picture of their past to counter derogatory stereotypes common in newspapers and in the theater of the time. Irish-American scholars gathered primary materials, compiled organizational histories, and popularized an Irish-American record that was compatible with the patriotic American temper of those days. The result was a series of books, usually bound in green and gold, that extolled both American and Irish patriotic achievements in enthusiastic and uncritical fashion. There is much important information in these books, but it is embedded in ethnocentric, super-patriotic declamations of Irish-American self-promotion. The same is true for most of what passed at this time for the history of the American Catholic church with which the Irish were so closely associated.[1] Thus, the true history of this group was masked by mainstream neglect and the apologetic needs of the Irish-Americans themselves. It was not until the mid-twentieth century that a number of works addressing Irish-American history in a new scholarly and more objective spirit appeared, followed by a number of localized studies of Irish-American life that provided a fresh and much more authentic view of the group's background and development.[2]

These studies confirmed the sweeping extent of Irish-American participation in the life of the country throughout its development. Studies of the Revolutionary War, the formative years of the republic, the mid-nineteenth century's industrialization and conflict, the later years of continued mass immigration, and the twentieth century's decades of social diversification showed that the Irish maintained a presence and a distinctive influence throughout these periods. By the late nineteenth century, the group had attained a status that showed a mature adjustment to American life, representation in complex echelons of power, and skillful use of organizational networks.[3]

John Higham, long one of our most respected historians of ethnic life, has explained one factor that helped produce this extraordinary panorama in American life. The decentralized nature of American society prior to the twentieth century allowed innumerable enclaves and networks to flourish within a national political unity. The sheer expanse of America both isolated ethnic groups and stimulated ethnic diversity. When integration of these ethnic enclaves and networks did begin to occur, the groups themselves were integrated into regional and national affiliations as well as into further association with the general society.[4] Thus, amid the tremendous complexity of American society Irish communities and organizations could maintain distinct cultural identities and mutual relationships even as their populations interacted with the broader mainstream of American life.

But just what was it that ethnic groups like the Irish maintained and transmitted concomitantly with their identity? It was their "tradition"—that is, information about themselves, a social heritage, a set of views, and a process to fulfill their own values, all of which resulted in an awareness of group affinity. Tradition, as Clyde Kluckhohn wrote, is custom given a "backbone of time."[5] Ethnic traditions are composed of a distinctive fund of historical experience and a particular array of symbols, usages, and attachments assumed to be part of the relevant heritage. Such a tradition is not a static mold of beliefs and behavior. Neither is it slavish repetition or simply arbitrary inventions. Rather, it is a changing heritage influenced by innovation, social differentiation, and responses to shifting conditions. An ethnic tradition is usually linked to a place, a people, and a legacy of recollections; for the Irish, this has meant reference to Ireland, its history, its internal social variations, and the phenomena of emigration. The Irish-American tradition has been a compound of folk and popular perception as well as objective reality.

The pertinence of this formation and conveyance of tradition has been obscured in various studies of the Irish that have focused on the dynamics of American social change. Over the last two decades, studies dealing with the social and economic mobility of ethnic groups, and the Irish-Americans among them, have been widely pursued. These studies have shown that the penetration of the Irish into the labor and entrepreneurial systems of the country was at first halting and troubled. As immigration continued through the second half of the nineteenth century, however, greater opportunities arose. Yet, gains for the Irish-born remained minimal in many places, and the sons and daughters of Irish immigrants progressed at a rate behind that of Germans, Scandinavians, and later-arriving Jews. The barriers of anti-Irish and anti-Catholic discrimination, limited cultural expectations, militant anti-labor practices, and other disabilities retarded Irish-American occupational mobility. When such mobility did ultimately occur, the difficulty of achieving social stability in the face of a swiftly changing and frequently disruptive American economy was a constant in the history of a group that continued to have a large working-class component.[6] Whatever the dimensions of this mobility, it has proceeded from a base of ethnic attachments that both retained and changed its character over time.[7]

The specific means used to maintain and stabilize group ties include the cultivation of individual identity within the group and the social manifestation and reinforcement of identity through association, distinctive group expression, and the exercise of group leadership. Identity can be fostered by family inculcation, communal association and communication, and attention to the surrounding society's portrayals of the group. Forms of association, whether occupational or civic, support personal identity, and communication provides a rhetorical and cultural expression for group purposes. The leadership that emerges from the group projects and symbolizes the group's identity.[8] The four sections of this book are organized to show just how these necessities of ethnic social continuation were provided by activities in the Irish community in Philadelphia.

The historical materials used to illustrate these social processes are diverse. They are, however, clear evidence of ethnic development, and they are compatible with the process of ethnic persistence explained in the Research Note at the end of the book. The materials selected for inclusion in this study all deal with the fundamental experiences related to the four factors of identity, association, communication, and leadership. These factors involve elementary processes that can be shown to exist in similar communities elsewhere, as the Conclusion of the book will demonstrate. The use of folklore material on family life, work life, and leadership, like the use of oral interviews, may perturb some very traditional historians who focus exclusively on written documents, but the use of such data is especially important in the study of groups lacking extensive written records.

The interpretation of the historical experience recounted in the book is aided by many of the endnotes and the specialized studies in the Research Note at the end. References from psychology and anthropology illuminate the ways in which the family and group affinity function in formal and informal groups. Sociology and ethnic studies afford insights into folk grouping, symbolic association, and directive organization, while studies in communication provide guidance in interpreting the underlying contents and styles of group expression and the utilization of various media. Analysis of leadership reveals the internal functions and representative roles of leaders and the exercise of power and mediation leaders assume. These references will, I hope, serve as signposts for further research into the intimate yet socially potent formulations of ethnic behavior.

Philadelphia is one city in which the Irish community has faced the drama of adjustment to urban life and has had to devise the methods for its social continuation. It is a city that has been the theater not only of the foundation of the American republic, but also of the unfolding of the industrial work life and democratic participation that have characterized much of the nation's growth. But it is a city with a peculiarly foreshortened historical image: the events of the founding of the nation are memorialized in the historic district where Independence Hall and other sites of the American Revolution are presided over by custodians of the National Park Service. And the city's history is further manifested in the cult of its upper-class, with the monuments of their lifestyle ranged around Rittenhouse Square and the Main Line belt of estates that extends for miles west of the city. Yet, the working class and immigrant experience that was the central historical engagement of the overwhelming portion of the city's population during a century and a half of industrialization has not been part of what is conceived to be "historic Philadelphia." It is to this uncelebrated dimension of the city that the Irish involvement with Philadelphia in large part belongs.

Sam Bass Warner, Jr., in his insightful study *The Private City: Philadelphia in Three Periods of Its Growth*, notes that the city changed so rapidly in its growth that the "Philadelphia of one generation barely resembled its predecessor."[9] Yet, within this powerful vortex of urban change, people had to find an equilibrium. They had to find forms of family and community association that would permit them to have some orientation amid the novelty and arduous work that the industrial order generated. Warner states that there are "other Philadelphias" besides the introverted city that he explores in his study, and one of these is the intensive network of Irish interaction that has been part of the city's past. The following chapters provide examples of the social forms in this

Irish subcultural world. It is the author's hope that readers will find their presentation both instructive and enjoyable. At the end of the book, a conclusion reviews the social life of this Irish community in terms of the role that communication has played in its development and continuation. Differing views about this interpretation can be pondered in the light of the statement by Warren Susman that "cultures can be arguments or debates themselves," a statement with which a people with argumentative gifts such as the Irish have could agree.[10]

1 Identity
Mind Yourself

How people think of themselves is at the root of ethnic differences. In Irish families, the cautionary instruction to "mind yourself and you'll mind others" is often heard from childhood. "Mind yourself" is an admonition to be conscious of who you are and what your responsibility is. The corollary, "and you'll mind others," is advice aimed at social obligations. These phrases signify the way in which all of us, whether of Irish or other groups, contract early in our lives into a consciousness of our identity.

How has a sense of Irishness been maintained by people immersed in the diversity of an American city? How is a subcultural identity experienced by personalities subject to all the vagaries and influences that present competing and contrasting identities in the American milieu? In a reconsideration of the classic *Beyond the Melting Pot: The Negroes, Puerto Ricans, Jews, Italians and Irish of New York City*, twenty years after its original publication, Nathan Glazer noted that even in the face of potent assimilating forces, ethnic subcultures can have the capacity to sustain themselves in conditions of social flexibility.[1] John D. Buenker has argued that the different levels of the American social system are sufficiently flexible so that subcultural identities can be cultivated without serious conflicts.[2] The human personality is so complex that all of us adopt and sustain various roles. For Irish-Americans to retain personal and family consciousness of their Irish heritage without any special disabilities has been both feasible and acceptable for some generations now since the decline of the more severe anti-Irish sentiments that were once in wide currency.

The ways in which Irish-Americans have nurtured their own tradition amid the pluralism of American life can be demonstrated by examining their cultural bonds and interaction. The subjective discovery of identity requires a consciousness of a history that binds one generation to another. Tutoring the young in historical information, however informally, is clearly a part of the identification process. Elaboration and reinforcement of the process continues through social interaction with kin and the ethnic community in "the culture of everyday life." But the personality mediates contradictions and conflicts, so that Irish-Americans must be able to reconcile their participation in the Irish tradition with their distance from Ireland, and their ethnic identity with the broad diversity of American life. Psychologically, this process is a continuous choosing and balancing of orientation, symbols, values, and attitudes. One of the wonders of social life is that it is carried out in the lives of children and busy adults and into the wintry years of old age. Social organizations and a consciousness of identity beyond family and the primary community extend the process of mediation in the broader society.[3]

The Irish-Americans whose experiences are recounted in the first part of this book have had to define identity for themselves and then manage that identity and make it viable in the general community of Philadelphia. The use of family stories to show how a sense of Irishness is developed is instructive because of the intimacy and informality such stories represent, for these qualities indicate the subtle and incremental ways through which people are infused with an ethnic sense of themselves. Family names, customs, diet, folk beliefs, music, and a variety of other factors enhance this process.

The experience of ethnic life through various organized groups carries the personality into wider social spheres. The Irish have sustained and expressed their identity through groups representing Irish county affiliations; nationalist causes, and religious, labor, and cultural collaboration. Maintaining such groups requires certain social skills, and the long history of the Society of the Friendly Sons of St. Patrick gives evidence of the use of such skills to deal with internal conflict and external change.

For a group to maintain its social position in a pluralist society, it must be attentive to the image it possesses in the general community, as may be revealed through such records as advertising, official public recognition, or even printed polemics. The popular media depiction of the Irish in cartoons and in the theater affords an opportunity to examine the group's attempts to monitor and influence portrayals of itself. Thus, the materials used in this part of the study provide examples of how ethnic personality formation, management of group life, and social images have developed.

Family Lore

Is there anything so Irish as a good story? It is not just that the Irish have produced a huge array of renowned short story artists, novelists, tale-tellers, and raconteurs that has exalted storytelling to an extraordinary level of skill among them. Perhaps of more significance is the fact that storytelling is still a living tradition for this people. It is not all just blather galore and miscellaneous pub talk. Rather, it is part of something ancient, human, and psychologically rewarding.[4] In all this exchange and recitation of encounters, adventures, and diversions is spiritual communing; and, of all the kinds and variations of storytelling, none is more familiar, memorable, and formative than the family stories that have been shared around the hearthside, the dinner table, or wherever the family is gathered.

It is the family that possesses the heart of mankind. Every culture is shaped by the bonds and sentiments of families. For the Irish, a people that in the too-recent past was steadily denied the rewards of a stable and fully developed society, the family has had to serve in a special way as a vessel of hopes and satisfactions. Indeed, because of the shared history of oppression, poverty, emigration, and repressed aspirations, the family became, some would argue, an obsessive focus of Irish emotionalism.[5] Whatever the relative status of the family in different groups, an imperative of formative family influence molds every ethnic tradition; yet, the fundamental role of the family is not usually the starting point for the analysis of Irish-American experience. Even such a classic study as Oscar Handlin's *Boston's Immigrants*, though it discusses the difficulties of housing and employment, does not do so from a family perspective, nor does it penetrate the pivotal subject of family consciousness and morale, around which immigrant communities composed their worlds. The fine work of R.A. Burchell on *The San Francisco Irish, 1848–1880*, which finds the Irish family a potent agency of stabilization, bases its analysis on census material and not family accounts. This same deficiency characterizes practically all of our studies of Irish-Americans, a lack of direct knowledge or description based upon the content of the family ethnic connection itself.[6]

In Irish families, as in all functioning families, there are treasuries of lore and recollection that are potent in their emotional influence. Each such treasury takes psychological precedence in the memoirs and imaginations of family members when they recall their upbringing and domestic experiences. Both models of behavior and critical informal instruction are imparted by these troves of memories. More often than not, these stores of memory are a great miscellany of symbolic people and events, trivia, and frequently distorted or romanticized remembrances. Because of their psychological intimacy, the family stories are seminal in establishing ethnic identity. Although there are differences in defining what an ethnic group and an ethnic identity are, scholars agree that a consciousness of a common past is a prerequisite of ethnic orientation. The formation or perpetuation of an ethnic social structure demands that both young and old people be made aware of their past and their identity.[7] Parental and other family discourse fundamentally imbues each child with a perception of self. Indeed, children are dependent upon this kind of direct information, and they categorize it readily. From it, they come to comprehend the manifesting marks of language that signify group life and status. Such discourse establishes the basis for interaction with others and provides a world view that confers both a tie to the past and a place in the present. In a complex society, a person may maintain a pluralism of roles as he or she grows, but this diversity does not extinguish the ethnic consciousness imparted through the intimacy of family colloquy and recollection.[8]

For the Irish, long noted as an especially verbal people, the transmission of identity through oral means has a distinguished history. Not only was Gaelic culture powerfully endowed with an oral tradition of memorization, poetic recitation, and oral presentation of everything from great epics to simple folk tales, but that tradition also interpenetrated family life and domestic entertainment. It persisted into modern times, and James Loughlin cites a roster of nineteenth-century nationalist leaders whose views were deeply shaped by family stories of eviction, oppression, nationalist example, and historic struggle.[9]

For those whose cultural lives were disrupted by the experience of emigration, this oral tradition was modified but not subverted. Emigration to America meant discovery of new dimensions of literacy, mass media influence, and social interaction, but the distinctive ethnic cult of storytelling and transmission of family lore persisted. This tradition provides a body of material for ethnohistorical analysis and also for an understanding of the way in which family stories support the continuation of ethnic life at personal and social levels. The family stories current in Philadelphia will be presented only in bare outline in this chapter, for the purpose of the presentation is to show the range and themes of Irish-American recollection and not the style and detail of recitation, though that in itself is a fascinating subject. The stories chosen for recounting here were selected both because they were current in the community and because they focused on life-shaping events or enhanced ethnic memory.

The content of the Irish family stories current in the Philadelphia community ranges across five broad categories of experience: life in Ireland, the process of emigration, adjustment to America, returns to Ireland, and stories savored for their special humor or peculiarity. The stories are almost invariably enriched by repetition. Unless dealing with truly tragic events, the stories usually are invested with a personalized style and often told with self-mocking commentary. For the families that share these reminiscences, the events recounted take on a nostalgic significance and an intergenerational instructive value that raises them above the level of simple remembrance.

Stories of life in Ireland commonly recall the poverty of those impelled to emigrate. Owen B. Hunt, a widely known raconteur who came to the city about 1910, was full of recollections of the hard life in his birthplace in County Mayo. He would show the scars on his shins from repeated burns suffered as a boy when he had to sit so close to the turf fire to keep warm in his family's cold cottage that the fire burned his flesh. He would tell of his wonder at finding books for sale at a fair, for books were entirely absent from his village. Maggie Jane McGinley, one of eight children of a widowed mother in Ballynabreen, County Donegal, remembered that her family subsisted for a long period solely on remittances from two aunts in America. Daniel Gallagher, also from Donegal, was one of nine children who lived on a tiny farm so hilly and rough that a horse could not be used to till it. The members of the Donegal Society in Philadelphia are clear in their memory of the fact that their organization was founded in 1888 by emigrants who had fled the most stark conditions of near-famine since the 1840s, conditions that drove the parish priest of Derrybeg, Father James McFadden, to become famous for his advocacy of the rights of his afflicted congregation against the privileged English landlords of the area. In many families, the children are still taught the old rhyme that recalls the poverty of Northwest Ireland: "I come from the County Donegal, where they eat potatoes skins and all."

The pressure of poverty suffused the memories of even the very young in Ireland two generations ago. Maggie Jane McGinley was sent off to relatives in America by her hard-pressed mother even though she was very young and unprepared for such a journey. Mary Kate Flannelly was also packed off "to the States" by her saddened mother, and she recalled that she had no idea what to expect and was very naive in her early years in the city. Frank Devlin, brought as a youth to St. Bridget's parish in the Falls of the Schuylkill, said that at home in Ireland he had, "not a shoe to stand in, not a shovel to dig with, and not a hat to keep the sleet off me skull." Margaret O'Callaghan from Shercock, County Cavan told of families so poor in her girlhood that their children came to her family's store with only an egg or two to barter for tea. Tom Hanson told of not even having chickens that would give an egg, so as a boy he trained his dog, Tiger, to swim among the duck nests at the edges of the lakes in County Roscommon and to return to him with duck eggs. But lakes, ducks, eggs, and all belonged to the landlord in those days, and the landlord's man came with the police and took away Tiger as a thief of a dog.

The epidemic character of emigration from poorer areas is clear from the family accounts. Peg Donnelly's two older sisters had gone to America, and she saw one friend after another leave her townland in the 1920s, so she too finally decided to leave. Bill Drake's brother had gone to South Africa and his sister to Europe before he emigrated to Canada and then to the United States. Of the eleven children of the family of Hugh Marron, who himself had worked for years in America before returning to settle down on a County Cavan farm, ten had emigrated by the time the father was in his sixties.

The degree of sympathy with Irish nationalism that has characterized Irish-Americans has been much commented upon, and often lamented by some observers. It is important to recognize that the source of much of this nationalist advocacy has its roots in the family memories of ordinary immigrants, and family stories of the harshness of British rule give rise to widespread antagonism. Among immigrants in the twentieth century, for instance, the "Troubles" of the 1916–1923 period are especially memorable. Una McCauley saw British troops shoot a young member of the Irish Republican Army on a Dublin street and heard a British officer say as he stood over the wounded youth, "Let the dog die." Her family was forced to emigrate after British troops burned the family's shop in Dublin. Bill Drake, of Oldcastle, County Cork, was a noted local athlete who played the ancient game of hurling, but the British banned the Irish game as an illegal pastime. Drake saw the "Black and Tan" British irregular troops shoot an unarmed man dead in the street in his village, and one of his own friends was shot by the British in retaliation for the escape of a prisoner. Tom Jordan of Carralavin in County Mayo had his home burned by British soldiers. Jordan, who fought with the IRA, had the satisfaction of seeing the estate of an English lord confiscated when the independent Irish state came to power in 1921. In a more recent context, Vincent Gallagher was almost run down, seemingly deliberately, by British troops in armored cars when he visited Belfast in the 1970s, and he particularly resented the incident when, as he recounted, he was "almost run over by a platoon of British soldiers in my own country." Stories like these are part of a huge lore of nationalism that is one element of the recollection of Ireland among the Philadelphia Irish.

The tales and recollections of the journey to America are legion, and they are often embroidered with detail, laced with humor, and magnified with the passage of time. Most of the stories deal with the actual journey and arrival in America; more intimate factors surrounding the emigration, such as intergenerational conflict, village loneliness, the lure of adventure and romance overseas, and the part that adolescent quest for status played in the process, are rarely spoken about. The stories are, therefore, travel tales that have taken a traditional form.

Kate Collum and a friend, both Irish-speaking girls, remembered arriving in Boston. Kate's brother had alerted immigration officials and forwarded money so Kate and her friend could journey to Philadelphia to join him. The girls were paged at the Boston dock but could not believe that anyone in America would know their names or be able to contact them, so they did not respond to the paging or get the money for their train fare. Somehow they found the Travellers Aid Society, were given fares, had destination tags pinned to their coats, and were ushered to the train station. They were awestruck when they were seated in the train near a black man, the only person of that complexion they had ever seen. They asked each other in Irish what was it in America that produced such a complexion and would they turn that way if they lived in the place.

Maire Curran recalled coming to the United States in a sailing ship, which she boarded in Ireland after being instructed by the crew to bring her own food and bedding for the voyage. This voyage, remembered by a very old woman, was probably one of the last of the historic emigrant traffic under sail. While this woman still lived, people were coming to America by jet plane, a truly striking contrast.

John McGettigan came to America the long way round. He had been sent to Rome to study for the priesthood, but that did not work out. He traveled to various U.S. cities and finally settled in Philadelphia before World War I. Emigration was still heavy then, and it was becoming possible for the first time for immigrant Irish wage-earners to return to Ireland for visits. John McGettigan went into the travel business and became the generator of a continuous traffic to and from Ireland. He sponsored hundreds of immigrants; loaned them money for their passage, interest free; and contrived to elaborate a network of receptions, referrals, lodgings, and job placements for the incoming Irish. He is widely remembered in the city for his long years of assisting new arrivals and also for his wonderful musical ability; for years he played fiddle and concertina and sang at dances, weddings, and christenings.

The protracted nature of some of the family emigrations is illustrated by the story of Mary Donovan. An Irish-speaking widow from Roscommon, she had to work hard to improve her English when she decided to "go out" to America. She left her two sons in the care of a brother, came to Philadelphia, and took jobs as a waitress. Soon enough she had her own tiny restaurant on Christian Street. She saved diligently, sent money back to Ireland to support her boys, and eventually, after ten years of work and thrift, was able to bring her sons to America to join her.

The vicissitudes of adjusting to America are apprised in family stories not in terms of the larger issues that are contemplated by historians, but in personal terms that involve the problems of daily life. Where to live, how to get a job and keep it, and how to behave in America are the themes treated. A good many of the Irish country girls who came out to Philadelphia in the earlier part of this century got jobs readily as "living-out girls"—servants, maids, and cooks in the households of well-to-do families. Maggie Jane McGinley was pleased to work as a serving girl because she got free room and board as well as wages and could therefore send practically all her earnings back to Ireland to her family. Margaret Sheridan from Cavan came first to Boston, then to Philadelphia. She married a man who became a chauffeur for wealthy families. After raising her eleven children, she joked about finally becoming a "career woman" when she took a job as a housekeeper in a local rectory.

After arriving in Philadelphia in 1922, Kate Collum got a job for six dollars a week cleaning the house, cooking and minding the children of her well-to-do employers. She later worked in a mansion called "Woodcrest," where twelve servants were employed. Margaret Lawless, who came as a girl to Philadelphia, was one of eight children. She was the daughter of a woman who herself worked for a time in America and returned to Ireland, and this was not uncommon. Some young women, like the three McFadden sisters—Julia, Mary, and Nora—did not take long-term servant jobs but put themselves through nursing school. Mary Harkin was enterprising enough to open her own dressmaking shop near Rittenhouse Square and become dressmaker to the wealthy women of the neighborhood.

Immigrant girls often softened their adjustment to America by maintaining ties with older women from their homeland. The households of Maggie Boyle and Sara Magee were well known to Donegal girls who spent their days off gossiping, cooking, and learning with the generous matrons whose homes became centers of social activity in the evenings. Singing, dancing, and incipient romances were part of this substitute domesticity among the immigrant girls.

The new life in the city was not all happy for these women. Peg Donnelly, who came to Philadelphia just after her brother, a policeman, was shot and killed on duty, found that coming to the same city where he was killed was hard for her. Margaret McKinney's husband never recovered from his injuries sustained in World War I, and he died leaving her with three young children to raise. Kate Collum's brother was killed by an automobile, and she had a great problem obtaining money for his funeral.

The presence of religion in the lives of these immigrants was so traditional as to be taken for granted. Their recollections ordinarily included references to going to Mass, being married in church, attending christenings, and being associated with priests and parishes. If the ceremonies of the church in their lifetimes were highly formalized and almost impersonal, their associations with their fellow Catholics and their personal consciousness of the need for principles of conduct based on the Ten Commandments, Jesus' teachings in the New Testament, and the virtues of the saints held out to them as models were usually deeply felt. Their fidelity to Catholic teachings, whether exaggerated in self-flattery or not, was part of their cult of Irishness.

For male immigrants, the stories of adjustment to America most frequently involve problems of employment. One man recalled finally getting a job, but found out he was working for an employer so cheap, as he put it, "that every nickel he made was a prisoner." James McGroary, interviewed at the age of ninety-two, came to Philadelphia in 1921. He worked successively as a gardener, a coal heaver, and in a machine shop and at Cramp's Shipyard. During the bank failures of the 1930s he lost his $1,700 in savings and returned to Ireland in 1934. James O'Brien, also interviewed at ninety-two, worked as a stoker in a boiler room for fifty-nine cents an hour, then later worked for the Philadelphia Transit Company where many Irish were employed. He and his friends vividly recalled stories of the bitter transit strike of 1909 when a general strike was declared in the city by the labor unions, and the transit company, aided by police, broke the strike amid widespread violence. Edward Curran recalled the work life of the Irish at the Baldwin Locomotive Works, where labor union activity was vigorously opposed by the company, which sent spies to the workers' gathering places to discover the names of those who talked of unions so that such labor sympathizers could be dismissed. It was a hard life of often menial and unstable employment but with the usual affirmations that work lives were well-spent if survival and family sufficiency could be assured.

With these stories of ordinary work life there is also a fund of stories about men who exceeded expectations and became notable examples of success. Men like Joseph McGarrity, who became a wealthy man but who continued to work zealously for Irish nationalist causes, and James Ryan, a day laborer on the railroad who became a wealthy building contractor, are well-remembered. These men were immigrants, but second and third generation success stories are even more widely known. The story is still told of Michael Francis Doyle, who as a young delivery boy was hectored from the front door of a Rittenhouse Square mansion when he tried to make a delivery there. He was treated rudely and told to go the rear entrance. He lived to become a wealthy lawyer and buy the same mansion. Thomas Cahill, child of an indigent family, became a rich coal dealer who endowed the first boys' high school in the archdiocese of Philadelphia. The stories of handsome Olympic athlete John B. Kelly are many, from his days as the bricklayer son of a big family in the Irish Falls of the Schuylkill neighborhood to his campaign for mayor of Philadelphia in the 1930s. These narratives of success reflect more than extollations of American opportunity. They are confirmations of the rise in status and the trust in hard work that have been part of the self-conscious Irish-American credo. They also proclaim the mastering of adversity and the victory of the underdog, two themes as venerable as the Irish storytelling tradition itself.

Another category of anecdotes and stories involves the experiences of emigrants who return home to Ireland for visits or to reestablish residence there. The theme is one that has been treated both poignantly and mockingly among Irish writers in such stories as George Moore's "Home Sickness" or Edna O'Brien's "A Rose in the Heart of New York." The returned "Yank" is the object of an entire genre of folk humor in Ireland. In the United States, however, the ritual journey back to Ireland to see the old homestead, to hunt for relatives and to see the places made memorable through family lore is an ethnic ritual. For many of those returning to Ireland it is a bittersweet indulgence. Air travel has for a generation made it possible for tens of thousands annually to engage in this exercise, and the tales of it are manifold.

Mickey Carr was a Gaelic speaker from Gortahork in Donegal who got only one chance to return to Ireland in 1969. He left his homeplace there early in the morning of his first day back and returned late in the evening to tell of his thorough elation that, for the first time in half a lifetime, he had spent an entire day speaking only Irish, a language whose poetry he dearly loved. Tom Marron's return was of a different kind. Absent for forty-seven years from the old country, he resolved to have one drink on the plane for every year he had been away. He did, and had to be taken off the plane at Shannon Airport on a stretcher.

Some of the tales of return are suffused with the pain of old memories and nostalgia, while others are quite peculiar. Bob Clarke went back to his townland and met his old schoolteacher, by then an aged scholar. They climbed to a height in Mayo and the old man pointed out sixteen sites far across the green landscape where there had once been villages which had been abandoned due to penury and emigration. Maurice English, a publisher, returned to his father's townland in Cork and wandered by a churchyard where he found a fresh grave with a headstone with the same name on it as he bore, Maurice English. Hugh Breen, a widely known figure in Philadelphia, could not go home to County Derry for forty years, though he owned land there the whole time and had sisters there. He had fought with the IRA in the 1920s, and his daring had earned him a reputation that made him still unwelcome in British-ruled Northern Ireland. When he finally did return, he had to be extremely careful in moving around his home area.

Patrick O'Callaghan returned to the farm in County Monaghan he had left as a youth. He had raised a family in America, and his brother had worked the farm in Ireland. His mother, who held title to the farm, offered it to him as the oldest son, according to the old country custom if he wished to return permanently. Bernard

Croke's relatives knew that he loved "boxty," a potato cake made with chives. On one of his visits to Ireland, he was treated to boxty for breakfast at one house, for lunch at another, and for "tea" at another, and he finally had to eat boxty again at a big public function in Derry. "Had I flown home that day," he recalled, "I'd have had to do it airfreight."

The whole emotional experience of "going back" has embraced generations of Irish-Americans now, and it has spawned not only a huge tourist industry, but also an extensive store of reverie, confrontation, and recall. Brian Friel's play *The Loves of Cass Maguire* deals feelingly with the deeper emotions involved in going back. Returning to Ireland is a rite of re-passage, a reversal of time and of lifetimes, and the tales it evokes are psychologically penetrating.

There is a collectivity of stories that is largely based in humor or in strange events and situations. Some of these stories deal with very traditional themes, such as the ghost story. Joseph Coogan recalled one such story that a County Wexford uncle would tell. Returning home late one night and seeing lights in the local church, he stopped and peered into the church. He saw a priest saying Mass at the shadowy altar by candlelight. He left puzzled by a Mass said at night with no congregation. Thoughtfully, he went his way home. Inquiring later, he was told by the old people of the parish, "Ah, sure, that was Father ———. He's dead these long years. He took money from the people to say Masses and didn't say them, so now his punishment is to return from purgatory in the dark night and say them alone." This is a venerable tale known in many different forms.

Tom Hanson would tell the story of Mickey Mannion, a notorious outlaw. Mannion was a robber and highwayman who was captured and taken to Roscommon town to be hanged. He was hung, but the rope broke and he survived. The authorities relented and did not hang him again, for they feared public reaction to such a sensation. Mannion was set free after stern admonitions. The local people were so superstitious that they shunned Mannion after his release: "The devil himself wouldn't take him," they said. Mannion returned to the authorities and begged to be hung again. His wish was granted, and he was hung until dead. But afterward, his shade, with a noose around its neck, would confront people on the misty roads of Roscommon. As they quailed in terror, the spectre would say in a dreadful voice, "I'm Mickey Mannion. Hang me again!"

Some stories circulate because of their zany humor. Joseph Coogan's family has a story of a Catholic relative who spirited the Protestant girl he loved away from an event being held at a Protestant Orange Lodge in Ulster. He got away with it and married the girl, but she remained staunchly Protestant her whole life. A tale of romance of another sort was recounted by Ann Leahy. Not long after arriving in this country, she accepted a friend's invitation to visit New York on a double date. It was arranged for them stay in a nice hotel. Off the foursome went to theater, dinner, and dancing. Very late, they returned to the hotel. The friend and her fellow casually paired off and disappeared into that girl's room. Shocked, Ann Leahy stood in the hall with her date, who obviously was bent on sleeping in her room and, indeed, her bed, a thought that horrified this moral immigrant maiden. After an hour or more of hallway colloquy and sparring, Ann looked at her watch and said, "Oh, now, time for Mass!" She marched the fellow off to St. Patrick's Cathedral for the earliest early Mass, where he knelt in moody disillusionment.

Patrick O'Callaghan left a tale with his family of his first working day in America. He had never been in a town of more than three thousand people before coming to America. In the great city, he suddenly found himself as a newly-hired delivery boy of sixteen with a horse and wagon hunting for addresses in what seemed an absolute maze of streets. At one point he backed his wagon into a big excavator's ditch. Later, told to deliver a package to the dumbwaiter in a hotel, he asked a kitchen employee, "Are you the dumbwaiter?" and was chased from the premises.

Tom Hanson's two grown sons were inordinately fond of Nellie, the old dog with which they had grown up. These sons, Tom and John, were very distressed when the dog became ill. John, who was studying in the medical field at the time, got books on dog anatomy and sicknesses and diagnosed that the dog had a lesion on the brain. The two brothers drank bootleg whiskey, as this was during Prohibition, and morosely contemplated poor Nellie's fate one night. Treatment by a veterinarian was beyond them, for they had no money. Feeling no pain themselves as they drank, they sadly considered their dog's affliction and decided to operate on the creature. Placing it in the kitchen gas oven, they anaesthetized it. John operated on the dog on the kitchen table and Tom assisted. The next morning, according to the story, Nellie was up and around with a bandaged head that was not too bad. Tom and John, however, had hangover-heads of terrible proportions.

For males especially, sports were a standard subject of discussion. Sports enthusiasts like William Lynch or John O'Riordan could talk for hours about the great days of Connie Mack's (Cornelius McGillicuddy's) baseball teams whose players were idols to local youth. Prizefighting was a sport with a long Irish participation in the city, dating back to the mid-nineteenth century. Not only were the feats of national favorites like John L. Sullivan, Jack Sharkey, Jimmy Broderick, and Billy Conn extolled, but local careers of boxers like Tommy Loughran, Eddie Cool, and Billy Maher were long remembered. The superb track champions Ron Delaney, Eamon Coughlin, and Marcus O'Sullivan on the great Villanova University teams were cheered from one record-breaking race to another. Mention of the football heroics of such players as Frank Reagan, one of the first Irish-Americans to gain celebrity at the University of Pennsylvania, and the "iron lineman," Bucko Kilroy, of the Philadelphia Eagles, could set off years of sports remembrance. Irish football games were sponsored by the county societies, and the Donegal Society had especially good teams. In the 1980s, games organized by new immigrants became a subject of dispute because of the fierce scatology and obscene language the heated teams hurled at one another. Whether it was the epic brawls set off by basketball games at St. Ann's parish in the 1920s or the victories of the track and swimming teams of the Shanahan Athletic Club in the 1940s, there was always athletic fare to be shared, and this accorded with the active working-class culture largely characteristic of the group. Sports were the stuff of family discussion and difference, and the attendance of memorable games by fathers, sons, uncles, and cousins became part of the verbal lore.

Why did these particular stories impose themselves on the memories of the families who told them? Why were they retained to become available for review? Some of the stories are personalized first-hand experiences and thus valuable to the tellers or their families. Others are symbolic of the emigrant experience, a phenomenon so broad in scope that it becomes comprehensible only when depicted in individual and family terms. Other stories are antic and peculiar and satisfy a human need for humor and curiosity. Currents of antagonism exist in the stories of working-class strife, and this, too, is symbolic of a long period of disadvantaged labor. There is little envious resentment of the successful Irish figures, such as John B. Kelly or Michael Francis Doyle, rather, there is a tolerant admiration. The different tales do show varieties of Irish identity in the city—the "greenhorn" immigrant, the serving girl, the hard-pressed worker, the successful bourgeois, and the nationalist advocate. The stories in themselves do not represent a social critique so much as they represent Irish storytelling forms such as the journey tale, the tale of trial and adventure, and the humorous account of novelty or diversion. They may be inaccurate in details or even substance, but the stories serve the needs of the tellers for shaping family knowledge and personal inheritance, selectively retold to fill out the details of life's events.[10]

Family stories such as these, elaborated, embroidered, passed from one generation to the next without transcription, are the very stuff of ethnic identity. They are part of a complex of "inner connections" in the personality not immediately discernible from social behavior alone.[11] The stories are remembered by a process of emotional signification: what people care about, what is emotionally significant to them, has a strong influence on what is remembered. There is extensive research to show that emigration and mobility have grave psychological risks for children.[12] The existence of a family lore of familiar, instructive tales is one way that emotional well-being can be fostered for children in such circumstances of migration and cultural dislocation. But to confirm one's identity, one must choose among various kinds of identifications active in the surrounding society. Part of this choice involves seeing one's proximate lifestyle in the perspective of other cultures and of history. Through family stories, the Irish-Americans can see themselves in relation to Ireland and in relation to family and ethnic history, with their own family settings as microcosms of that history.[13]

Although some scholars see group identity "as a ready-made set of endowments," others believe that a participatory function is involved in the "listening" that children and adults perform in absorbing and personalizing family lore. Certainly, the complexity of the oral history narrative is elaborate enough to convince us of the subtleties involved in even the simplest cultural transmissions. Wording, prose, verse, style, plot, and informal dramatization are all parts of the process.[14]

At the far end of the life cycle, the recounting of family stories continues to serve the personality. Studies have shown that there are biases in the memory process that reshape and distort, and even erase, autobiographical recollections. People use memory as a support for their image of themselves and suppress experiences that trouble that image.[15] The existence of well-worn family reminiscences, shared and mutually corrected and recognized, provides a sort of mental buffer for the aged. The old ones are the sources and purveyors of memories that help to preserve their identity,

maintain their self-esteem as their powers decline, and perpetuate
certain facts and myths required for coherent individual and family functioning. This all testifies to the wisdom of the old Irish saying that "memory is the mind." Thus, it is not only the Irish
tradition that is nourished by the companionate reminiscences of
family tales, but the essential nature of the human family at large.[16]

Friendly Sons

To be a participant in a tradition and to be conscious of one's ethnic heritage carries with it a disposition to join with others of like
background. A singular illustration of how Irish-Americans have
shared their tradition is revealed by the Society of the Friendly
Sons of St. Patrick for the Relief of Emigrants from Ireland in
Philadelphia. It is one of the oldest ethnic organizations in the
country and is an invaluable example of Irish skill in balancing
contradictions and of doing so for over two centuries. The sheer
extent of the organization's existence over twenty-one decades provides a unique case study in the dynamics of ethnic identification.
Through more than two hundred years of fraternity and charitable
association, this society has repeatedly had to revise its orientation
in relation to the trends of American community life and changes
in Ireland. In doing so, the society has been a notable demonstration of the complexities of ethnic identity. It has steadily had to
balance internal differences over Irish nationalism and religion,
two influences that have brought great turbulence to the life of Ireland itself and that continue to do so today. By exemplifying in an
adaptive fashion various features of Irish-American identity, this
organization has provided a "time theater" of ethnic transition. It
has been one of the public galleries of Irish identity with its diverse and able membership drawn from the city's changing spectrum of community life, and it is an illustration of identity in an
organized dimension.

On March 17, 1771, twenty-four men sat down in a tavern in
Philadelphia and formed the Society of the Friendly Sons of St.
Patrick, an organization that continues to the present day. The motives of the founders were in the first instance charitable, for by
1771 Philadelphia had long been a haven for Irish people who left
their native land "dressed in destitution." The founders of the society were moderately successful men whose names would become
associated with the establishment of the American republic in succeeding years. They were all men of commerce, born in Ireland or

of recent Irish forebears. Thus began one of the most notable ethnic organizations in the history of the nation, an organization that not only has helped to preserve the identity of the Irish in an increasingly diverse society, but has also, for over two centuries, carried out a mediating function among the Irish themselves, as well as between them and the elements of the larger pluralist polity in American life.

The position of the Irish in an American culture dominated by Anglo-Saxon leadership and orientation has been one of subcultural minority status for most of our history. As such, the Irish required some public institutional forms that would establish their own image and assist their social adjustment in relation to the dominant groups in community life. The Friendly Sons of St. Patrick provided such a vehicle, and, more remarkably, sustained that function over a very long period of time. How this function of maintaining identity was performed reveals for us the persistence and changes of adaptation that are frequently overlooked amid the simplistic assumptions that characterize our approach to ethnic history.

Membership in a group such as the Friendly Sons was always a mark of identification with Irish background and an association with others of that background. In the colonial world in which the group was founded, ties existed among the emigrant Irish merchants around the Atlantic trading world. These took the form of Hibernian Societies in some places or just informal groups in others. Ties of birth, ancestry, marriage, and affinity linked Irish merchants and soldiers in Spain, Portugal, France, and the West Indies with those in New Orleans, Charleston, Baltimore, Philadelphia, New York, and ports in Ireland and England. These ties not only aided commerce among the Irish, but, as the era of revolutions approached in the eighteenth century, they provided a network for communication that would foster conspiracies against England.[17]

From its outset, the Friendly Sons projected itself as a public organization and devised various symbols to identify its members. Its meetings in taverns in Philadelphia were noted in the local press and known to leaders of the community. A medal with the image of St. Patrick was struck and presented to each member, and a membership scroll was later designed. The chief public event of the year was a St. Patrick's Day dinner of March 17, and quarterly dinners were required by the rules. Prominent Philadelphians were invited to these gatherings, and in 1782 George Washington was a guest of the society at its New Year's Day dinner, at which he accepted honorary membership in the society.[18]

During the American Revolution, the society provided both military and political leadership to the rebel cause. Its members became officers in Washington's command, organized their own military companies, collected significant funds to support the Continental cause, and participated in the ferment that helped to shape the nation's new government. Generals Stephen Moylan, John Shee, Edward Hand, and Anthony Wayne, and Commodore John Barry were all members who distinguished themselves in the patriot cause. Indeed, the society's early membership reads like a roster of Revolutionary stalwarts. The only member of the society ever expelled was deprived of membership for his British allegiance during the Revolution.[19] By its support of the American cause, the society not only set forth the identification of the Irish with revolutionary principles and American patriotism but also reinforced the identity of the Irish as a distinctive group in American life, a group antagonistic to the new Republic's enemies and one that had created a notable record for itself.

As time went on, the society attentively fostered its own tradition, extolling its early patriot days and maintaining the memory of the revered founders. The society seriously respected its founders' traditions, keeping to the annual round of dinners and referring constantly to its Americanism. The membership varied in size over the years, and in 1790 it was necessary to seek a broader membership through association with a group called the Hibernian Society, a name similar to that used by groups in Charleston and New Orleans.

Prominent members like Blair McClenachan and Mathew Carey were controversialists engaged in the rough-and-tumble politics of the Federal and Jeffersonian periods. A letter written by Thomas Jefferson attests that he wished to refute allegations that he was critical of members of the society, an example of how political leaders respected the group. By 1820, the society had clearly institutionalized itself in the life of the city, and, in a limited way, in the nation. Hence, it was entirely appropriate for an honorary member such as Andrew Jackson, the son of Irish parents, to have framed and hung in his fine home, the Hermitage in Tennessee, his certificate of membership in the society.[20]

It was an affirmation of a valuable common identity that the society offered its members, who were largely drawn from the commercial, professional, and political class of the city, not from the artisan and laboring class. The society permitted the expression of an Irish-American identity that represented talent and high community standing, for just this kind of an image was needed to counter the two most serious problems of popular perception that were threats to the acceptance of the Irish in American life. The first obstacle was the prejudicial image of the Irish transmitted through Anglo-Saxon views and interpretations of the history of Ireland. A long record of struggle with Ireland had imprinted upon English opinion and tradition a deeply unsavory view of the Irish, and this view had wide currency in America, especially among the Anglo upper class. Second, the continued migration of impoverished and uneducated Irish people to America presented a distinctly unappealing and frequently shocking display of misfortune.[21] From Ireland's most stricken areas came rural laborers and displaced tenants who were afflicted with disease, depression, and degradation. Such images served to further the traditional Anglo stereotypes characterizing the Irish as a failed race and tended to undermine the social acceptance of those Irish who were more successful, difficulties that became acute as immigration increased after 1820. An organization like the Friendly Sons provided a medium through which the more successful Irish could present an image of themselves that was not grounded in dependency and alien ways but was based on independence and competent achievement in American terms.

The fact that the character of the Friendly Sons was charitable was also significant in affirming the responsible nature of its Irish members. The organization's contributions to the relief of immigrants testified to the fact that those in the society recognized Irish immigrants required assistance, while also demonstrating to the Irish community itself that these leaders and successful men were not estranged from the city's larger impoverished Irish population. Their charity provided credibility for the members whose businesses had to function in the city and also demonstrated the cultural unity of the Irish, no matter what differences of class or worldly goods distinguished them.[22]

An Irish nationalist testimony was presented by the society as well. From the beginning, the members had opposed England's rule in America, and they were articulate in their opposition to England's rule in Ireland. This was less explicit for the founders of the society than for the following generation of men who took part in the activities of the United Irishmen, a revolutionary society that strove unsuccessfully to liberate Ireland with the aid of

France. These emigrés, driven into exile by repression attending the failed rising of 1798, brought to America a fiery dedication to revolutionary republican principles. Mathew Carey and others were relentless partisans of Irish liberation. The nationalism they shaped was a key factor in the launching of the very long Irish-American tradition of aid for the old country's revolutionary aspirations. For Philadelphia leaders with political interests, identification with Irish nationalism was also important in gaining the electoral support of the growing Irish population, and the Friendly Sons offered a platform from which to proclaim that identification.[23]

As important as these affirmations of identity were to the internal opinion and self-image of the Irish community, the function of the society as a mediating influence between the Irish and the broader Philadelphia community was of almost equal significance. Not only did the society provide patriotic credentials for a group whose loyalty to the United States was insistently questioned as nativist sentiment grew along with heavy immigration, but it provided an example of civility and respectable social deportment in contrast to the raucous and agitated behavior of the poorer sections of the Irish population. One of the areas for demonstrating this civility was in the unified and tolerant fraternity formed by both Protestant and Catholic members of the society. In the early years of the republic, interreligious relations ranged from benign to uneasy. The constitutional guarantees of freedom of religion did not dispel the intolerance, envy, and evangelical frictions that created difficulty in a religiously pluralistic society. Notorious among the religious hostilities as the nineteenth century proceeded was that between Irish Catholics and Irish Protestants, the hostility inflamed by English policies that purposely set one group upon the other in Ireland was transferred to America. The collaboration of Protestants and Catholics in the Society of the United Irishmen in the 1790s ended, and the areas of conflict grew. Yet, the Friendly Sons were able to maintain an organization that included both religious groups and to do so within a framework of genuine mutual respect and esteem. This fact displayed to the predominantly Protestant community in Philadelphia the best features of Irish liberal thought. It also refuted those Protestant and nativist propagandists who sought to characterize the Irish Catholics as a whole as a threat to liberty and to the religious values of American life. The succession of Protestant and Catholic presidents of the society gave the Irish Catholics themselves a model for judicious relations in the general community, a model much needed in a group that had experienced centuries of religious persecution in Ireland.[24]

The tolerance evidenced by the society was not limited to religion but extended across cultural and ethnic barriers as well. Even at its first meeting in 1771, the society had as guests and honorary members six prominent non-Irish Philadelphians. As early as 1793, the group's custom was to invite to its dinners representatives of the St. George Society, the St. Andrew's Society, the French Benevolent Society, the German Society, and, at a later date, the Welsh Society. Thus, common philanthropic concern and American fellowship did help to overcome the difficulties of intergroup association even in decades of high tension.[25]

While there were public debates about the dangers of pauperism and the cost of supporting indigent immigrants, the society continued its voluntary charitable work. The burden of poverty was so widespread that no single organization could deal with it effectively, but the role of the Friendly Sons gave evidence to the general community that the Irish were concerned to help care for their own. In a time when the role of government was very limited in dealing with social problems, this private initiative did place a portion of the city's Irish leadership in public view as ministers of a responsible and humane obligation. It must be recalled that in 1844 the famous anti-Irish and anti-Catholic riots of the city were a sensational display of antagonism toward the same kind of immigrants the Friendly Sons were assisting.[26]

The steadily declaimed patriotism of the society served in a special way to mediate the position of the Irish in the city. As far back as the furious controversy surrounding the Alien and Sedition Acts in 1798, the public had been treated to the depiction of the Irish as dangerous radicals and a threat to American institutions. The increasing immigration in the 1830s revived such fears. By the 1840s, Protestant religious revivalism had fueled an unprecedented wave of anti-Irish sentiment. As the Civil War approached, the identification of the Irish with the Democratic party, the party of secession, caused the group's patriotism to again be challenged.[27] As each of these waves of anti-Irish feeling crested, the Friendly Sons could firmly proclaim the patriotic origins of the group and the significance of its continuous loyalty to American principles.

Members of the society were often on different sides of political issues. The meetings of the society, however, offered a neutral ground where men of different political persuasions could come

together. It was also a network wherein those with moderate political objectives could discreetly ply their ambitions, another device
through which the Irish could mediate with the general community. Those in search of some political aid sought access to the society, and the members often acted as intermediaries to make
possible the appearance of political figures at its gatherings. James
Campbell, the first Irish-Catholic cabinet member in American history, could rise to prominence partly through identification with
the society, as could scores of others in the nineteenth century. In
the second half of the nineteenth century, when the Irish were the
largest minority group in Philadelphia, the value of having a
readily available pool of Irish contacts in organized affiliation was
a resource that few leading politicians could ignore.[28]

The history of the society in the period of the Civil War and
the Gilded Age that followed provides a record that bears the mark
of increasingly American influences. The service of members in
the Civil War was memorialized in the most eulogistic fashion.
Orations, toasts, resolutions, and commemorations saluted valor
and death upon the battlefield in a romantic and refulgent rhetoric
that cascaded through the society's affairs right up through the
1890s. The organization was caught up in the great era of America's
impulse to join organizations. Its history in the late Victorian years
is rife with the pretentious and ornate style of the time. Its dinners
became huge and elaborate feasts with orotund addresses and self-
congratulatory recitations. In 1887, the menu of the annual meeting
included oysters, turtle soup, pâté, salmon, beef, chicken, terrapin,
seven wines, four desserts, and cognac; and the governor of Pennsylvania gave his address of welcome to the honored guest, President Grover Cleveland. The president's remarks included this
tribute to the Friendly Sons, also called the Hibernian Society at
the time: "I say, long live the Hibernian Society and long may its
benificent and benevolent objects be prosecuted. When another
centennial day shall be celebrated, may those whose names are
then borne upon your membership roll be imbued with the same
spirit of patriotism and join as ardently and actively in the general
felicitation as do those whom I see about me here today."[29]

This period for the society was probably the most important
since its establishment, for it was the period during which the social mobility of the Irish was taking place on a broad basis. There
had always been Irish people who moved among the non-Irish with
ease, but the 1880s and the 1890s were a time when the ranks of
such people grew rapidly as more and more Irish took advantage of

education and the economic and social opportunities that opened
to them. The society was in the forefront of this movement; and
lawyers, physicians, judges, journalists, businessmen, and civic
figures increased its membership. It is not surprising, therefore,
that the society would, by 1893, be holding its meetings in that
temple of bourgeois success and proper Philadelphia dignity, the
staunchly Republican Union League Club. By 1902, it even accorded a reception in honor of members of the Grand Lodge of Free
and Accepted Masons, a group long considered anti-Catholic.[30]

The liberal and revolutionary nationalism that had been part
of the ideology of the early members of the society had as one of
its features the leadership of Protestant Irishmen. When nationalists like Theobold Wolfe Tone and Archibald Hamilton Rowan
visited Philadelphia, they were as likely to consort with Irish Protestants as with Irish Catholics. As the nineteenth century progressed, this Protestant commitment was diminished in the face of
rising Catholic political activity until, in the 1860s, the Fenian
Brotherhood established a new basis for Irish nationalism. Unlike
the old nationalism that derived from the French Revolution, the
Fenian Brotherhood was nourished in the radical ideology of the
nineteenth-century revolutionary underground that included diverse strains of conspiracy. The Fenian Brotherhood, with its creed
of protest violence, alarmed many American observers, and its
intrigues in the United States proved very disturbing. The brotherhood was succeeded in the late 1870s by another radical network,
the secret Clan na Gael (Children of the Gael). Although some Protestant nationalists were involved with the Clan na Gael, it was
predominantly Catholic. Only a few of the members of the Friendly
Sons of St. Patrick were attached to either of these organizations. The proprieties of American life had converted most Irish-
Americans to a moderate rather than a revolutionary view of Irish
nationalism.[31]

Thus, while the nationalism of the early 1800s could be shared
fully by Protestant members of the society, this was much less true
in the period after 1860. Irish Protestants and their distinct Scotch-
Irish tradition in America had been massively challenged by the
huge Irish Catholic immigration of the mid-nineteenth century. So
threatening were the poverty, religious growth, and radical nationalism of the immigrant Catholics, even though only a small cadre
shared the credo of radical nationalism, that Irish Protestants increasingly characterized themselves as Scotch-Irish and stressed
their ties to Britain and to the British Empire, partly as a result of

the alienation in Ireland between Catholics and Protestants. Hence, they were put at a distance from the older Irish nationalist tradition. In an organization like the Friendly Sons, it was made more difficult to pretend that there was unity about the future national status of Ireland. One member, Martin I.J. Griffin, was a publisher and historian who denied the existence of a Scotch-Irish identity. The result of these developments was that strident Irish nationalism became tendentious in the society and moderated in favor of maintaining fraternal ties and collective philanthropy. It was moderated to such an extent that the society could extend its best wishes to the St. George Society year after year even at the height of furious nationalist campaigns that were producing unparalleled political tension in Ireland under Charles Stewart Parnell.[32]

It may have been this internal tension about nationalism that induced the society to publish a flattering history of itself. The decision to publish a history of the organization in the late 1890s was an important cultural landmark in the life of the organization. A short booklet on the society had been prepared in 1844 by Samuel Hood, but the publication that would emerge in 1892, compiled by John H. Campbell, an editor and total-abstinence enthusiast, would be the first full description of the society available to its members and the public. This publication established in a definitive way the record of the society's past and was a substantial support for its traditions. The book itself was in imposing volume of 570 pages with picture plates of notable members, an ornate green and gold cover, and a biographical directory of all members from the organization's inception. It was a true Victorian achievement, a book that was representative of a whole category of publications that enhanced the reputations of groups seeking to confirm their status in American life. Prepared by a history committee of the society, the book was a very sturdy work of research, especially in its recapturing of details of the lives of men who had long since passed from the scene. It not only recounted the events of the society's past in a dignified fashion but also proclaimed American patriotism on almost every page. Celebratory praises, boastful declamations, and catalogs of soldierly achievement were mingled with the accounts of the society's benefactions in behalf of immigrants. A whole separate section of the book was reserved to recite the deeds of the Irish Brigade in the Civil War. The volume unrestrainedly expressed the virtues of masculine dominance and bourgeois propriety. As such, it proffered a message to the non-Irish leaders of the community. It professed in assertive and effusive terms the assured status of that echelon of the Irish who composed the Friendly Sons. Blending their tradition with that of the American mainstream, it refuted with biographical evidence the stereotypic depictions of the Irish that were fixtures of the stage and cartoon press at the time. Although the book did not sell as well as anticipated, it performed its function of further elevating the society's image among the Irish themselves and among leaders in the general community.[33]

With this history endorsing the dignity of the society, the group could again orient itself toward charitable works. The restrictions on immigration in the twentieth century altered the role of the society as a charitable organization. Irish immigration into Philadelphia diminished, and the conditions both in Ireland and in the United States pertaining to immigrants were a far cry from the harrowing days of the mid-nineteenth century. The need for the society to aid immigrants directly lessened. As a result, the society made annual contributions from its funds to groups such as the St. Vincent de Paul Society and others that provided aid to all kinds of needy people. As its direct charitable role declined, the Friendly Sons increased its civic and cultural activities. In 1895, the Society began a series of presentations to the city, the first being a statue of Commodore John Barry, Irish-born father of the American navy, placed eminently beside Independence Hall. In 1922, a memorial to General Stephen Moylan, the first president of the Friendly Sons, was donated to the city for a park in the then heavily Irish area of North Philadelphia. In 1927, a plaque commemorating early members was dedicated as part of the restoration of St. Mary's Church, an eighteenth-century Catholic parish in the oldest part of the city. Gifts to groups other than Irish were made, such as a donation to the Russian Jewish Relief Fund in 1905 and a gift to victims of the Johnstown flood.[34]

In 1915, the members "rejoiced that definite progress had been made toward self-government" in Ireland as a result of the agreement of England to a limited form of Home Rule. Men like Michael J. Ryan, attorney and orator, who became president of the group in 1916, were long-time workers for the Home Rule cause and supporters of a basically conservative parliamentary evolution in Ireland's status. The declaration of an Irish Republic in 1916 in Dublin by radical nationalists of the Sinn Fein movement and the tragic repression that followed their rebellion caught the members unaware, as it did most Irish-Americans. The society's history deals uncertainly with this series of events, stating that indignation was expressed, but the epochal Easter Rising of 1916, a pivotal happening for modern Ireland, is accorded only token recognition. This omission is reflective of the conservative consensus the society represented. In Philadelphia, a whole network of Irish nationalists led by Joseph McGarrity, wealthy head of the Clan na Gael, were deeply involved with the armed insurrection of 1916 and the subsequent Irish guerrilla war for independence. They were not for the most part, members of the Friendly Sons, and they formed a separate and quite differently disposed element of the Philadelphia Irish community.[35]

As the new Irish state emerged from the guerrilla war and fierce British repression, the society oriented itself toward the leaders who had risen from the revolutionary underground. In 1919, Eamon De Valera, sole survivor of the 1916 rebel leadership group, was smuggled into America to seek support for the infant Irish republic. In October 1919, the society joined other Irish groups in feting De Valera in a series of banquets and rallies that became a euphoric outpouring of the Irish community. The society, however, was not in the lead in organizing these gatherings. The achievement of a form of government called a "Free State" and the signing of a treaty with England in 1921 brought some stability to Ireland, but a civil war between Free State adherents and those strongly committed to a fully independent republic cooled American sentiment about Ireland's affairs. At length the Friendly Sons in 1928 welcomed William T. Cosgrave, head of the Free State, at a special banquet and a series of local events, and honorary membership in the society was conferred upon him. Thus, the society confirmed its approbation of the Irish settlement that had been effected after generations of struggle and the bloody strife following 1916.[36]

Beginning in the 1920s, the society provided a platform for officials of the independent Irish state to address an Irish-American audience in Philadelphia with attendant publicity in the local media. Irish ambassadors to the United States and cabinet members of the Irish government, heads of Irish universities, scholars, churchmen, and representatives from Northern Ireland all took the platform at events of the society to discuss the problems and prospects of the Irish people. Irish officials recognized the need to maintain a favorable bloc of opinion in America concerning difficult subjects pertaining to Ireland's development, such as explanations of the small country's neutrality during World War II, the persistence of British-imposed partition of the country, and the cultural gap between Ireland and the United States. The society provided a vehicle for presentations about Irish politics, education, and economic development to a segment of Irish-American opinion that was interested, more informed than the general public, and conservative enough so that there would be no untoward challenges to the views expressed.[37]

There had been, of course, a lengthy record of American politicians addressing the society: everybody from General Ulysses S. Grant to President Grover Cleveland had availed themselves of the privilege in the 1800s. The opportunity to speak to the Friendly Sons was especially sought by one generation after another of Philadelphia and Pennsylvania political figures. In the days of nationalist agitation, this was important to those members anxious to influence American leaders in behalf of Ireland's claim to independence. Hence, a long line of governors, congressmen, and officials of every level of government, as well as representatives of the army and navy, discussed American and Irish subjects before the group. John F. Kennedy, while still a senator in 1957, told the members, "I feel strongly the ties of common kinship. All of us of Irish descent are bound together by ties that come from a common experience." In saying this, he asserted a truth of Irish-American life that persisted beyond the personal political advocacy that had become such a lasting feature of the society's oratorical tradition.[38]

At the St. Patrick's Day banquet in 1959, the Irish ambassador to the United States, Frederick Boland, said in his address:

The new generation of Irish men and women, the first generation of Irishmen born into freedom, is taking over control of affairs in Ireland, and there is a new spirit of enterprise and confidence and dynamic purpose in the air. We have much to be thankful for. Our standard of living is high by European standards; our institutions of government compare favorably, from the point of view of stability and facility and probity, with any democratic country. We have good housing, much improved public health standards, a sound educational system, no illiteracy, and very little crime. We have a rich and fertile soil. Our labor relations are good, our industry and industrial exports are expanding, and we have managed to provide out of our own resources sea and air communications which can match any in Europe. But, we have no illusions. We know that if we are to achieve, the level of economic and social well-being we want, we must work, save, and invest and take risks. But being convinced as we are of the ability of our people to meet these challenges, and relying on their great resources of character and determination which have been so often and so severely tested in the past, we face the future now with courage and sober confidence, resolved not to rest until we have achieved that kind of Ireland united, peaceful and prosperous, of which our ancestors dreamed and which is the aim of every good Irishman to bring about.[39]

The sober confidence and courage of Irish leaders would be profoundly challenged ten years later when the British government of the six partitioned counties of Northern Ireland would be plunged into tragic discord. The Protestant-dominated Northern Ireland government proved to be unequal to the disorders that began in 1969 as a result of Catholic and nationalist dissent and British Unionist and Protestant repression. The government fell apart and was replaced by direct rule from London, and a revival of Irish Republican Army and Ulster Defense Association violence and British army violence.

Various members of the Friendly Sons sought to have adopted resolutions expressing nationalist views of the conflict. The society's historian, Owen B. Hunt, was one of the proponents. The officers of the society, however, in deference to the differing views within the organization about the Northern Ireland problem, avoided going on record about the conflict. As bombings, assassinations, torture, hunger strikes, and ferocious denunciations continued year after year in Northern Ireland, the society studiously avoided taking any position that would align it with any faction. Instead, it made contributions to the Corrymeela Center, an ecumenical education facility in Ireland and invited speakers identified with moderate views and ecumenical activities, such as James Humes, director of Policy and Planning of the U.S. State Department; Reverend Douglas Baker, a Protestant clergymen; Reverend Patrick Brady, a Catholic priest; and Reverend Fred Pierce Corson of the World Council of Churches. Thus, the society continued its mediating role even during these years of intense stress, when Irish-Americans were continually being accused by British and Irish officials of fueling the violence in Ulster. Not until 1981 during the Belfast prison hunger strikes that claimed the lives of ten men did members adopt a resolution relating to the conflict, and this occurred only after considerable debate. The resolution was put in the form of a letter to President Ronald Reagan stating, "The Society of the Friendly Sons of St. Patrick in the long tradition of American support for civil and human rights throughout the world, respectfully urges you to communicate with the governments of Great Britain and Ireland that a prompt end to this grievous situation may be achieved, and thus resolve this struggle so that peace may return to the land of our forefathers."[40]

This measured statement reflects the moderation that had come to characterize the venerable old society. Its membership had always represented men of property and considered views, and its founders had included gentlemen, sea captains, merchants, a physician, and an attorney. A review of the membership rolls before the American Civil War shows that 84 percent of the members were in white-collar occupations or professions and that the average property holding was valued at $51,740 at that time. Over a century later, in 1951, a similar review of members showed the group dominated by attorneys, contractors, manufacturers, bankers, business executives, and political office holders. An examination of members' occupations in 1981 showed that 20 percent were attorneys, among whom were seventeen judges, while twenty-eight members were physicians. The society represented only a portion of the Irish in the city and therefore did not reflect a socially diverse representation of that community.[41]

Some would contend that the Friendly Sons was, for most of its history, simply an assimilationist, super-patriotic liaison of convenience for middle-and upper-class businessmen and public officials. Certainly it was predominantly a group for merchants and business and professional men, and an exclusively male association. In these respects, it fits into the pattern of American organizations to which "joiners" flocked in a society where fluid relationships were the norm. However, it was also a vehicle for affirming Irishness in a particular way with its emphasis on charitable activities, interreligious fraternity, and concern for Ireland's well-being. Whatever other functions it served and continues to serve, these concerns were paramount. The attachment to Ireland is so clear and so persistent among its members and in its records of activities that the role of the society in this regard is conclusively confirmed. More than a local group dedicated to casual fellowship and the assertion of status, the society has been and is the projection of a notable kind of Irish aspiration toward unity and the retention of historic bonds.

The history of this society is a remarkable example of the calculated cultivation of identity and the modulation of that identity with respect to American opinion and changing conditions in the United States and Ireland. It is a record of repeated adaptation to cultural and political changes and to ethnic issues. Despite its skill in dealing with the delicate issue of balancing religious difference, the organization was never able to bring women into its councils. The group's conservative nature remained dominant, contradicting the stereotype of the Irish that depicted them as sponsors of radical associations. Yet, in its mediation between the Irish and the general community, it illustrates with remarkable constancy the influence that minority cultural forms have exerted on the maintenance of pluralism and social harmony in this country.

Paddy Portrayed

Just as Irish families counseled the young to be mindful of their behavior, and just as the Friendly Sons of St. Patrick sought to project a reputation for charity and tolerance, so the Irish in the city sought over a long time to ensure that the image of the group would not be unfavorable to their social acceptance and civic standing. The particular problem of the Irish was that, in a predominantly Anglo-Saxon culture, their group had long been characterized in a derogatory fashion, and this derogation was imported into America under British auspices from colonial times forward. As is evident in the history of such organizations as the Friendly Sons of St. Patrick, this legacy had far-reaching social and civic implications. Richard Ned Lebow has written that "by the nineteenth century the major characteristics attributed to the Irish—indolence, superstition, dishonesty and a propensity to violence—had remained prominent in the British image for over six hundred years."[42] This inheritance of imagery was used in Britain to explain the complex history of conflict between the two peoples and came into use in America to explain the problems attendant on mass immigration and the social and cultural differences represented by the Irish.

In a study of the Irish in the theater, Maurice Bourgeois sums up the time-honored stereotype of the Irishman as it prevailed in the nineteenth century:

> His face is one of simian bestiality with an expression of diabolical archness written all over it. He wears a tall felt hat (billicock or wide-awake) with a cutty clay pipe stuck in front, an open shirt-collar, a three-capped coat, knee-breeches, worsted stockings, and cockaded brogue-shoes. In his right hand he brandishes a stout blackthorn or a sprig of shillelagh and threatens to belabour therewith the daring person who will "tread on the tails of his coat." For his main characteristics (if there be any such thing as psychology in the stage Irishman)

are his swagger, his boisterousness and his pugnacity. He is always ready with a challenge, always anxious to back a quarrel, and peerless for cracking skulls at Donnybrook Fair.[43]

This was the view of the Irish that they had to contend with when confronted with the problem of adjustment to American life.

How people see one another in a democracy is crucial to the success of their society and to the success of the people themselves. The popular media are perhaps the chief influence in how groups of citizens are perceived beyond those impressions derived from direct everyday experience. In his study *Paddy and the Republic*, Dale Knobel has shown how extensively ideas of Irish inferiority and satires of the Irish were spread in the first half of the nineteenth century.[44] The problem of prejudiced views about minorities has been a continuing challenge to democratic life because of this popular stream of damaging derogation. If a society of unprecedented mixture of peoples is to work civil and coherent social views among groups are necessary.

Irish immigrants presented a complex challenge to early America. The new country needed their labor, and, after the Revolution, it was committed to democratic principles that countenanced the participation of this category of persons in civic life. Yet, the Irish were largely Roman Catholic in the nineteenth century, not Protestant as was the dominant leadership, and they also bore social problems as a result of their shattered history in Ireland. But certain advantages prevented them from being subjugated: they spoke English and were disposed to be politically active, their numbers were too great to permit them to be driven off like the Indians, and they were soon dispersed too widely to permit them to be segregated like blacks. Gradually they circulated actively in American life, challenging existing codes and institutions. Some of the earliest cartoons of the Irish stem from the resentment of the group's penetration into community life. As Irish immigration increased after 1830 and Protestantism experienced one of its periodic revivals, tension increased, as did anti-Irish feeling.[45] The generation of immigrants resulting from the Great Famine in Ireland in the mid-1840s brought with it destitution, disease, family disorganization, and mass concentrations of Irish in major centers of the country's life. The stereotypical image of the Irish as slum-dwelling, uneducated, comic, and servile people who were incurably violent was stimulated by this demography of misfortune.

Although the service of the Irish in the Union army in the Civil War brought some moderation of the hostile views about them, this really did not dispel the derogatory image applied to the group. The acceptance and progress of some Irish was always offset by the arrival from Ireland of others less presentable and by the turbulence and distress of those in the urban ghettoes. In the 1880s and 1890s, thousands of Irish families achieved "lace curtain" status and moved into better housing areas, but cartoons of the Irish as brawlers, clumsy servants, and generally undesirable characters continued to appear in the media. Those who succeeded in upgrading their lives were often seen as overly aggressive and as crass imitators of their betters, while those who failed were classed with the sub-human and apelike creatures of cartoon invention that had long been featured in the British and American press.[46]

The power of literacy was limited in the nineteenth century by economic and cultural restrictions on education. The freedom to see was frequently an important substitute for the freedom to read: in a frontier society, in cities crowded with immigrants, and in a society that was fluid and rapidly expanding, people tended to garner ideas in crude form by responding to images. This is one reason the cartoon became an enormously popular and influential medium for the portrayal of public issues and the depiction of group characteristics. And just as American culture bore within its mentality certain assumptions about blacks, Indians, and Jews, so it also came to portray the Irish in the "cartoon culture" of newspapers and magazines as having recognizable traits that betrayed mocking assumptions and prejudices about the group. The power to depict, however, is not the power to explain, and the cartoonist is disarmed by the complexity of social life. As a result, cartoons regularly contain contradictions and anomalies—along with the mockery and hostility, the Irish did benefit from their association with humor and comedy reflected in cartoons. Frequently, Paddy the threat was complemented by Paddy the amusing fool.[47]

In a metropolitan community such as Philadelphia, the public had access to most of the major publications circulating in the nation, and this was especially true of mass-produced illustrated magazines and journals after the Civil War. The city itself was a major publishing center. Illustrations transmitting derogatory and satirical views of the Irish were so extensive that scholars have been able to compile an entire archive of such material. The Balch Institute in Philadelphia has a large collection, including John Apple's ingenious work for the Anti-Defamation League of B'nai B'rith in which he gathered anti-Irish, as well as anti-Semitic, cartoons that appeared in St. Valentine's Day greetings, newspapers, posters, labels, and a wide variety of other visual materials.[48]

Some of the more notable examples of the anti-Irish cartoon tradition in Philadelphia can be cited beginning in the early period of the nation's visual expression. The Irish as a disruptive political element are shown in an 1810 cartoon featuring one "Billy O'Dunn" as part of a satire directed against Thomas Jefferson's allies in the city. Another cartoon of the controversial Matthew Lyon, a congressman, shows him as a wild, uncontrollable Irishman wrecking a political meeting. The increased presence of the Irish in the 1830s and 1840s brought a spate of anti-Irish and anti-Catholic publications with such titles as *Priestcraft Unmasked* and *Liberty versus Romanism* and often including lurid illustrations of an inflammatory character. The famous anti-Catholic riots in Philadelphia in 1844 were depicted in cartoons showing murderous Irish riot scenes.[49]

New printing techniques of the second half of the nineteenth century greatly expanded cartoon production. *Harper's Weekly*, with cartoonist Thomas Nast, led in portraying the Irish as a threat to American life and values in the 1870s. Nast was highly gifted, and his cartoons depicting the Irish as ape-like, corrupt, violent, and religiously depraved were fierce satires. In 1881, a book titled *Solid for Mulhooly* was published satirizing Irish political-machine life in Philadelphia. The book was so popular it was reissued in 1889 with scathing drawings by Nast.[50] One showed Mulhooly, the fictional politico contrived for the book, in his birthplace, a pig trough complete with frolicking pigs. The infant Mulhooly roisters in the trough, swinging a whiskey bottle. Such cartoons had long been traditional and became even more popular, continuing into the twentieth century. Some appeared in the *Saturday Evening Post*, that homely and very popular weekly published in the city by Edward Bok. These often showed Brigid, the clownish Irish maid, enacting follies or having tantrums in domestic situations.

Irish efforts to contradict and correct these cartoon images were intermittent. As early as the 1780s, Irish Catholics formed a society in Philadelphia to defend their religion against "calumny and slander." But views of the Irish were part of a strong Anglo cultural tradition, and, in 1823, Mathew Carey wrote of the "most vulgar and rancorous prejudices" common in the minds of English and American readers concerning Ireland. The *Catholic Herald*, the city's first Catholic newspaper, was founded to refute calumnies against Catholics and their Irish attachments. A mid-nineteenth century Irish leader, Father Patrick Moriarty, was a controversialist who combatively refuted anti-Irish rhetoric and became extremely popular in the Irish community for his prowess in this regard. As late as 1924, the members of the Society of the Friendly Sons of St. Patrick were at pains to repudiate the old canard that "the Irish are incapable of governing themselves."[51]

The depiction of the Irish in the theater was as distressing as the stereotypical cartoons. Despite how they were portrayed, though, the Irish themselves were an integral part of the American theatrical scene. Thoroughly represented in the early minstrel circuit, in the Victorian melodramas and musical reviews of the commercial theater, in vaudeville, and in the serious legitimate theater, they functioned as producers, actors, musicians, writers, and theatrical publicists throughout the country. Irish entertainers readily portrayed the stereotyped figures in plays by John Brougham, Edward Everett Rose, and Dion Boucicault.[52] The need for employment overcame any scruples that the thespians may have had, and this caused a split among the Irish, with some willing to tolerate the stage Irish satire because it was presented by Irish people and others hotly protesting the presentations.

Despite the attempts of some people to explain away the participation of Irish theater people in the demeaning of their own group, increasing numbers of Irish found the portrayals of their character and background to be offensive as the commercial theater expanded in the 1880s and 1890s. The strutting of comic buffoons and ignorant dupes across the stages of the city brought a desire for some alternative. One option was to seek to construct a theater circuit designed for the Irish themselves and done on an amateur basis through Irish organizations and the Catholic parish dramatic societies that flourished in the major cities beginning in the 1870s. These made possible the projection of an image of the Irish that, while not always free of humorous satire or stereotypical foibles, was a decided improvement over the commercial theater's stage Irish depictions. The hunger of the Irish for respectability led them to join groups that taught elocution and encourage literary interests, and such groups often had dramatic companies as part of their programs.

An example of such an effort is the Enterprise Catholic Young Men's Association of Germantown, a district of Philadelphia. Founded in 1871 in a parish that had been established in 1850, the organization produced plays steadily and successfully until the 1920s. Boasting a one thousand-volume library, the association prided itself on the oratorical and dramatic talents of its members. The parish of St. Vincent's was heavily Irish, and the Enterprise Association was almost totally Irish. Through the 1880s, its plays often included those of Dion Boucicault, and the entire effort had a thoroughly ethnic spirit and orientation. The parish had a fine hall and stage, but the troupe of players from St. Vincent's visited other parishes and even filled the city's huge Academy of Music in downtown Philadelphia for benefit performances. Edmund Falconer's *Eileen Oge*; Joseph Pilgrim's Irish musical reviews *Rory O'More*, *Robert Emmet*, and *The Irish Tiger*; Henry A. Jones and Henry Herman's *The Silver King*, and other standard Irish plays of the time were the repertory. Shakespeare's *Julius Caesar* and a whole roster of Victorian farces and melodramas were also presented from year to year. By the 1890s, the group was presenting four plays a year, and in 1905 it produced seven, alternating these with "musical evenings" on the parish stage. Some plays were given eight or nine performances. The records of the organization note the names of the players who became actors and actresses in the legitimate theater and some who went on to play in early motion pictures.[53]

One incident in the long campaign against offensive stage portrayals of the Irish illustrates the heated feelings involved: on March 30, 1903, at the People's Theater in the heavily Irish Kensington district, a riot broke out when two hundred Irishmen disrupted a performance of a farce titled *McFadden's Row of Flats*. Eggs and vegetables were thrown at the stage. A free-for-all combat ensued. Women fainted. Some performers became hysterical. Police poured into the theater as the affray continued, and, following a roaring melee, nineteen men were arrested. The newspaper account of the affair noted that a similar uproar at a local theater had greeted a play called *McSwiggan's Parliament* in 1887, and subsequent reports blamed the riot on the Ancient Order of Hibernians. An official of the Irish American Club decried posters which depicted Irishmen with green whiskers advertising the People's Theater performance. Pinkerton detectives were hired by the theater owners to trace Irish conspirators, and a newspaper account stated, "These kinds of protests occurred in the city from the 1880s to the 1900s, although they were not always so violent."[54]

The sensitivity of the Irish to the stage Irish stereotypes did lead them to overreact to offensive portrayals. Thus, when the Abbey Theater brought Synge's *The Playboy of the Western World* to Philadelphia on tour in 1912, the Ancient Order of Hibernians and other groups, believing the portrayal of rural Irish people to be prejudicial, organized boycotts, pickets, and protests. Owen B. Hunt, a vigorous local figure who had been born in rural County

Mayo in Ireland, recalled campaigning against stage Irish presentations even after World War I.[55]

Just before World War I, a positive effort was devised by two
young theatrical troupers to mount productions that would be free
of anti-Irish bias and more modern than the kinds of plays offered
by the Enterprise Association and other amateur groups. Mae Desmond (Mary Veronica Callahan) and Frank Fielder formed a legitimate theater stock company, the Mae Desmond Players. Between
1917 and 1927, this troupe presented hundreds of plays calculated
to be "uplifting" and to avoid the old stereotypes of the tawdry
commercial theaters. The troupe played to audiences in Philadelphia and elsewhere and developed a faithful following. Drawing
talent from local acting groups and the commercial theater circuit,
the Desmond Players aimed to provide theater that was balanced in
its presentation of Irish characters and that was also in accord with
Catholic moral sentiments. Melodramas, mystery dramas and
comic plays, musicals, and some of the old favorites among Irish-
Americans, but in updated versions, were produced. Although the
Irish plays of the group were romantic to a fault, Mae Desmond's
plays banished the Handy Andy Irish fool and the drunken brag-
gart from the boards. The Irish Catholic community, in effect, developed its own entertainment circuit with groups such as the Mae
Desmond Players and the parish amateur troupes that added to local cultural life.[56]

Beginning in the 1920s, of course, the movies became an intimate part of the leisure life of America. The medium became crucial for democratic processes of intergroup understanding and
cultural education. The idea that movies were and are designed for
entertainment alone is not sustainable. No invention so potent, so
popular, and so reflective of social attitudes and conditions can be
realistically seen as mere entertainment. The movies not only reflect the cultural context, but also help to shape it. They do reflect
the group attitudes of the broader society, and they perpetuate and
transmit group attitudes. In the case of the Irish, the long history of
dramatic and representational imagery stored in American social
psychology came into play in the new motion picture industry.

The revelation that drama, melodrama, and light entertainment, as well as that new promotional suffusion, "glamor," were all
to be part of the film industry drew Irish entertainers, actors, and
actresses, like others in their profession, to the magic realms of the
silver screen. They were to play a large part in installing the Irish
in the Hollywood pantheon of make-believe. By the 1920s, the

Irish were so broadly dispersed in the American population that they were ready to become a symbolic constituency in the country's motion picture life. The stereotypes about them had been familiar for so long that they were a natural group for inclusion in the panoply of films. Their ubiquity gave them a familiar role similar to that of the Indians in cowboy movies.[57]

Although the film industry took up the role of extending the long tradition of Irish imagery, the very general market for films required a softening of the Irishness of the group when portrayed on the screen. Too close a correspondence of the film images to old country manners and identities would produce problems of intelligibility for a general American audience. While retaining Irish names and basic identity in the film characters, the film makers played on a wide variety of Irish-American types and the wide diversity of Irish-American experience. The films had to develop recognizable stock types and situations by which Americans could perceive group characterizations placed in familiar settings, and this they did with the rich lore of Irish-American presence.

The film industry created new thematic types and enhanced old ones. The Irish soon found themselves portrayed as gangsters by Jimmy Cagney and Lloyd Nolan, as soldiers by Pat O'Brien and Victor McLaglan, as adventure heroes by Errol Flynn and Tyrone Power, as humorous priests by Bing Crosby and Barry Fitzgerald, and as cowboy tough guys by John Wayne and others. Roles as Irishwomen went to Maureen O'Hara, Geraldine Fitzgerald, Ann Sheridan, and Sarah Allgood in melodramas of domestic sentiment and vapid triviality. The lack of substantial dramatic connection between the movies and the larger issues and values of life led the Catholic clergy to be especially critical of Hollywood's products, and they communicated to the Irish-Americans a wary attitude toward motion pictures. The conservative Catholicism of Philadelphia was a good breeding ground for this censorious view. A public relations man from Philadelphia, Joe Breen, was appointed chief "enforcer" of the sanctions imposed by the Hollywood Production Code, written by two Irish-Americans—Martin Quigley, a trade journal publisher, and Daniel Lord, a Jesuit priest, as part of an effort by Catholic leaders to oppose "movie morality." The code was a combination of conservative rural, Protestant values and equally conservative Irish-Catholic strictures, a thicket of cautions, guidelines, and proscriptions aimed at insuring that virtue triumphed and vice was penalized and that sex would be mildly suggestive but never prurient. The ultimate application of this moralist viewpoint occurred when Philadelphia's irascible prelate, Dennis Cardinal Dougherty, who was offended by a salacious bit of billboard advertising, officially forbade all Catholics in his archdiocese from attending the movie *The Moon Is Blue* under pain of mortal sin.[58]

The conflict with the mainstream culture about the morality of movies was lost by the Catholics as standards became even more elastic after the 1960s. The Irish, or at least some of them, continued to find fault with the way they were presented in films. Many found the depiction of Irish village life in the popular film *Ryan's Daughter* to be offensive. The Federation of Irish-American Societies intermittently called for boycotts of publications and products because of its unhappiness with how Irish people were depicted in articles and cartoons. And St. Patrick's Day greeting cards and caricatures showing the Irish as drunks and clowns rankled many Irish-Americans. In a symposium at the Balch Institute for Ethnic Studies, William Brennan, the president of the United Irish-American Societies in Philadelphia, stated that sensitivity to such presentation was still a distressing issue for his group in the 1970s. He quoted Kathleen Hoagland, editor of an anthology, *1000 Years of Irish Poetry:* "Over a period of centuries, through clever and bitter propaganda, even the minds of a whole nation can be impressed with a sense of inferiority."[59]

What transpired over this long course of controversy was a differentiation of Irish-American responses to the distorted depictions of the group. Irish theater people, advertisers, editors, promoters, and others who stood to profit from Irish stereotypes found it expedient to propogate them. Another segment of the group, especially in the period of organizational expansion and social striving from 1880 to 1920, fought the depictions in favor of a code of respectability and religious sensibility. Still others among the less educated and less socially self-conscious accepted and enjoyed the stereotypes that to them represented humor, vitality, and raffishness. Thus, it was not unusual for Irish saloons, restaurants, businesses, even Irish-dominated schools, to decorate around St. Patrick's Day with mocking and absurd decor that included leprechauns and dancing colleens. Finally, some Irish-Americans were sufficiently self-assured or unconcerned that they refused to take any of the portrayals seriously and were able to distance themselves from such considerations.

Television ushered in an even more affecting age of media presentation, and as the Northern Ireland troubles erupted beginning in 1969, television presented images of the Irish as violent and uncontrollable radicals and agitators. Such images were a shock to most Irish-Americans, who had been only vaguely aware of the festering Northern Ireland situation. The whole perception of Ireland had been transformed by modern tourist advertising under the policies of the Dublin government. The Irish airline, *Aer Lingus*, and the official tourist agency, *Bord Failte*, had conducted a skillful campaign to present the country as mildly prosperous, progressive, yet rich with storied ruins and exciting scenery. Their campaign had worked: Ireland's image by the 1960s was one of a tourist fairyland for Americans. The tremendous popularity of Irish literature also uplifted the image of the Irish, so that, by the second half of the twentieth century, they were seen to be a gifted if sometimes querulous nation of jolly and hospitable people with charming speech patterns. The tragedy of Northern Ireland changed all that, and the action reports of bombings, vicious killings, and intractable hatreds in Ulster tore a huge hole in the posters showing Ireland the Beautiful.

Nightly, Irish-American families in the early 1970s beheld television interviews and coverage that showed fierce antagonism, horrible civilian casualties, and absurd political wrangling in the Northern Ireland cockpit. The image presented was one not only of furious violence and guerrilla mayhem, but also of religious bigotry, political incompetence, and deprivation and agony in Belfast and Derry. This was the image projected for their children of the land of their forebears. The television presentations largely omitted the role of Britain in producing and sustaining violence and adding to the "no compromise" stance of the dominant faction. Television reportage shredded the carefully cultivated picture of respectability, lofty literary discourse, and cultural coherence that the Dublin government and the Irish-Americans had fostered.

As the television networks exercised their skills in on-the-spot coverage of the Northern Ireland conflict, Irish-Americans were both bemused and irritated by the grim visual recording of the struggle.[60] It diminished their view of themselves as inheritors of an Irish tradition liberated from exploitation and the bitterness of the past. Network presentations contrived fictional treatments of Irish-American gunrunning to the Irish Republican Army, and these provoked at least one delegation to visit a local television station, WCAU-TV, to strongly protest the showing of

Irish-Americans as mindless collaborators in violence. A dispute arose over whether the annual St. Patrick's Day parade would include proponents of militant views about the Northern Ireland problem.

In the early 1970s, newspaper coverage of the events in Northern Ireland was extensive, and feelings ran high. An organization that supported militant activists in Northern Ireland, Irish Northern Aid, sponsored a steady round of picketing, protest, and other efforts to oppose British policy in Ulster and American government silence about human rights violations there. Letters to the editors of the newspapers showed strong opposition to Britain and disgust at the U.S. State Department's defense of British policy of military repression of the Catholic population in Northern Ireland. The views of the militants had gained a broad sympathy among a larger section of the local Irish than had been the case when the first violence erupted in Northern Ireland. Along with the newspaper articles and correspondence came a spate of cartoons that pictured the Irish Republican Army and other Irish as mad bombers, violent predators, and even as rats preparing to blow up civilians. Some of these cartoons were by local newspaper cartoonists, while others were reprinted from syndicates or other newspapers. Editorials that favored British sovereignty over Northern Ireland and acceded to Britain's contention that all the uproar there was merely an internal British problem brought furious protest. At one point, a picketing and protesting crowd of hundreds surrounded the building of the Evening Bulletin, one of the city's major daily papers, to object to that newspaper's editorial position and coverage of Northern Ireland matters.[61] The morbid scenes of hunger-strike deaths, the British army round-ups and internments, and the circumlocutions of Irish and Irish-American politicians all produced a psychology of distress among the city's Irish articulate in defense of the group.

The picketing of the British Overseas Airways offices and similar activities diminished in the late 1970s, but the protests in print about how the American media dealt with the Northern Ireland issue continued. Various Irish organizations and local universities sponsored conferences and symposia, and a continued flow of dissenting letters and op-ed articles contrasted militant views with more moderate sentiments concerning peace and reconciliation. The latter opinions came to form the framework for editorial and general coverage about the problem.[62] Throughout this period, the Irish in Philadelphia had been treated to one more instructive episode of how fragile their image of respectability was. The image of

Ireland and things Irish had been transformed from one of achievement and pleasantness to one of murderous disorder. Of course, the reality was different; most of Ireland was utterly pacific, and the Ulster furies were contained in a small area of the island, but the media coverage made it seem otherwise, much to the chagrin of tourist industry officials. Most Irish-Americans were only marginally related to concerns about Northern Ireland, but for those who did have attachments to the area and who were concerned, the media presentations were searing and the mental reactions very disturbing, for they recalled a protracted history of abuse and detraction that was too long and too acute to be disregarded.

Efforts by the Irish in the city to counter prejudicial imagery of their group persisted also. The Center for Irish Studies, formed in 1983 as a liaison among college and university teachers concerned with Irish studies, took steps to counter stereotypes that same year by adding a photograph exhibit to their lectures and research. The exhibit depicted the history of the Irish in the city through immigrant scenes, work life, educational and religious events, notable figures in the city's Irish-American past, and scenes from contemporary Irish-American activities. The exhibit broke attendance records at the Balch Institute for Ethnic Studies.[63]

Another enterprise launched in 1985 by the same center involved the compilation of a teaching kit titled "Images and Indignation: How Cartoons Shape Our Views." The kit included cartoon reproductions drawn from over a century of stereotyped portrayals about the Irish. Designed for use in schools and colleges, the kit was prepared with a grant from the Pennsylvania Humanities Council. The teaching guidelines and interpretive materials in the kit were translated into a Spanish language version, as well as an Irish language version for use in Irish-speaking schools in Ireland.[64] This project was just one of many that presented a positive picture of the Irish to the general community. Folk music concerts, cultural competitions called *feisanna*, exhibits of Irish art treasures, lectures of the Irish American Cultural Institute, and conferences on Irish subjects were all consciously aimed at asserting a distinguished cultural profile for the group, and these activities related to the broad problem of the tradition of negative depiction that had affected the Irish over the decades.

The long preoccupation of the Irish with their image in the general community demonstrates the persistence of intergroup relations difficulties even for ethnic groups that are considered to have "succeeded" and risen in status in this country. Although the Irish protested for several generations about the mocking imagery, it was too strong to be exorcized and could only be ameliorated over a long period of time. Not only did the general community have a flawed view of the Irish, but many of the Irish themselves shared the view and even collaborated in its propagation in the theater and elsewhere. The enjoyment of satirical and self-mocking presentations when they were humorous undercut the group's ability to oppose such characterizations with unanimity. Moderating influences functioned slowly as rising education and broadening tolerance conditioned interethnic relations, but, even in the period after 1969, the Northern Ireland troubles raised old images again. The problem of establishing a favorable image for ethnic groups is one of the most complex and subtle long-term difficulties in democratic society, and the Irish represent one of the most interesting cases of the perplexities involved with it.

The problem of social image was bound to have both a personal and a social impact on Irish identity. This was an ethnic group that had emerged from a culturally fragmented society, a background that produced an ample quotient of insecurity that emigration did not diminish.[65] In the United States, Irish people, having been removed from their native folk communities in the old country, were judged by the images that the media made of them, not by the context of their traditional culture. Hence, those images were of powerful significance for them. As the group raised its cultural and social aspirations in America, the image of the Irish as a cavalcade of buffoons despite social advancement produced intense frustration. The decline of Irish immigration and of the demographic strength that it represented, as well as the displacement of the Irish from political leadership in urban areas in the second half of the twentieth century, revived a paradigm of their earlier minority status. The eruption of the Northern Ireland problem and its media depictions added to the sensitivity expressed by at least a notable proportion of the group in the city.

The reaction of some of those identifying themselves as Irish was to extoll the value and dignity of their cultural and historical tradition, to assert their achievements as ethnic Americans, and to contradict detractors while protesting unfair portrayals. These responses to the nagging problem affecting their identity thus constituted a latter-day version of earlier anti-defamation activities that had become an inherent feature of American ethnic-group life. But, in a city where the 1980 census reported that over half a million people designated themselves as being of Irish extraction and where the suburbs contained another 200,000 such people, unanimity on such a subject was not possible. While some abandoned all hopes of being designated in any respectable fashion and others enjoyed a cult of Irishry full of clownish contortion, a core of people continued protests. Whatever the reactions of this population, as the twentieth century moved toward its end, Irish-American identity continued to be trailed by an antiquated but still-active legacy of representational deformity, as well as deliberate propaganda emanating from London to abet British rule in Northern Ireland.[66]

2 Association

Show Me Your Friends

The organizational life of the Irish in the United States is one of the keys to their longevity as an element in our pluralist mosaic. Although early nineteenth-century political experience in the campaigns of the oracular Daniel O'Connell contributed somewhat to Irish organizational activities in America, the promotion of group associations on the scale that followed increased immigration in that century could hardly have been imagined by those who considered the Irish a hapless and disorganized people. Michael Funchion, editor of the broad-ranging survey *Irish-American Voluntary Organizations*, has classified the kinds of associations the Irish have formed over the past two centuries in this country.[1] These include immigrant aid societies; fraternal and beneficial associations; organizations of people from various Irish counties; nationalist, cultural, and educational groups; businesses; and political, labor, and religious organizations, some specifically Irish and some simply dominated by the Irish as members or leaders. This organizational tradition, so impressively manifest in American life through several generations, has been shown by Dale Light and David Noel Doyle to have taken on sophisticated forms to accommodate the diversity of Irish-American class dispositions as the group changed its social make-up.[2]

The organizations maintained by the Irish-Americans performed a variety of functions that met class and ethnic needs. Membership in an Irish group enabled the individual to express feelings and kinship that helped to offset the isolation so often induced by immigration into the impersonal settings of urban districts. For the ethnic group at large, associations made possible combinations for mutual self-interest. These associations also served as bridges to the broader society, and, conversely, they served as structures through which the general community could have access to the Irish-American subculture.[3] In more concrete ways, the Irish groups allowed identification with familiar symbols and common goals with strong emotional implications. They made possible forms of mutual assistance and protection not available in the general society and were the vehicles for a social interaction that was marked by pride and shared understandings within a traditional idiom. Furthermore, they served the functions of distributing power within the group, disseminating information, and acting as agencies of social change. In so doing, they encouraged the rational formation of goals and opinion, especially on emotional issues such as Irish nationalism, and thus performed a certain socially-therapeutic role.[4]

In this section, three kinds of organizations illustrate Philadelphia versions of this organizational capacity. The first is a working-class association, informal in its beginnings but later shaped by labor union activity. The daily laboring life of longshoremen was the essential basis of this worker affiliation that spanned a whole century when the Irish dominated the waterfront work of Philadelphia. In a far different world from that of the port workers, the Irish attorneys of the city formalized their long-standing informal ties in the second half of the twentieth century, and their liaison at the professional and political level is of great interest in a time of revived ethnic consciousness.[5] A third kind of association, one that is characteristically American, is that of social reform exemplified by the idealistic life work for urban social justice of Anna McGarry and her associates in the Catholic Interracial Council. Each of these organizations represents a distinctive Irish-American affiliation facing the problems of this ethnic community. They reflect three features of Irish-American life long recognized in the history of the group: in the case of the longshoremen, the struggle to survive in a harsh economic climate; in the case of the attorneys, the animations of ambition and politics; and, in the case of the Interracial Council, a constructive religious idealism.

The relative autonomy of these associations within a pluralist culture is difficult to assess. John Higham notes the "permeability" of organizational life in America that confers a certain ambiguity on it.[6] Strict social science categories simply will not suffice in delineating it. The Irish organizations dealt with in this section have played multiple roles, reflected diverse and often subtle influences, and formed support systems for an ethnic identity and cultural tradition in an urban society characterized by complexity and continual interaction.

Dockers on the Delaware

One of the strongest ways in which a person's sense of belonging can be reinforced is for the daily work group with which he or she is associated to constitute a binding endorsement of the individual's personal and ethnic identity. Most people spend more time interacting with their daily work groups than with their immediate families. Even for those whose work experience is broken and uneven, the work group is powerful in providing a sense of social belonging and a style of behavior that shapes immediate experience. For the Irish longshoremen on the waterfront of Philadelphia, the work group was also an ethnic association. The dock world was their world, and they served it with the strength of their backs. Longshore work was Irish work for over a century, and all of the traditions, mores, and memories that went with it reinforced the Irish affinity fostered by years of mutual labor among men of one's own background.

Ever since the opening of trade routes across the broad Atlantic, Irishmen have labored on the wharves of the major ports on both sides of the ocean. Ireland itself, of course, possessed ancient ports, and, as maritime trade expanded, Irish seamen and port workers went with it to harbors in the farthest reaches of the Atlantic.[7] In the nineteenth century, the great dispersion of the Irish population because of deprivation and British injustice brought thousands of unskilled workers from rural Ireland to the same ports made familiar to seafarers from northern Europe over several generations. Even in the early part of the nineteenth century, the Irish were part of the work force in the leading American ports. The Irish have been a persistent force in the dock world of Philadelphia from the days of sailing ships to the days of container ship cargo technology that has drastically reduced port labor in the twentieth century.

Throughout the port's history, dockworkers in Philadelphia shared with their brothers in other shipping centers the misfortunes of wharfside labor that had been a part of port life since ships first congregated in sheltered estuaries to transfer cargo. Heavy and dangerous labor, irregular employment, exploitation, intimidation, crime, and violence were all part of the port worker's lot long before transatlantic trade routes flourished. In Liverpool, Bristol, and London, the Irish had long been laborers loading England's commerce. As their numbers increased in the 1800s, they clashed with English dockworkers over the right to handle cargo. In some places, the Irish were the diggers who expanded the ports, excavated canals, and cleared channels.[8]

In planning Philadelphia, William Penn had specifically charged his Quaker confreres to find a site where, "it is most navigable, high, dry and healthy; where most ships may ride of deepest draught of water and load and unload without lighterage."[9] These instructions given in 1681 emphasize the belief of the colonists that no settlement could survive or grow without an adequate port.

Thus, from the foundation of Philadelphia, an active port had been the chief asset of the city on the Delaware. From the beginning of the city also, the Irish had been represented in the population of the port area. In 1767, the *Pennsylvania Gazette* was advertising that Garrett and George Meade were importing choice Lisbon wines. The Meades were an Irish family with ties to Spain and the Caribbean. Magdalene Devine imported cloths, and John Shea was a busy merchant at the same time. In 1785, the *Pennsylvania Evening Herald* advertised wares imported from London, Liverpool, and Amsterdam by J. Gallagher of Second Street opposite the Friends Meeting House, and James Byrne, jeweler and silversmith, offered imported items also. In any given year in the 1700s, there were numerous such notices giving evidence of the activity of Irish people in trade and port connections.[10]

The presence of Irish sailors in the port was part of the early Irish association with shipping in Philadelphia. At least 116 Irish-owned vessels were registered at Philadelphia between 1734 and 1776. David Noel Doyle records that ships' masters in Philadelphia sought Irish seamen and servants. The crews of Philadelphia ships were drawn not only directly from Ireland, but also from the Irish in the city and from the Irish who had been sent to the West Indies.[11] Sea captains like Irish-born John Barry were able to readily gather Irishmen into their crews during the Revolutionary war. In Philadelphia, some sailors would stay ashore and drift into dockside labor. Immigrants were a continual addition to port labor since, after arriving penniless on Philadelphia's shore, they would be drawn to whatever unskilled waterfront work they could find. There is no reason to believe that what Earl Niehaus has noted of New Orleans was not also true of Philadelphia: "wharves were a principal place of employment for the 'lower order of Irish peasantry'."[12]

In 1810, a delighted Moravian maid visited Philadelphia and was awed by the busy port. She wrote, "O beautiful Delaware! and the multitude of ships lining the wharves up and down as far as we could see! some of them so large that their bowspirits projecting at an angle over the streets extended nearly to the upper windows of the opposite warehouses."[13] What was true in 1810 continued to be true for generations. The ship traffic into Philadelphia was great, and the tonnage of cargo handled grew steadily. So did the influx of Irish immigrants. By the 1830s, they were the chief ethnic group filling unskilled occupations in the city. In 1836, Philadelphia longshoremen joined in a strike that tied up all the Atlantic coastal ports, the first recorded strike in what was to be a long history of labor conflict. The turbulence on the waterfront became endemic. In 1850 and 1851, the dock men in Port Richmond carried out a strike after being represented in negotiations with employers by what historian Bruce Laurie terms a "gang." This instance is notable because it throws light on a fact of work life with broad significance in the nineteenth century. Informal work groups were the vehicles for resolving many labor questions in the absence of formal labor unions.

Four out of ten Irish workers in the city in 1840 were hod carriers, laborers, draymen, and stevedores. The informal social bonds of men like the dock workers were the chief form of their labor cooperation and protection, and these bonds were steeped in ethnic affinity. Laurie states that for the Irish unskilled workers, "cohesion and segregation typified their religious and social life."[14] Further, "the commonality of their experience and the political context that greeted them in Philadelphia enforced both group cohesion and a strong sense of ethnicity."[15] Laurie concludes that Irish gangs, cliques, and work groups served as "surrogate unions" to protect workers both from displacement by other casual labor groups, notably blacks, and from abuse by employers.[16] As David Brody remarks, "Ethnic identity was a shaping force for labor solidarity." Indeed, one of the distinctive features of American labor at this time was that worker identity was defined more in racial and ethnic terms than in terms of class. Alan Dawley found that there was in the nineteenth century "an orientation away from class consciousness and toward a view of labor as one interest group in a pluralist society."[17]

Through the 1840s, the conditions in Ireland continued to bring a steady tide of Irish to the port. The year 1850 is, therefore, a good year in which to examine their presence on the docks of the city. An investigation of the manuscript forms of the census of 1850 shows only seventy-four stevedores for the whole city, of whom about one-fourth have recognizably Irish names.[18] Port labor, however, was largely casual labor, and the formation of work gangs to unload and load vessels followed an informal pattern that would persist for well over a century. A man need not be designated at stevedore to work on the docks, and the census identifications are clearly marginal in relation to the huge work force required to keep a port the size of Philadelphia functioning.

A wide variety of occupations connected to the port are listed in the 1850 census for the riverfront First and Fifth wards in Southwark in South Philadelphia, and some examples will indicate the diversity of activity in which the Irish were involved along the docks. The occupations of waterman, wharf builder, rigger, mast maker, sailmaker, and painter all appear beside Irish names, as do sailor, caulker, ship carpenter, and "mariner." Waterman is one of the most common occupations listed. These were boatmen who plied the river transferring all kinds of cargo and equipment in small boats. Before the days of heavy cranes to manage cargo there was a great deal of off-loading into small boats to land lighter commodities. Onshore, the draymen and carters—occupations in which the Irish were the most common workers listed in the census schedules—were engaged in hectic hauling to warehouses, mills, and outlying locations. In the First Ward, men born in Ireland, with names like Patrick McCardy, Michael McNamee, and James Kelly, were listed as carters, and most were in their twenties. John McDevitt, however, was a skilled craftsman who, as a coppersmith, would have had much work related to ship fittings. The more skilled trades such as ship carpentry were not frequently practiced by Irishmen. The names for those in such trades indicate that the men doing shipbuilding and skilled maintenance were more often of Scandinavian background, and, according to the census, these workers were often from Newfoundland, Yankee shipwrights from Maine, and men from the Jersey coast or the Chesapeake.

The extent to which the port formed its own occupational world is indicated by the concentration of port workers and tradesmen in the streets of the waterfront. In the Second Ward in 1850, for example, on the 400 block of South Front Street, there were a shipbuilder, a mariner, a rigger, a ship carpenter, and a sea captain in residence. Swanson Street in the First Ward was the home ashore for sailors like Henry Ryan and George Magee. At 229 South Third Street, a boarding house had as residents Michael McGinnis, his brother Patrick, and a collection of other Irish stevedores. Again, much of the labor in the port was casual labor and, as such, was composed of the kind of people most likely to remain un-

listed in any census or directory or merely listed as "laborer."
Still, by 1860, the number of Irish listed among stevedores rose to
37 percent.

From the 1880 census, it is evident that the concentration of
port workers was still in the streets within a few blocks of the
river. In this riverside area, tiny row houses on narrow streets,
blind alley courts, ramshackle wooden warrens serving as boarding houses, gin mills, warehouses, factories, and supply lofts were
crammed together along the Delaware. Riggers, sailors, and stevedores lived on Reed Street near Front beside 35-year-old Michael
Haggerty; his wife, Maggie; and his two daughters, Kate and Ellen.
Old stevedores like Irish-born David Dedam from Swanson Street
may no longer have been able to work and may have had to scrab-
ble for odd jobs. At 945 South Front Street, William Grace and his
brother, John, both born in Ireland, lived with William's wife, Margaret, and his six children. Supporting a wife and six children as a
stevedore in 1880 cannot have been an easy task, but large families
were common among the stevedores who were married. Although
stevedores like James McGinley of 112 Carpenter Street had seven
children, it appears from the 1880 census that most men in this
occupation were not married. Single male immigrants were the
most available labor supply for this kind of work at this time. The
places where the young workers lived were often simply "flop
houses." Even in the twentieth century, old-timers remembered one
place where one's rent paid for a dormitory cot and hot soup, and
the tough old Irish woman who ran the place would cheat without
mercy. When the lads came home drunk or exhausted and fell
asleep before getting their soup, they would wake up and ask for it.
The landlady, who would rub fat on their faces while they were
asleep; would reply, "Sure, wipe your face. Ye had your soup when
you first came in, and that's the proof of it."

The port of Philadelphia was supervised by the municipal government from its inception. In 1803, the Pennsylvania General Assembly established a Board of Wardens appointed by the governor
to regulate licensing of pilots and wharfage rates. Gradually, this
board came to oversee new pier construction and such matters as
fining those violating port rules. In 1854, control of the wardens
was transferred to the Philadelphia City Council. In 1859, the city's
Department of Wharves, Landings and Markets let contracts and
hired workers to keep channels open and add wharves. The Civil
War and the industrial growth of the city brought continual port
expansion, and, in 1874 alone, eleven wharf extensions and twenty

dredgings were undertaken by the port wardens. In addition to the thirty-two apprentices paid by the wardens, gangs of laborers were involved in this work, and most of these would have been Irish diggers and haulers working in the mud of the river, for the concentration of Irish directly adjacent to the South Philadelphia docks increased between 1850 and 1880. Such laborers earned an average weekly wage of $7.30 in 1880 when they worked, but, because of weather conditions and other irregularities, such laborers could be unemployed for weeks at a time.[19]

One of the persistent features of work around the docks was the high rate of accidents. Longshore work is dangerous even under modern, more controlled conditions, but, in the 1880s, few elements of ships or docks were standardized, knowledge of cargo weights and stresses was limited, and cranes and unloading gear were primitive. The workers were often unskilled and not well-acquainted with their tasks, so the probability of injuries was increased. The admissions book of the Pennsylvania Hospital in 1880 lists Irish-born workers in dockside occupations who were hurt and treated at the hospital. Stevedores, laborers, and seamen treated at the hospital were usually part of the port's work force, and fractures were the leading cause of treatment among them. Fractures of the fibula were the most common misfortune, and contusions of all kinds were the second most frequent injury. Knee breaks, wounds, fractured skulls, burns, and heat exhaustion are all listed among the reasons for admission of the seventy-one Irishmen in the 1880 sample drawn from a total of 1,509 patients, of whom about 400 were Irish-born.[20] It was, of course, normal in 1880 for many injuries to be treated at home or by local physicians outside of hospitals; thus, one hospital sample certainly does not reflect all of the physical problems inflicted by in-port work, but it does indicate the kinds of injuries incurred by the heavy labor required in longshore work.

In the early twentieth century, more and more machinery was introduced in loading operations on the docks. Sailing vessels became a rarity, and cargoes became even more diverse. Philadelphia's port included wharves that were specialized for handling coal, lumber, grain, produce, steel, and sugar. The Port Richmond piers handled huge tonnages of coal brought for shipment from upstate Pennsylvania by the railroads. The wharves of the Schuylkill River on the western edge of South Philadelphia had declined as ships got larger and canal shipments down the river diminished. Nevertheless, there had been large Irish work forces on the Schuylkill docks for seventy years before that river ceased to handle a heavy volume of general cargo.[21]

Although the Irish dominated the dockside work force, they shared its burden of labor with others as the nineteenth century drew to a close. Blacks were also clustered in the courts and alley-like streets close to the wharves, and they increased their presence on the docks as the twentieth century opened, often doing the worst work that the more experienced Irish would try to avoid. In the 1890s, Edward McHugh, who had trade union experience in England, successfully organized a portion of the local longshoremen, and his union probably included some blacks. By 1910, there were, according to one source, 3,063 dockworkers in Philadelphia, 1,369 of whom were black, although these figures seem low for such a large port as Philadelphia. At that time, the foremen for the dock gangs were practically all Irish. Peter Curtin was foreman for Murphy, Cook and Company, the largest of the port stevedore firms. John J. Walsh was the leader of the radical Industrial Workers of the World on the wharves, struggling to organize the exploited dockers against powerful opposition by the shippers.[22]

In a remarkable series of oral history interviews carried out for the Philadelphia Maritime Museum, a ninety-year-old black man who had spent two generations working on the waterfront recalled how he became the first black work gang leader on the docks:

> One day Macnamara and Mr. Dugan came on the ship where I was working . . . Yes, sir, gents, what is it? . . . "We're gonna make a gang boss out of you, so how long do you think it would take you to get a good gang together?" I said, "About ten minutes!" "You mean you could go out there, you could hire a gang of men, and they'd be sufficient to get producen [sic], stow cargo correct and all that?" I said, "Why certainly . . . I'd be a dumb man to start with to walk down, hire men that wasn't goin' to do your work. . . . That be a lost cat right there."[23]

Implied in this colloquy is the assumption of superiority on the part of the two Irishmen, and their lack of confidence in their black acquaintance. It was common practice for employers to play blacks against whites to prevent any unity that would lead to labor organization. Intimidation and fighting of all kinds were native to the waterfront, and conflicts between blacks and whites, between one company's workers and another's, and even between one gang leader's men and another's were all part of the violence on the wharves. Established dock gangs fought those composed of recently arrived "greenhorns." Irishmen from County Mayo fought with those from Donegal, very often in competition for desperately needed work. It was all part of a very physical world. Men worked strenuously with their hardened bodies, and brawls and rough-and-tumble punch-outs were not thought to be unusual and were often regarded as nothing more than playful encounters. These were hard men who had a strength that later generations can only regard with awe. Philadelphia contractor John Donovan recalled that, in his boyhood at the beginning of this century, many of the fights could turn vicious, with boat hooks and cudgels used to inflict serious injuries.[24]

The period prior to World War I was one of rapid expansion and change for Philadelphia's port. The opening of the Panama Canal, the increased capacity of ships, improvements in port machinery, and expansion of the U.S. Navy Yard all meant growth in activity. In 1913, a huge new drydock at the navy yard was begun. The Pennsylvania Assembly, at the urging of Senator James Mc-Nichol of Philadelphia, raised the city's debt limit to finance port improvements. Philadelphia Congressman Michael Donohoe from Port Richmond pressed in Washington for an even bigger U.S. Navy shipyard.[25] A deeper channel upriver to Trenton was opened. In one week in 1913, some 4,500 immigrants arrived from Italy. For the same year, the total of immigrants landed at Philadelphia broke records by exceeding 26,000. The secretary of the city's chamber of commerce, Napoleon Bonaparte Kelly, effused that eleven steamers were being loaded at once for Europe. In May of 1913, the port shipped two-hundred thousand tons of sugar and 3 million bushels of grain. Nitrates, wool, tobacco, and wood pulp were among the port's $90 million in exports.[26]

This prosperity for the port was shared by the port workers only in that they were less subject to unemployment. More cargo meant more back-wrenching labor in dangerous conditions for wages as low as the shippers and port companies could make them. Congressman Donohoe had campaigned for more municipal control of the port, which he claimed was "in the grip of private business."[27] John J. Walsh and the black stevedore Ben Fletcher battled to organize the longshoremen through the Industrial Workers of the World. Their Marine Transport Workers Union led a strike to obtain bargaining recognition in May 1913, and their strike succeeded. That was just one of the organizing wars of waterfront labor that were to last for decades.[28]

One of the I.W.W. organizers said of the violence that accompanied the unionization efforts: "You must bear in mind that there was nothing but the mounted police along the waterfront with their clubs and guns, and it was murder to organize whites let alone Negroes."[29] John Sloan's drawing *The Pennsylvania State Police in Philadelphia*, which portrays the mounted police clubbing strikers, dates from this period. In a city whose politics were thoroughly dominated by conservative Republican business interests in concert with notoriously corrupt machine bosses, the treatment of strikers was never gentle, and, on the waterfront, it was brutal. During the general strike of 1910, in which the port workers joined, wage loss, arrests, and blacklisting took a heavy toll. When World War I began, the nation's dependence on shipping to aid the Allies and later the American Expeditionary Force in France gave the longshoremen increased power. The I.W.W. radicals saw the war as an imperialistic folly. Their leaders and the long-suffering stevedores led a general strike of all port workers in 1918. Under wartime powers, the federal government imprisoned John J. Walsh, Ben Fletcher, and other I.W.W. leaders. Many believed they were deliberately railroaded into prison after shippers pressured the government. Six years later, Walsh was still in prison after others had been released[30].

Of course, the full vulnerability of the dock workers' situation cannot be grasped unless the total environment is taken into account. These were men with very limited or no schooling. Their work life was constantly disrupted, and, even when employment was available, it ranged across a bewildering variety of piers and cargo-handling tasks. The piers were generally filthy and thronged with rats. In 1914, typhoid fever spread through the river wards because of a lack of sewers. Intermittently, "wars" were declared on the rats, with bounties of five cents for a live rat and two cents for a dead one. The housing conditions of the longshoremen were at the slum level or worse.[31] Occasionally, through pilferage or some lucky overtime, some extra benefits would be secured, and a family party or work mates celebration would be held. Still, the heavy work, the dangers of being crippled or maimed, the inclement weather, the fighting, and the improbability of a better future for most was hard to face even for toughened men. The pattern of short-term rewards and immediate goals and satisfactions prevailed.

To cope with such conditions, the longshoremen developed strong mutual ties to their workmates once they were able to become part of a circle of fellow dockers. These ties were frequently organized around family relationships, since, among the big Irish families, brothers, cousins, and in-laws would look out for one another in finding work, taking one another's parts in disputes, and lending money when times were bad or when injury or illness prevented a man from working. When men work in dangerous conditions, they choose their co-workers carefully, since their lives often depend on one another. The reliability and morale of the work group was critical in many situations. Sometimes ties were related to friendships that grew up in the small streets where the dockers lived. As Irish Catholics, the workers attended local parishes, and these were another medium for contacts and relationships. The special terms and parlance of the docks and the ill-treatment by the shipping companies and the police reinforced their informal solidarity. Consciousness of their Irishness was a binding influence as well; they had common roots and a folk inheritance and spirit deriving from their Irish identity. Their families had survived in Ireland against grinding adversity and had survived immigration and poverty in America, and there was usually a confidence that they would survive the dock world they inhabited.

A work career that could represent many of the Irish dockers of Philadelphia is that of Patrick Nolan. Born in 1901 in Butte, Montana, of parents from County Mayo, Nolan landed his first job in the copper mines loading ore cars. In 1926, he left Butte and worked in Chicago as a laborer, saving enough money to go to Ireland. He married a Mayo girl and brought her to Philadelphia after working as a laborer on construction of the Empire State Building in New York. In Philadelphia, he worked for the Publicker Brewery on their grain unloading dock. In 1933, he went to work for Murphy, Cook and Company, the port's largest stevedoring company. Each day he would go to the "shape up" at Pier 40, and, if lucky, become part of a gang of about twenty men to load general cargo, wood pulp, steel, grain, or sugar. He recalled steel as being the most dangerous cargo to load, but grain dust was also perilous because inhalation of it in poorly ventilated holds could cause unconsciousness, and, because of its combustible nature, it could cause terrible explosions in the holds of ships. In 1934, Patrick Nolan joined the International Longshoremen's Association to seek better work conditions. World War II opened opportunities to work at the New York Shipyard in Camden, New Jersey, and at the Midvale Steel plant, but in 1945 he returned to the docks at the Franklin Sugar Company. His labor of almost half a century on the Philadelphia docks ended when he retired to his tiny house on Watkins Street near the waterfront.[32]

Some of the Irish were employers of stevedores themselves. George Kelly, after working as a bargeman, came to own his own pier on the Camden side of the Delaware in 1868, and he worked crews of marine mechanics and longshoremen until selling his interests to Murphy, Cook, and Company after World War II. Kelly and his family were waterfront leaders for four generations. Their "hiring corner" at Front and Catherine Streets was well-known. Dan and Pete Meehan held the street corner at Second and McKean Streets for their "shape ups" and favored men from Donegal, while County Tyrone and County Derry men were hired more readily at Front and Moore Streets by compatriots active there. Saloons were often the focus of hiring agreements and deals for labor. The I.L.A. saloon at Snyder Avenue and Water Street was operated by "Skinny" Dougherty, who, if a patron entered in a business suit, would have him pushed back from the bar while a chorus of voices, led by Dougherty, would shout, "Workingmen first!" Jack Gallagher's saloon at Front and Mifflin Streets, Pat Garrity's at Front and Reed Streets, and Tyrone-born Jer Stuart's at Water and Porter Streets were all longshoremen's haunts. Charlie Kelly, called "The Divil" and wharf boss for the German-American Line; George Kelly, "The Harp"; and William Kelly, "The Chief," could all be met and negotiated with for jobs, and their word was ever their bond.[33]

The competitive world of the docks made longshoremen steadily conscious of the danger and ugly nature of much of their work. A stevedore named Robert Callen recalled:

Very few people are aware of how strenuous the work is that the longshoremen do. Most of the work was put on trays in the hold of the ship. The hold of a ship consists of a hole approximately sixty foot in depth. That's a sixty foot climb down the ladder and it was straight up. You had to be physically able to do that. And once you got down in the hole you had to be physically able to do the work. And the work was not mechanized like it is today. It was brute labor. It was hard, it was dirty, and it was the only way you could support your family and the only way you could make a living.

The only ones able to do the work were the ones physically in good shape. Many of the cargoes we handled were dirty and obnoxious. We often come up with the story that when you worked wet cowhides you never had any trouble getting a seat on the trolley going home. Many of the people who handled these hides had to be worried about anthrax and developing diseases associated with the hides. You always had plenty of flies around to keep you company with the hides. And then you had other obnoxious cargoes like ores, spiegel iron, lead residue, chrome ore, magnasite.

John Quinn described the usual work gang procedure:

> Longshoremen work in gangs. When you got hired you found out whose gang you would be working in, what ship you would be on and where she was docked. A lot of the companies had trucks they would drive the men to the pier in. When men got to the pier they found out which hatch in the ship they were working. The gang is made up of the holdmen, who work down in the ship's hatch; wharf-men, who work out on the pier; and the deckmen and winch runner who together operate the machinery for lifting the cargo in and out of the hatch.

In this kind of work arrangement, the holdmen, though termed "unskilled," had to have a keen knowledge of just how to compose cargo loads. Both the immediate safety of the cargo handlers and the ultimate stability of the ship depended on correct loading. A longshoreman named McGinniss recounted, "The hatch foreman hired you 'cause you knew how to do it. . . . He didn't have to holler at you how to do it . . . . He'd say you're gonna use slings on them bales and not hooks. . . . The men down in the hole did the thinkin'."

John Quinn remembered that "most of the gangs had some hard-core operators down there that kept things rolling. They would find out what was next. If the foremen wasn't up there, they would yell up to the hatch tender, 'We can only use two or three more drafts. You better find out what else you got up there.'"

The dangers of the work were increased when shipping companies tried to reduce the "turn around time"—the time it took to unload and then load a ship and get it to sea again. Often future employment depended on who won the races in moving cargo. Joseph Brennan recalled:

> Each gang tried to outproduce the other gang . . . If we done a little better than you, we was in for the next ship. And then we start fighting. In them days we used to put maybe ten, twelve thousand feet of lumber an hour out. And then the first thing you know it was fifteen thousand, and then it was eighteen thousand and then it was twenty thousand. And they would offer each gang maybe five or ten dollars, a little bonus, if you done a little better the next time . . . They was cutting one another's throat all the time.

Under such conditions it is not surprising that accidents were common. Joseph Brennan remembered: "I've seen some, you know, cases where people get killed. Their parents, wives, never got a dime. They just bluffed them out. [Employers] had a habit if you got hurt, if you broke your back, or your leg, they'd get you a water-boy's job. It wasn't no work. You just put a bucket out during the day . . . till finally they would dump you altogether."

If the work was dangerous, it was still preferable to no work at all. John Quinn stated: "Years ago, it was tough getting work . . . Every workday as many as five thousand men would come down here to the docks along Delaware Avenue hoping to be put to work loading or unloading a ship. Men were down here in the morning before the sun came up, at lunch, after supper, and even in the middle of the night."

Robert Callen recalled, "My father was a longshoreman. He'd have a ship. Sometimes a month, three weeks would go by before he got another." Joseph Brennan said that work shifts could last forty-eight hours, "and you had to stick with it, because the man would ask you 'if you're tired, go home!' and you wouldn't get the next boat."

E.J. Hobsbawm has commented that working conditions on the docks in England remained primitive right into the twentieth century, and the same is true for Philadelphia, as these interviews testify. Hobsbawm's analysis of dock work in other respects applies as well to the Philadelphia port workers' response to rationalization of their work—the setting up of criteria that would exclude old workmates, relatives, and those within the ethnic network of affiliation. The dockers opposed it. Their ethnic work ties were not only a defense against exploitation; they were a protection of working men's social bonds.[34]

One of the few men who consistently tried to alleviate the harsh employment conditions on the docks was Father Dennis J. Comey, a Jesuit priest who conducted a labor school in Philadelphia beginning in 1943. As a "waterfront priest," he served as mediator in dozens of disputes over the years and served on panels of the American Arbitration Association dealing with port problems. He was first involved with a dispute concerning the hiring of longshoremen to handle explosives at double regular wage rates. Because of bad weather on the river, the work could not be completed, so the shipper sought to pay only at regular wage rates. Father Comey also had to deal with conflicts concerning different interpretations of work rules, such as just when a ship hold where chemicals were being handled was ventilated adequately. Through the 1950s, he worked to curtail shakedowns and payoffs related to hiring and cargo moving. A man like Dennis Comey would persevere to bring about decent conditions on the docks, but the greatest changes came as a result of new technology.[35]

John Quinn saw World War II as a turning point: "Many men from the waterfront neighborhoods went off to war. Suddenly, there was a shortage of longshoremen who were knowledgeable enough to do the war effort work safely. Because of the extreme importance of the port to the war effort, the International Longshoremen's Association signed a contract with the shipping companies promising not to strike. But once the war was over, the men returned to their jobs with a new determination that they would be treated fairly." Gradually, through a rank-and-file effort, gains were made in safety provisions, pension, and vacation provisions, an orderly hiring procedure to replace the "shape up," and stronger bargaining rights for the union.

As the work conditions on the waterfront at last improved, however, the entire nature of port cargo handling was being changed by technology. After World War II, the forklift truck that lifted cargo stacked on pallets came into use. Cargo was increasingly packaged in larger units to permit forklift handling, units larger than a man could lift. Steel containers grew in size, and huge new cranes and finally rail cars and ships themselves were designed to utilize containerized cargo that came in forty-ton units. Such a unit replaced a twenty-man longshore gang that would work four hours to unload such a tonnage of general cargo. The displacement of workers proceeded swiftly.

In the 1960s, the union sought a guaranteed annual income in the face of rapid displacement of longshoremen by mechanized cargo handling systems and eventually won such an income plan. But the Philadelphia port was declining at a fast pace. Big local industries that shipped finished goods were failing after 1970 because of foreign competition and changing technology. Baldwin Locomotive Works, Midvale Steel Company, and dozens of other major manufacturers shut down or migrated elsewhere. Shifts of industry to the "Sun Belt" drastically curtailed the Delaware port activity.

There were still Irish workers on the docks, but they usually rode forklift trucks or operated cranes rather than manhandling cargo. They still knew who they were. In 1981, when hunger-strikers were dying in British prisons in Northern Ireland, Irish-American labor leaders threatened to boycott the handling of British goods in Philadelphia.[36] The trend in the port, however, was clear: employment was declining rapidly.

Families that had worked in the port for five generations were now forced to seek employment elsewhere. A whole work tradition faded from the waterfront and with it the Irish longshore group that had dominated the docks throughout most of their history. As the dock worker's world changed, its history would grimly remind many to ponder the question, "What forces are there in society that compel workers to earn a livelihood amid such persistently inhumane and cruel conditions over more than a century and a half of port labor?"

The record of Irish labor on the waterfront represents a period of bitter struggles. Often divided among themselves over which men could get which kinds of work or any work, Irishman competed with Irishman in crude battles of job competition. Employers and gang bosses set one faction against another to divide the work force. To this amorphous and buffeted array of hard-pressed men, labor organizers brought messages of mutual interest and solidarity, but they brought messages of mutual interest and solidarity, but they brought them into a dock world of confusion, illiteracy, and desperate self-interests. It was a setting overborne by employer antagonism. The injunctions of priests to workmen were most often to serve and suffer as God's children in a sinful world. The injunctions of judges were that combinations of workers were nefarious conspiracies against society. Practically the only social ties these workers had other than through the distresses of their common predicament were some vague affinities of the social abstraction called class and the even more elemental bonds of ethnic identity.

Thus it was that through work groups such as that of the longshoremen, the Irish-American working-class tradition was sustained. The kinship born of toil enhanced that deriving from a common ethnic heritage. What was true of the longshoremen was true for laborers, hod carriers, brickmakers and bricklayers, iron workers, and railroad men. There is some validity, therefore, in the reply of the big man in County Roscommon, who, when asked if he was curious to visit America, said, "Ah, not at all. Me whole family was out there, and it was them that built it and kept it running for years, and it took the skin of them doin' it."

Loquacious in the Law

In contrast to the physical labor of the docks, the intellectual work of the courts formed a different dimension of Irish association in the city. Attorneys mentally weighed issues of legal import, while the dockers weighed cargo burdens with their backs. Dockmen made their own law, the law of work. Attorneys served the courts in the work of law. The dockmen struggled at the bottom of the working class, while the attorneys joined the middle class.

For the Irish living under Anglo domination in early modern times, and again as a minority within American society, the process of adjustment to Anglo-Saxon law has not been without its strains. Two things were required to permit the Irish to gain confidence in the law of the Anglo master: a change of culture and a class of advocates who could deal with and interpret that legal tradition for them. Development of the law itself in a complex American society required a movement of modernization. In this adaptation, the lawyers, and especially the Irish community's own lawyers, played an indispensable part as guides, models, and leaders. They led the Irish through the maddening mazes of immigration law, property law, criminal law, and labor law that institutions of the new world of America spun forth in endless webs of enactment and regulation.

Always in an ambiguous role, the lawyers were both the agents of the larger society and the protagonists of the changing Irish subculture. In the nineteenth century, they were frequently the defenders of the Irish underclass in the criminal entanglements of many from the minority group. They were also contenders for the freedom of religion and education of the group in hundreds of court cases involving freedom of assembly, the acquisition of property for religious uses, the custody of orphans, and the institutional rights of schools and religious orders. As the Irish achieved affluence, the lawyers represented those who became propertied and powerful in their own right. In Philadelphia, renowned as a forum for legal jousting, the Irish became a notable element in the ranks of bench and bar, entering into the Philadelphia legal tradition with energy, drawing on their own Irish backgrounds for resources of ingenuity and rhetoric to create careers of distinction. Thus, within the collegial circles of the bar, the Irish established their own set of connections, lore, and contentious dignity.

Even in the early days of the republic there were some Irish in the law in Philadelphia. Jasper Moylan, half-brother of one of Washington's generals, Stephen Moylan, was in practice in 1782.

The Moylans were a Catholic family, but Irish Protestants such as John Shee were attorneys also. In the 1790s, David McGehen, James Kelly, Daniel Delaney, David Moore, Edward Drury, and Mathew Henry were all handling cases. One of the first members of the Bar Association when it was established as the "Law Association" in 1802 was Francis McShane, and lawyers of Irish background were a continuous part of its membership all through its early decades.[37] An estimate of their representation in the membership reveals that they made up less than 5 percent of the total number of Philadelphia attorneys for many decades. For those entering practice after 1840, new opportunities for notable careers were opening. Heavy immigration, expanding industry, and greater elaboration of American law increased the need for and the status of lawyers.

Dennis W. O'Brien, born in Reading, Pennsylvania, in 1818, went on to attend Harvard University and to be admitted to the Philadelphia Bar in 1853. He became an assistant district attorney and was a judge of the orphans court in the 1870s in the city. Lewis Cassidy was very successful in civic and political life. Charles O'Neill entered the profession in 1843 and later was a congressman for many terms. John Barry Colohan, born in County Galway, admitted to the bar in 1843, was an engineer and very active in railroad development. James Campbell joined the bar in 1833 and became successively a court of Common Pleas judge, attorney general of Pennsylvania and the first Irish Catholic to sit in the cabinet of the United States when he became postmaster general in 1853.[38] These careers provide a record of success at a time when the Irish in the city were a group largely regarded as unacceptable in the upper reaches of Philadelphia society, and behind their rise doubtless lies many a tale of shrewd calculation and devious application.

Daniel Dougherty was more successful than most attorneys of his generation. Born in 1826, he was admitted to practice in 1849. Although a Democrat, he supported Lincoln, helped found the Union League to support the Union cause, and became renowned for a clarion address in support of the Union at the outbreak of the Civil War. thereafter he was extremely popular as an orator. Dougherty was at one time a member of the committee that admitted new members to the bar after examination of their knowledge of the law. It was the custom then to require rote answers to a great store of chronological and historical questions. The procedure was, apparently, tendentious and even whimsical. Dougherty opposed this procedure and argued for a more rational examination based upon the actual needs of legal practice. His was one of the first voices raised in behalf of reform of the old method of legal education that was becoming increasingly outmoded in the 1870s. He continued his practice until 1892, a much-admired figure in the Irish community.[39]

In the second half of the nineteenth century, the careers of Irish advocates were attuned to the needs of the large Irish population and to the industrial Philadelphia that was expanding on every side. Thus, William H. O'Brien became a fixture in the Irish community because of his handling of tangled affairs relating to estates in Ireland. Michael J. Ryan became a public official on the strength of faithful Irish voting power, and Dennis F. Murphy worked his way up through the courts as an intermediary for Irish litigants and constituents. William F. Harrity, the son of Donegal parents, was both an active political figure in the Democratic party and an attorney for a wide array of financial and business institutions in the city. Anti-Irish prejudice was extensive in the 1890s, when Theodore Roosevelt could refer to his Irish political foes as "sodden, vicious, disgusting;" and, in Philadelphia, lawyers had to make their way against such bias.[40]

In the twentieth century, the Irish began attending law school in larger numbers, and, by the 1920s, they were taking an ever broader part in the city's legal affairs. The peculiar local pattern of Irish-Catholic participation in the Republican politics of the city, so different from the heavily Democratic Irish orientation elsewhere, enabled some to obtain comfortable practices and connections with Republican political sanction. Cornelius Haggerty was a member of the Board of Revision of Taxes; Thaddeus Daly was on the Civil Service Commission; John P. Connelly, a trial lawyer, was city solicitor; Judge Harry McDevitt was a power in politics for decades. If the Irish had been excluded from such posts for much of the nineteenth century, they made up for it in the twentieth.[41]

Other lawyers achieved notability because of their mastery of increasingly complex areas of the law. Bernard O'Connell was an expert in negligence law, and Robert H. Boyle was an expert on wills. Still others fought and fought hard for social betterment through the law. W.F. Brennan worked for years to obtain and then have enforced pioneer child labor laws. Thomas Cogan was the city's first "public defender," assuring representation to those too poor to be able to pay for it. Michael Francis Doyle was distinguished by his encyclopedic knowledge of international law.

Doyle was symbolic of the emergence of the Irish as a major element in the city's legal fraternity. He was one of five children in a family that was comfortable if not affluent. He received his law degree from the University of Pennsylvania in 1897. His preceptor was William F. Harrity, a man with wide affiliations in politics and business. Doyle won local renown in a case that forced the U.S. War Department to continue a practice of allotting army clothing contracts to widows and daughters of soldiers after the government tried to alter this old practice. The clever young lawyer coming to the aid of widows and orphans was a good public image, especially when the lawyer and many of the widows and orphans were Irish.

Doyle's work as a specialist in international law grew as his keen mind absorbed more and more knowledge of this field. His income grew as well. He was able to purchase the former home of John Wanamaker at 1503 Rittenhouse Square, the elite area of residence in the city. His intensive cultivation of Catholic religious activities also aided his business by providing contacts and access to clients. As a strong supporter of the Democrats and of Al Smith and Franklin Roosevelt, Doyle repeatedly sought federal honors and preferment when Roosevelt became president. He was part of the Irish generation that moved from Republican to Democratic affiliation during the New Deal upsurge in the politics of the city. At length, in 1936, he was appointed by Roosevelt to the World court at the Hague. Until the end of his life in 1960, Doyle remained the very image of the successful and intently Irish-Catholic Philadelphia lawyer.[42]

When men such as Doyle were active in the legal profession of the 1920s, the profession was still dominated by the codes and privileges of Philadelphia's Anglo upper class. Nathaniel Burt, chronicler of the "perennial Philadelphians," details the extent to which the law was the traditional preserve of the upper-class families of the city. But, despite exclusionary practices among the major law firms, a number of Irish moved up in the legal-political realm, including Vincent McDevitt, Thomas McBride, John Patrick Walsh, John Boyle, Francis J. Myers, James Lafferty, and others who held various public offices or had notable careers. Thomas McCabe was one of the few who, after experience as general counsel to the Pennsylvania Supreme Court, became a champion of civil liberties.[43]

In the 1920s, Jews and Catholics, among others, were simply not welcome in the stately, oak-paneled offices of the prestigious leading law firms. There was a revival of anti-Irish and anti-Catholic sentiment at the time, first because of the Irish drive for an independent Ireland, challenging the England that Anglo-Americans revered, and later because of the candidacy of Catholic Al Smith for president.[44] The new competition of more Irish lawyers also prompted resentment. The prominence of such figures as James McGranery, who later became attorney general of the United States under Franklin Roosevelt, heralded the full emergence of the Irish members of the bar. Although some Irish began to make their way into the lofty reaches of tradition-bound dominant firms, the more expedient course became the formation of predominantly Irish firms. After World War II, prejudices waned and all kinds of random influences eroded most of the segregation of the profession, but there remained clearly identifiable ethnic attachments and differences of style.[45]

Both politics and the law require highly developed skills in mediation. Satisfying the conflicting demands of constituents and achieving acceptable verdicts for litigants invested those in the law with these skills. The Irish, as speakers of English in polyglot immigrant areas of the city, became the representatives and interpreters of the laws of the land for more recent arrivals. The Irish lawyers were, as well, mediators for their own group in labor disputes, family fights, religious disputes, and political feuds beyond number. Whether in ward meetings, conference rooms, or courtrooms, they plied their knowledge and wiles to arrange compromises in conflicts in which definitive victories were not attainable. In a conservative profession in a conservative city, such was their role. Nevertheless, this did not stifle the advocates' propensities for flamboyance, eccentricity, garrulity, or fierce competitiveness. The stories recounted among them include not only the usual lore of courtroom histrionics and legal wit, but also examples of Irish dedication to views seen by others as radical. William B. Hanna, president judge of the Orphans Court for thirty-one years, boasted, "I have fathered more orphans than any man in the world." Michael Francis Doyle journeyed to London to seek clemency for the doomed Roger Casement at the trial preceding Casement's execution for aiding the Irish rebellion of 1916. Judge Robert Bolger defiantly defended the antique will of Stephen Girard that excluded blacks for Girard College even in the 1950s on the basis of the hallowed principle of the sanctity of wills. William Fitzpatrick, while a member of the local American Civil Liberties Union, took issue with its pleadings against Catholic nuns wearing religious garb while on public school property. He obtained evidence showing that female Pennsylvania Dutch fundamentalist teachers in public schools believed the lace caps they wore to be religious garb, but nobody pleaded against them. The other civil libertarians on the board were aghast at their own contradiction.[46] Mayoman Austin McGreal, an intrepid attorney, could tell such stories with uproarious delight.

As their practices and prominence grew, the Irish lawyers learned well how to act the parts of gravity and pomposity required of them. In 1936, the Irish were rewarded with the election of one of their number to be chancellor of the Bar Association when Francis Bracken was chosen for the post. But the law was more than its practice. An understanding of the law naturally led to a concern for its framing and administration. Election to legislative and judicial offices was an avid interest with the law fraternity. For the Irish, this was an avocation, if anything, even more acutely pursued. Not all their attorneys had rewarding practices. As a result, many were only too eager to plunge into the electoral wars in order to achieve the prestige and temporary security of public salaries. In the days when the city neighborhoods were more self-contained, each one had its local lawyer with his modest office and neighborhood clientele. From this network of community ties, such an attorney could readily build a political following. For center-city lawyers, the chance to seek election as the favorite of some economic interest was always there. Thus, the Irish attorneys like others, sought elected positions along with real estate brokers, former military men, saloonkeepers, and building contractors, holding themselves forth as champions of the rights of their own group and as guardians of the public interest. As the Irish grew in influence, lawyers became embedded in the political and judicial makeup of the city "as thick as raisins in a Christmas pudding," as the saying went.

The attorney who entered politics was responding to the need for representation of Irish voters who had grievances. The exploitation to which the group was subjected in the 1800s inspired resentment among the Irish and intermittent attempts to obtain improvements. Using the ballot box to elect those who would support legislation to improve working conditions, seek public health advances, extend educational opportunities, and insure a voice for protest was a method the Irish learned well. An elected representative who was trained in the law was presumably better able to work for such gains.

The Irish organizations in the city recognized this fact and advocated greater Irish representation. The Donegal Beneficial, Social and Patriotic Association, for instance, placed this resolution in its minutes early in the twentieth century:

> February 21, 1909
>
> At a meeting of the Donegal B.S. and P. Association held on the above date at Industrial Art Hall, the following resolution was adopted:
>
> Whereas, there are in the City of Philadelphia American citizens of Irish birth and descent numbering about one-sixth of the population, and they are entirely without representation on the Benches of the County Courts, whilst nearly all other nationalities and races are and have been recognized by appointing and electing powers of the City; therefore be it
>
> Resolved: that immediate steps be taken by us in the various Societies of which we are members to have their attention called to the conditions so that petition and demand may be made upon the Governor of the State of Pennsylvania to fully consider the rights of so many and to appoint a person or persons of Irish birth, nationality or race who in his good judgement might be a credit to the State and County to fill one or more of the positions on the Bench which are probably to be created in the near future. We hereby request all the various Irish organizations interested to join in our petition and demand and we also pledge ourselves that we shall work and act in every way in our power to the end that the present unjust conditions may be remedied and the present opportunity may not pass without our obtaining the recognition so long denied us.
>
> Resolved that a Committe of Three be appointed to act in conjunction with similar committees from other Irish Societies to help to carry this resolution into effect.[47]

Higher motives of public service were usually mingled with practical considerations that went far to confirm the ties of lawyers with politics. Lawyers were involved in numerous public functions as agents and trustees of government. This meant fees for legal services. There were insurance contracts to be drawn, investigations to be carried out, and court-assigned responsibilities to be performed, all of which brought fees. As a result, legal connections with the party in power provided entry into a realm of professional opportunities that could not otherwise be obtained. Sometimes major law firms informally delegated one member to seek a public office. More often, an enterprising attorney would be spurred by his own ambitions to individual effort and prompted by the vanity and vitality that have always been part of political enthusiasm.

As government relentlessly expanded its role in the twentieth century, the involvement of citizens and corporations with the law proceeded apace. Previously, lawyers had done well by virtue of being close to big business. As time passed, the law itself became big business. Access to huge fees depended upon which firm was chosen by elected officials to handle city bond issues, deal with city insurance matters, and represent public and semi-public agencies. The legal business of the city extended far beyond the city solicitors's office and the work of the district attorney and the common pleas courts. The toppling of the hoary Republican regime in city hall by an astute political machine under the Democratic party accompanied a period of reform in the 1950s. The Irish were a key element in the Democratic coalition, but they were not strong enough in numbers and votes to dominate the blacks, Jews, Italians, and other groups that formed the Democratic party's ethnic constellation. Instead, they often served as figureheads, guides, brokers, and mobilizers for the other groups. It was a complex function full of pitfalls.

Under the leadership of such figures as Judge Eugene V. Allessandroni, Italians in the city had been organized for political purposes for some years. Lawyers of Italian background formed a group called the Justinian Society to further their interests. Jews had two lodges of B'nai B'rith for their needs or professional association, plus the Locus Club, a center-city dining facility similar to the older Philadelphia Club and Racquet Club that survived as symbols of the days of Anglo dominance. Although after the 1950s increasing emphasis on legal skills led to broader recruiting by the major law firms, patterns of ethnic solidarity in the composition of firms still remained. Token representation of new ethnic groups in old firms slowly expanded so that by the 1960s there was much freer recruiting and representation among them.

For many years, a St. Thomas More Society existed for Catholic lawyers. The society held an annual Red Mass at the Cathedral of St. Peter and Paul, at which the assembly of judges in their robes was impressive. It was, however, a religious and nonpolitical group. Choice of Catholics for judgeships had been important for several generations because of the sensitivity of the Church about administration of family law, adoption policy, and other matters. Although the Democratic party reigned in full power over Philadelphia in the 1960s, it was a pluralist party. Influence in it and in the city's legal circles depended on more than religious identification. The St. Thomas More Society was not an appropriate vehicle for the Irish to maintain their tradition of political activism. This became very clear when a newly elected governor of Pennsylvania, Milton Shapp, a prominent Jewish businessman, appointed a large number of judges in 1971, and the Irish were alarmed to note that they were not recognized in the selections to the degree they thought appropriate.[48]

It was at this point that Thomas White and other lawyers of Irish background became serious about plans for a legal society that had been discussed for some time. White was born in County Derry and was one of a large family that had grown up in an industrial section of Philadelphia. His father had been involved in the Irish war of independence in the 1920s, and Thomas White was conscious of the old tradition of ethnic loyalty through which the Irish had advanced themselves in American life. In 1976, he led discussions toward the organization of what was to become the Brehon Society. Other founders of the group included Judge Joseph Glancey, a popular figure who became president judge of the Municipal Court; Michael Stack, intermittent candidate for political office; Thomas Leonard, future city controller; Dennis Kelly of the public defender's office; and Joseph T. Murphy, an active attorney. The first meeting of the organization took place in May 1977.[49]

The utility of such a society could hardly be overestimated. It was the kind of medium that led in many directions and enhanced all kinds of political possibilities and social ties. The society made possible the redefinition of the Irish as an ethnic bloc and as a political influence, and it countered the influence of other groups and permitted the promotion of numerous causes. Some of the earliest efforts of the Brehon Society were devoted to relating to others in the legal firmament. In 1977, a reception was held for Chief Justice Michael J. Eagan of the Pennsylvania Supreme Court. A schedule of luncheons was arranged so that new members and guests could be invited, and guests often included members of other ethnic groups who could be impressed by the solidarity of the Irish attorneys present. The first president of the society, Thomas White, worked energetically to extend its influence.[50]

Under the second president, Dennis Kelly, the group took a more studied interest in the nominating committee of the Philadelphia Bar Association. Thomas White was able to secure a judgeship. In 1979, the society sponsored a lecture by the district attorney of Dauphin County, and the choice was a good one, for the lecturer, Leroy Zimmerman, soon became attorney general of Pennsylvania. Letters to Brehon Society members kept them informed

about those in the society seeking office as judges or other local
and state positions. In 1979, a reception was held for Justices
Henry A. O'Brien and John P. Flaherty of the Pennsylvania Supreme Court.[51] The Society had become a fixture in the political
and legal orbit of the city.

Most Irish lawyers still represented small firms and individual
practices. As a result, there was a higher interest among them in
positions on the bench than, for instance, among Anglo-Protestant
upper-class attorneys. By 1979, seven out of fifty-five Court of
Common Pleas judges were of Irish background. Three Irish judges
were on the family court, but none were on the orphans court.
Four of the twenty on the municipal court were Irish, as were one
of five on the traffic court. In a city with a strong Irish tradition,
this could not be said to be an inordinate representation, though
both the president judge of Common Pleas Court and the head of
the municipal court were Brehon Society members. This representation indicates that, even after several years of activity by the
Brehon Society, the position of Irish lawyers in relation to the judiciary was conditioned by considerations of ethnic balance and
limitations of political power that dictated a broad spectrum of legal office holding in the city system.[52]

The more convivial side of the society was not neglected, and
such events as a St. Patrick's Day party, a Christmas party, and an
Irish musical fete in Fairmount Park were held. A hospitality suite
was set up at the annual Bench and Bar Conference. Although the
bylaws of the society provided that membership be open to "any
person of Irish lineage who is a member in good standing" of the
bar, it was also thought to be important that an associate membership be established for law students. Women lawyers had been admitted to the organization from the beginning, and their numbers
grew as more entered the profession through the 1970s. By 1980,
there were three hundred members of the Brehon Society. An estimated seven hundred members of the Philadelphia Bar were of
Irish background, about one-tenth of the total membership. Thus,
not all the Irish lawyers of the city were Brehons; some had little
interest in Irish affairs or local politics. Still, the fact that so many
Irish attorneys were affiliated was very significant for the informal
exchange and professional association that their ties implied.[53]

Aside from local political interests, many of the members of the
society were concerned about the problem of Northern Ireland and
the administration of justice there. Issues relating to U.S. policy toward the Northern Ireland conflict had been of interest to Brehon

members as well. In February 1979, Ruairi O'Bradaigh of the Sinn Fein party, political allies of the militants in the Irish Republican Army, was able to address the society at a downtown hotel. Later the same year, a member of the Dail, the parliament of the Republic of Ireland, and also of the European parliament, Neil T. Blaney, addressed the Brehons. Blaney was known for his strong nationalist views on Northern Ireland. The society sent a letter to the U.S. State Department protesting the U.S. policy of denying visas to nationalist spokesmen from Northern Ireland.[54]

As the Northern Ireland problem went through one tragic year after another, American opinion remained confused and alienated by its violence. British spokesmen continued to assert that Americans had no role to play in what they characterized as an internal British problem. Any American group interested in the subject was likely to be accused of supporting terrorism or being dupes for the Irish Republican Army. The leaders of the Brehon Society were not deflected from their interest in the Ulster situation by such difficulties. In fact, their persistent concern was quite singular and probably without parallel among American professional organizations. Neither clergy nor physicians nor teachers showed any such organized interest.[55] In 1980, when the widely respected James Cavanaugh was president of the society, further prestige was added to the efforts of the group to clarify Northern Ireland issues.

Jack McKinney, a journalist and strong proponent of the Irish nationalist viewpoint, addressed the society, as did Jack Sharkey, a city detective who compared police methods in Northern Ireland with those in American communities. Gerhardt Elston, president of Amnesty International, spoke to the Brehons about the investigations of his group into the practice of torture by British forces in Northern Ireland. The Society protested the awarding of an honorary degree to Prime Minister Margaret Thatcher by Georgetown University because of the record of her government in violating human rights in Northern Ireland. Members of the society also played a role in securing the release of Pearse Kerr, a young man who had been detained without charge by the police in Northern Ireland. Kerr was a Philadelphian and an American citizen, and his case resulted in considerable publicity in the city.

Through the early 1980s, the Brehon Society continued its round of local activities, but it did not lose interest in Northern Ireland issues. A number of its members toured Northern Ireland at the time that the American Bar Association held a festive meeting in London in 1985. Some visited Long Kesh prison, and the accounts of interviews and conditions in Belfast were of keen interest when the delegation returned. The society sponsored a debate between Father Sean MacManus of the Irish American Caucus and William Kelly of the Ford Motor Company, one of the companies with plants in Northern Ireland, about unfair employment practices in Northern Ireland. One of the judges who was a member of the society testified at congressional hearings in Washington about changes in American extradition laws that were aimed at apprehending fugitives from Ireland. These activities highlighted the strong feelings in the city's Irish community about the turmoil in Ireland and provided a model of the way in which Irish-Americans could publicize issues and try to influence opinion about them. Public pressure was a very traditional activity for Irish-American leaders, but this was distinctive in that it was being conducted by a group of legal professionals.[56]

In 1980, a professional political action committee of the society was formed under Frank Moran. Interest in judicial elections and in judicial appointments remained high, as did interest in the elections for leadership of the Bar Association. Reaching out to other groups was a continuous practice of the society. A luncheon was held to honor Rabbi Theodore Lewis, a man born and raised in Dublin who was head of the Touro Synagogue in Newport, Rhode Island, the oldest synagogue in the nation. Rabbi Lewis addressed himself to the record of religious tolerance in the Republic of Ireland. In the contest for vice-chancellor of the Bar Association in 1981, the Brehons, by informed agreement, supported a candidate named Marino, a member of the Italian Justinian Society, a support that was expected to be reciprocated at a later date.[57]

Why, in a period when Irish influence was said to be declining in other American cities, did the Brehon Society emerge in Philadelphia as a professional expression of ethnic solidarity? One reason may have been the late development of Irish leadership in a city long ruled by Anglo elements using politics as the instrument of their dominance. While most major cities had Irish mayors in the nineteenth century, Philadelphia only reached this stage in 1964 when James Tate became mayor in the wake of the overthrow of the century-old Republican regime that was the agency of Anglo sovereignty in the city, although the upper-class elements astutely avoided politics themselves while sending their emissaries to hold control. The elaboration of Irish-American professional life might have been retarded as a result of this situation until the mid-twentieth century, though this theory is debatable. Dale Light has shown that, if anything, Irish-American organizational life in the city was rather highly developed. By the 1880s, the city was a veritable hive of Irish groups.[58] The growth of the Brehon Society must be traced to more proximate causes.

The contention within the Democratic party for positions and patronage was the primary factor giving rise to the Brehons. The Democratic party was an uneasy balance of restive blacks, rising Italians, old-line Irish, activist Jews, and a mélange of other interests. After Mayor James Tate was succeeded by former Police Commissioner Frank Rizzo in 1971, Italians received numerous offices in city hall that they had never had political access to previously. This was a shock to the Irish similar to the appointment of non-Irish judges by Governor Shapp. As Rizzo's term waned, former Congressman William Green sought and was elected to the mayor's office. With an Irish Catholic again in that position, and with the Democratic City Committee headed by David Glancey, brother of Judge Joseph Glancey, a founder of the Brehons, the times were opportune for an Irish consolidation of political interests.

The bar itself changed greatly in the 1970s. Legal business expanded even though the city's economy generally declined. New lawyers, including many more women, competed actively for positions with established law firms. The membership of the Bar Association grew from 4,000 in 1965 to 5,900 in 1975. Such expansion required more careful attention to liaisons if traditional patterns of influence were to be maintained. The Brehon Society was one kind of response. The organization reflected the fact that several generations of Irish in the city had made their way to law schools, and a survey of the 20 percent of the members of the bar in the Friendly Sons of St. Patrick shows that they went to the University of Pennsylvania Law School in many cases but also to law schools at Temple, Columbia, Yale, Harvard, and Notre Dame universities.

The Northern Ireland crisis was another factor working to focus Irish interests. Thomas White, the key figure in the establishment of the Brehons, was north-of-Ireland man and felt strongly about the injustice of British rule there. The Jews had Israel as a pole of their ethnic concern. Blacks had the continuing struggle for equal opportunity. The Italians had the charismatic leadership of Mayor Frank Rizzo to contradict rising black political aspirations. Consciously or not, the Irish were given a new ethnic orientation by the Northern Ireland crisis. The Brehon Society meetings, addressing themselves to the subject repeatedly, presented the most intelligent and reasoned analysis of the problem in any forum in the city.

Finally, tradition itself was a stimulus to the organization of the Brehon Society. The Irish community in the city had a rich history of organized effort and social activity ranging over two centuries, and the lawyers were doubtless conscious of this fact. Although the Society of the Friendly Sons of St. Patrick was venerable organization that had many lawyers as members, it was firmly nonpolitical. Another group, the Irish Society, a fusion of political and labor union leaders founded in the 1970s, was very political but could not meet the specific needs of attorneys. If the Irish members of the bar were to maintain their status, enhance their political potential, and cultivate their mutual professional interests, the Brehon Society had to be organized to stake out their position among the legion of practitioners in the city.

This society, so adroitly developed, was a testimony to an Irish-American political acumen that had become almost habitual. In a profession increasingly changed by specialization and large computerized law firm practices, the human dimension of local ethnic association was important. The functions of the Brehon Society were carried out within the framework of pluralist exchange with other ethnic groups that reaffirmed the role of Irish lawyers as mediators in their community. The society was a clear example not only of the continuity of ethnic influences in the city's life but also of the situational nature and utility of modern ethnic organizations in meeting the needs of their constituencies at a variety of levels in a complex society.

It was a bombshell revelation, therefore, when newspaper headlines in 1986 announced that fifteen judges in Philadelphia courts had been accused of accepting bribes from the local roofers' union during 1985. The chief informant in the case was Mary Rose Cunningham, herself a judge who had been accused and then was induced by the Federal Bureau of Investigation to tape-record incriminating conversations with other judges and a union official. She had been quite active in the Brehon Society and was its vice president. Two of the ten judges charged in the scandal, Thomas White and Joseph Glancey, were prominent in the society. Another accused judge, Thomas Dempsey, was a society member. Black, Italian, Greek, and Jewish judges were suspended from the bench in the scandal as well. For the Brehon Society, however, it was a hard blow to a carefully cultivated image. For Glancey and White, the evidence pointed not to any actual crime but to "the appearance of impropriety," but the newspaper publicity tarred all those involved with the broad brush of misconduct.

The local judiciary was caught in a maelstrom of publicity. The news media did not at any point directly charge the Brehon associates with criminal involvement, but the implication was unavoidable in public opinion. Not all the Irish judges on the bench were tainted: indeed, one, Judge James Cavanaugh of the Superior Court of Pennsylvania, had flatly and curtly rejected a union "gift." Nevertheless, the unsavory side of big city politics was once again depressingly detailed in the tape-recorded revelations and the testimony about the judges. The scandal revealed that the expansion of the courts over the years had eroded the prestige and scrutiny of judges, and it had also opened up more and more temptations to violate professional ethics.

The publicity in this behind-the-scenes drama of the courts showed clearly the crude character of judicial administration in the city. Much of the scandal derived from the simple fact that judges had to run for office in electoral contests, and they had to raise the money to do so. One columnist stated that it was a premise of Philadelphia politics that you couldn't get slated in the city without labor union support and contributions.[59] The roofers' union, which had been led by a very tough boss named Johnny McCullough, had a record scarred by many violent incidents that brought its members before the courts on charges, so it was important for the union to have "friends in court." The old neighborhood bases of political power in Philadelphia had been changed by suburbanization and the decay of many traditional ethnic areas. The activist role of political action committees, construction contractors, municipal unions, and even the bar itself had replaced the support that used to come from the neighborhood level and the ethnic residential blocs that voted for their favorite ethnic sons. In view of these changes, the Irish attorneys and judges had turned to the new networks of supporters, and the raw trading of "gifts" for influence had continued as before. The old practice of all judiciary nominations and funding being controlled by the city committees of the political parties had broken down in the 1970s. The Brehons were the result of that new competitive situation. The Brehon Society, born largely because of political considerations, had been severely wounded in its leadership by political dealings.

The entanglement of the Irish leaders was part of the price to be paid for the hazards of political competition for power in an urban arena rife with difficulties. The old image of political corruption that accompanied the rise of the group to power in the major cities was once again brought to the fore. All of the patient and skillful work that had for over a decade been devoted to reasserting Irish professional prominence, political ability, and ethnic pride had been compromised in a swift revelation of improprieties. William Fitzpatrick, president of the Brehon Society at the time of the scandal, was sure the organization would continue, but he recognized the toll that had been taken by the imbroglio.

As an organization, the Brehon Society was notable among Irish associations since it was organized at a professional level. Almost all Irish groups in the past had been derived from the origins of members from localities in Ireland, from considerations of mutual aid and fraternity, or from more utilitarian working-class interests. The society carried on a dialogue about the thorny Northern Ireland problem without being labeled "extremist" as had many other groups. It also represented a latter-day attempt to mobilize Irish-Americans politically in a period of fluid "network" politics. The fact that its leadership was wounded in a political scandal showed clearly the insecurity of any group's hold on power in the whirligig of big city politics. If the Irish of yesteryear were insecure because of limited education, immigrant disabilities, and discrimination, their grandsons and granddaughters in the Brehon Society were plagued by a different kind of insecurity—the hazard of their careers because of legal competition and the perils of a political system that was laced with illicit forms of support.

Mrs. McGarry's Crusade

The work of Anna McGarry and her fellow Irish-American proponents of interracial justice can only be understood in the context of the Catholic tradition of social reform. In the nineteenth century, various organizations such as the Hibernian Society sought to aid impoverished immigrants. The mission of the Total Abstinence Brotherhood, launched in the 1850s, continued its opposition to alcohol abuse right into the 1950s with the preaching of Monsignor John Keogh. The nursing and health care services of the heavily Irish Sisters of Mercy and Sisters of St. Francis preceded their teaching in schools. Ardent labor reformers like Leonora O'Reilly struggled against child labor exploitation in the early twentieth century, and institutions for youth such as St. Joseph's Home for Industrious Boys helped youngsters adrift from families. The work of Sister Mary Scullion in sheltering the homeless and that of Sister Frances Kirk in behalf of children in besieged Northern Ireland brought this Philadelphia Catholic effort into the 1980s. Each of these reform efforts had strong clerical and lay backing and was supported notably by the Irish in the city.

The issue of race was acute in the old neighborhoods for generations. Living close together in the worst areas, competing for jobs, contrasting strongly in their views of themselves and one another and in their views of their respective grievances, blacks and Irish people were rarely companionable. Riots, antagonism, and unease blighted their relations. Catholic church work to reduce these tensions began only very slowly, and it was not until previously Irish parishes became all-black in the 1940s that priests and a few leaders began to understand the depths of black deprivation. Catholic social teaching slowly created a circuit of reform-oriented people in the 1930s, and, although old Dennis Cardinal Dougherty, who headed the archdiocese, would remain distant from their endeavors, their work to change attitudes and stimulate improvements for blacks in a largely segregated city continued.

The religion of the Irish Catholics in the view of the twentieth century reformers did have the capacity to counter racism by animating strong codes of sacrifice and good example. It was religion taught in a rigorously rational manner, insistent on methods of specific conduct. If God created all men equal in His eyes, then that meant blacks too, and the premise was sufficient to lead people to advance stubbornly toward fair treatment. Such general principles of social justice were abstract, and they were set against an emotionalism and negative racial imagery that were gradually revealed to be far more subject to inflammation than pious teachers imagined. In the face of the resentment aroused by interracial activity, most Catholics avoided even thinking about it. Some of the oldest Irish neighborhoods, such as the parishes bordering black ghettoes in North and South Philadelphia, had for decades been notorious for juvenile racial clashes. It was in such areas that Anna McGarry would work for years, and her personal activity to encourage equal opportunity in employment, education, and housing induced a core of the Irish Catholics she met to join with her in defying a racial alienation that had become part of the lifestyle of their ethnic group.

Some organizations result from long and hard experience, such as the unions of the dockmen. Some result from mutual political and ethnic interest, like the Brehon Society, Others are formed because of the determination of some individual to make a change. The reformers grouped around the interracial work of Anna McGarry were the latter kind of constituency. Few tasks are more

difficult than organizing people in behalf of something they fear
and resent, but it was McGarry's lifelong work to do just that. She
was a community organizer of extraordinary skill and persistence,
and her work to promote interracial association, credit unions, fair
labor practices, and housing improvement was marked by a commitment to justice that she developed from her Irish-Catholic background. As an organizer, she learned her skills firsthand in
addition to studying the writings of social reformers of many persuasions. She worked among Irish people who were still full of
memories of their own struggle for decency and advancement,
while they were being displaced as a group from many areas of
Philadelphia life by massive black migration that transformed the
racial patterns and codes of the city.

The work of Anna McGarry knew many important political figures and
prominent leaders, she was never very close to them in her personal life. Her closest friends were her black neighbors and the
ghetto people and other activists she knew best from her work
combating discrimination. McGarry lived in the heart of the huge
North Philadelphia ghetto, probably the only white woman for several miles in an area of slums, public housing, distress, and crime,
an area referred to by most white people in the city in the 1950s as
"the jungle." From her tiny row house in the ghetto, she resolutely
built a network of Irish Catholics who contradicted the racial views
of the overwhelming majority of their ethnic confreres in the harsh
inner-city world of segregation and mutual hostility. Throughout
her career, she dealt with rejection by her contemporaries, intimidation by officials, and the most intense kind of antagonism by
those who feared the coming of an interracial society.

The work of Anna McGarry, often the subject of stormy opinions among the Irish, did much to effect a change in their image in
the city and moderated their reputation for being the group most
antagonistic toward black advancement. By doing so, it altered the
position of the group that had for long been trapped in a duel of
social conflict with blacks. It provided young Irish-Americans with
an example different from that of people with racist attitudes they
knew only too well. Through the publicity accorded her work, the
general community could share knowledge of this example. McGarry's work decreased the exclusiveness and ethnocentrism of the
Irish, and reduced the proprietary attitudes of the group in relation
to the institutions in which they were influential, that is, the labor
unions, churches, and political circles. This was an admirable contribution through an organizational medium that required tough
convictions and astute behavior.

The long record of antagonism between blacks and the Irish in American cities is documented in various places. It was not so much that the Irish were more racist than other Americans. In fact, a good case could be made that they were less so.[60] The central consideration in the matter is that for most of the nation's history, the Irish, like the blacks, were steeped in the miseries at the bottom of the country's social system. Like blacks, they were assigned to the least desirable jobs, housing, and living conditions in most communities through the nineteenth century. Lack of education, competition for employment, and the social inflammation that derives from being frustrated and exploited deeply troubled both groups. The groups being placed so close together in big city slums resulted in a long history of combat and hostility.

It was not until much later in their span of American experience that most Irish-Americans were brought to think seriously about this situation. For a group moving beyond disabilities and into a more satisfactory position in the pluralist society of the twentieth century, it did become inconvenient at times to be labeled as anti-black. For people with a more developed conscience and a sense of social justice, the legacy of antagonism was a challenge. The reputation of the Irish-Catholic community had to be rehabilitated in race relations, for the group's works of charity and education were so broadly manifest and aided so many people that it was glaringly incongruous to have blacks alienated. The works of reconciliation were slow to emerge, and they had to await the mid-twentieth century, but they provide some fascinating portraits of Irish-American idealism and commitment to justice. Through such works, the image of the Irish-American community was considerably altered, and an organized effort was begun among the group to promote interracial justice.

Anna McGinley McGarry was born in the big Irish community in North Philadelphia in 1894. The area combined the "lace curtain" Irish in handsome three-story brick houses on the wider streets, with the less successful working class Irish in the smaller row house streets. These streets crisscrossed in solid urban density from Spring Garden Street to Allegheny Avenue East and West of fashionable Broad Street. Though there were mills in the area, it was extensively residential. The most prominent features of its skyline were the tall steeples and towers of its ornate Catholic churches: St. Michael's, St. Malachy's, St. Francis Xavier, St. Elizabeth's, Most Precious Blood, Our Lady of Mercy, and the Jesuit Church of the Gesu. St. Malachy's parish, where Anna McGinley grew up, was a workingman's parish of factories, warehouses, and railyards. Anna attended parish schools and a business school conducted by nuns. She married Frank McGarry in 1917, just before he was called into the U.S. Army and sent to France with the American Expeditionary Force. He was stricken in a mustard gas attack in the trenches and returned home an invalid. He never recovered and died in 1921, leaving Anna a widow with an infant daughter, Mary.[61]

As a young widow McGarry took a number of clerical jobs to earn her way. She was deeply religious, but the ritual Catholicism of weekly Mass attendance and a whole roster of devotional practices did not satisfy her. She sought more than individual discipline: something with a social meaning that would be part of the daily life of the working people around her who toiled in the mills, lofts, coal yards, truck depots, plants, and wharves of the city.

The Great Depression of the 1930s struck the lives of working people with devastating years of unemployment and insecurity. People of all backgrounds reached out for some set of ideas that would restore coherence to life and explain the defects of the economic system that had visited such tragedy upon millions of workers. An intellectual explanation of the problems of modern society based on the teachings of the popes and Catholic thinkers had been growing in the Catholic network of the country.[62] A counterpart of this social thought was an activist movement of practical organization and service. One of the most notable of the organizer-agitators involved with this movement was Dorothy Day, founder of the Catholic Worker movement for social justice and ardent defender of the rights of the poor. It was from such people as Dorothy Day, Monsignor George Higgins, Father Richard McKeon, Father Richard McSorley, and others that McGarry drew her social ideas and patterns of argument in behalf of social justice. During the 1930s, she became part of a widespread circuit of people propagating ideas of social reform, and foremost on her agenda was the relief of blacks from exploitation and the renovation of attitudes and practices that excluded blacks from full economic and social participation in community life.

Father Edward Cunnie was pastor of St. Elizabeth's parish in North Philadelphia. Originally founded by German families, the parish had become increasingly Irish and then increasingly black. Father Cunnie became fast friends with McGarry, and together they worked to counter the bitterness stemming from the movement of black people into the all-white streets of St. Elizabeth's. Becoming aware of the larger social implications of the racial problem, Father Cunnie joined with McGarry in forming the city's first Catholic Interracial Council in 1937. Through her affable and persistent efforts, McGarry was able to draw into the council a number of local figures who had access to city-wide leadership circles, including Judge Gerald Flood, Magistrate John Coyle, attorney Robert Callaghan, and a small representation of black Catholics who attended local parishes. She was able to involve blacks like Martin Fields, Gertrude Wallace, James Finley, and William Bruce, an official of the Laborers' International Union of North America. McGarry was the key to the engagement of these professional whites and black Catholics with a movement that was viewed by many people as dangerously radical and by most as a misguided idealism that was a threat to the "natural" order of segregation and repression of blacks.

The need for some Catholic efforts to overcome anti-black feeling was certainly widespread. The pastor of one parish in North Philadelphia campaigned actively in his community against the entry of blacks. He visited the local saloons one after another, haranguing all who would listen about the misfortunes that would follow a black presence in the area. In the building trades, in which tens of thousands of Irish found employment, the Irish dominated the skilled trades. Efforts of blacks to obtain more than a few token jobs in hod carrying, bricklaying, iron work, plumbing, or carpentry were generally opposed by white workers. In the 1930s, when contractor John B. Kelly hired more than a few blacks as bricklayers, a trade he himself had once followed, there was consternation among his Irish workers. The worst jobs of excavation, heavy loading, and cleaning up on job sites were known by the Irish in the skilled trades as "nigger work." In most other areas of life, blacks were carefully segregated. They were simply not served at center-city restaurants and other public facilities. For black Catholics, only two special churches existed in the city, one founded by Mother Katherine Drexel and one called St. Peter Claver's, a mission established through a benefaction of an Irish Catholic. Some black Catholics, however, had begun attending local geographical parishes by the 1930s and were accepted with wary uneasiness. The exclusionary and discriminatory customs of the Philadelphia community simply placed blacks in such a separate category that they were largely invisible in the formal life of the city and relegated to an urban half-world of poverty and anonymity.[63]

It was against such conditions that McGarry set herself, and she did so with a zeal that was to last a lifetime. In appearance, she was modestly attractive. She had one of those round, open, smiling faces that would be considered "typically Irish." She was fair, freckled, and gifted with a delightful blue-eyed vitality that made her seem especially friendly. With an easy laugh and an assured and amiable disposition, she was able to deal with people on an affable basis even when they stubbornly opposed her. As she matured, she became more like those thousands of Irish mothers throughout the city whose talents of reminding, coaxing, guiding, reproving, and encouraging held families together and moved them every day beyond reluctance to action. Although she was only about five-feet-three-inches tall, there was an unmistakable firmness about her manner. She could not be ignored or evaded. Her direct gaze and thoroughly purposeful presence placed her at the center of the groups that she joined. Persevering, articulate, and shrewd, she would challenge anybody in behalf of what she though was right. The force and integrity of McGarry's character made her career unusual and paved the way for a transformation of Irish Catholic practices in race relations and a later and greater change in the practices of her city.

McGarry was not especially close to the Irish-born organizational network in the city, nor was she part of the structure of county societies and nationalist groups that sponsored annual rounds of Irish dances and activities. The Irish in Philadelphia were so diverse, with such a long history of organizational elaboration, that Irish-Americans could relate to the Irish community in dozens of different ways. But McGarry's birthday was on St. Patrick Day, and she knew her own very well. She could speak with feeling and no little bit of heat about the contradiction of the social misfortunes of the Irish and what she saw as their diversion from the obligation that they had to aid blacks who were caught by the same prejudice and neglect that the Irish had fought to free themselves from all through the nineteenth century. McGarry was seen as Irish, too, by those in the general community. Her looks, her name, and her background committed her to being a representative of the Irish community, whether she always intended to be or not.

In the mid-1930s, she organized a group of college students into an Intercollegiate Interracial Council. The archconservative Dennis Cardinal Dougherty, who headed the Philadelphia Archdiocese, had advised Father Cunnie to begin interracial work only

with younger and more educated people. Such work was so unpop-
ular that it was inadvisable to begin with just any group of Catholics, the cardinal believed. McGarry was in touch with the chief
Catholic activist in interracial matters in the country, Jesuit Father
John LaFarge, who had a keen sense of how difficult interracial situations could become. He had lived through many rough encounters in his work for blacks. After successfully holding meetings at
the various colleges in the area and winning to her side a number
of young aides like Daniel Kane, Father Gerard Murphy, and attorney Joseph Stanton, McGarry took the next step of forming a council open to all. Although she had never attended college, this
proved no barrier to her action among students and educators. She
placed first priority in these early years on education in principles
of social justice and gradually influenced a widening circle of
thoughtful people. The years before World War II were a time of
testing methods and cultivating contracts. Visitors of all kinds were
welcomed in the McGarry household, and her home became a regular stopping-off place for touring French worker priests, agrarian
reformers, labor organizers, and interracial activists.

From 1940 to 1945, Philadelphia drew tens of thousands of
blacks to labor in its booming war industries. Tensions rose fitfully
as blacks moved into unaccustomed areas of the city's life. To make
more labor available, President Franklin D. Roosevelt had, at the
urging of the black national labor leader A. Phillip Randolph and
others, issued an executive order requiring fair employment practices in war-related industries, the beginning of profound changes
for the nation's major industrial centers. It further stimulated black
migration from the South, and, for cities like Philadelphia, it meant
a sweeping change in traditional racial patterns.[64]

Even under the restrictive conditions of wartime housing
shortages, blacks began to move into more white neighborhoods. In
North Philadelphia, this meant that big, heavily Irish parishes like
Our Lady of Mercy on Broad Street were faced by substantial racial
change. Along Broad Street were the Irish-American Club, the Ancient Order of Hibernians building, the Tavernkeepers Association,
and various halls where Irish events were held regularly. The
Irish families, largely steady and conservative working people, believed their neighborhoods would be ruined by black residents.
Under the conditions of crowding and exploitation that created
turmoil among blacks, the Irish did have much to be concerned
about. Problems of overcrowding of housing, adjustment to a new
urban environment, continuing poverty, and long-standing social

disabilities were all too evident among many hard-pressed black families. The Irish, many of whom had serious problems of their own, and many others who were only too conscious of having but recently escaped from the world of disability that blacks still inhabited, were deeply distressed by black encroachment.

The long war years brought all kinds of pressures to life in the city, but few were more notable than the racial crisis resulting from the employment of blacks in jobs on the city's transit lines, where they had never been hired previously. The wartime labor shortage had place transit officials in a tough position. They had to run more vehicles than ever to serve the far-flung local war industries, but most of the men who could have driven vehicles were in the service. A federal court decision in 1944 directed that blacks should be hired for transit jobs. The Philadelphia Rapid Transit Company began to hire blacks as bus and trolley drivers, and the reaction of the white members of the transit union was swift and bitter. The union was heavily Irish and had a stormy record in its fight against dreadful treatment over the years by the transit magnates who successively owned the system. The Transport Workers Union protested that the driving jobs would be wanted by men returning from the war. It was a stab in the back, they contended, to give their jobs to blacks while the men were on the battlefronts. The transit workers went on strike, even though some members refused to walk out. The city was in an agitated state, for three shifts of workers had to reach factories and shipyards daily, and having no trolleys and buses operating created a chaotic situation. Buses and trolleys operated by blacks began to be attacked with stones and sabotaged. Some said the union provoked the disorders while others said the turmoil was due to rumors and fights on overcrowded vehicles. At any rate, violence spread and local gangs of youths harassed and attacked the transit facilities. The city's transportation system ground to a halt.[65] Federal authorities wanted no interruption of war production. Under wartime powers, they sent troops to the city to ride on and protect subways, buses, and trolleys. The city took on the aspects of an area under military occupation.

Throughout this time, Anna McGarry was in the thick of talks with transit officials and workers, and she knew some of the union officers personally. Transit workers had been putting in very long hours to meet the increased wartime schedules. The racial dispute triggered a whole roster of grievances, but McGarry was respected by and could talk to both sides in the conflict. Firmly, adeptly,

with tireless tact and tough, personal honesty, she was able to expand communication between the irate workers and transit officials, police, and federal representatives. After long and fiery
sessions, some accord was finally reached: blacks stayed on the
job, and the union was assured that the transit company would not
try to overturn existing hiring rules. Everybody who had watched
McGarry work through this crisis had to recognize that she had
unique skills of persuasion and negotiation.[66]

In the years after World War II, Philadelphia scrambled to accommodate itself to the social changes the war had produced. In
1948, after a vigorous campaign, a Fair Employment Practice Act
was adopted and a commission appointed by the city government
to enforce it. The law forbade discrimination based on race, religion, or national origin in employment. One of the five commissioners in charge of investigating and making decisions about
discrimination complaints was Judge Gerald Flood, one of the
city's most respected jurists and a friend of Anna McGarry. Flood
and the other commissioners agreed that McGarry would make a
very good staff member of the commission, and she was hired.

In many areas of employment, blacks were unwelcome, and
McGarry worked hard to set forth the facts of such conditions. Several restaurant chains avoided hiring black waitresses but did em-
ploy blacks in kitchen work. The managers feared that the white
public would resent being served by blacks. These same chains
employed large numbers of Irish immigrant women both for
kitchen work and as waitresses. The restaurants were not union-
ized and preferred unskilled Irish immigrant girls from rural backgrounds who were unacquainted with unionization, spoke English,
were comparatively docile, and could be employed for relatively
low wages. One survey showed that of the 503 waitresses employed by the Horn and Hardart chain, only three were black.
Schraffts and Stauffers also favored Irish girls. An informal but effective system of job referral existed for the Irish girls, and many of
the managers of the restaurants were Irish as well.

McGarry pursued her dialogue with the restaurant representatives. As public facilities, the restaurants were loathe to cause any
controversy about their policies. There were, of course, lawyers
and executives of the city, the restaurants, and various civil rights
groups involved, but it was McGarry with her contacts with the
Irish work force who was responsible for keeping their trepidation
and resentment under control. She could be seen in the restaurants
daily talking to the waitresses, the women who worked at the

steam tables, and the kitchen workers, explaining and reassuring. Slowly but definitely, the hiring practices changed, and jobs for blacks became more common in food service. This retail breakthrough was important because of its visibility, and the commission was commended for the progress it had brought about.[67]

In 1951, a new city charter absorbed the Fair Employment Practices unit into a new Commission on Human Relations, with a mandate to eliminate discrimination and segregation in housing and public facilities as well as in employment. The commission was unequal to the task, but its programs of education and investigation would go far to relieve dangerous tensions. Although the Irish had been dispersing throughout the Delaware Valley for some time, several older neighborhoods were still identified as Irish in the city—Kensington, the Schuylkill area known as "Ramcat" in South Philadelphia, and an old industrial district called Swampoodle.[68] McGarry knew people in all these areas, and her contacts would be very valuable as conflicts erupted year after year in these neighborhoods, for racial change was coming to them and through them on a steady basis.

There were two areas of social contact in which race relations tended to be explosive in these tough old districts. One was the area of housing change. When blacks entered a previously all-white block, there was usually resentment, and it was fairly common for white neighbors to gather, for juveniles to vandalize the houses and cars of blacks, and for intimidation and sometimes rioting to take place. The other area of contention involved teenage groups who tried to keep blacks out of local playgrounds or clashed with them on the streets. In the Schuylkill district, a neighborhood with a long record of racial conflict, white adolescents threw shards of glass into the public swimming pool and closed it rather than share it with blacks. After-school conflicts at transit exchange points were not unusual. To the whites in the old mill district streets, the row houses they owned were their biggest investment. Black entry created panic, and homes were put up for sale in a flurry that made so many simultaneous sales impossible and created harmful price competition. Conditions approaching hysteria accompanied these situations, and McGarry was involved in resolving dozens of them each year.[69]

Her technique was to search out sources of local information through parish contacts, labor union acquaintances, and activists of all kinds and to construct an accurate picture of community feelings, rumors, leadership, and the circumstances of conflict. Having done so, she would work to neutralize hostility. She appealed to practical motives for the most part, stressing the uncontrollable threat violence represented and the need for rational control of events. She firmly defended blacks' rights to move where they chose, and many people hated her for that reason. When dealing with her own, the Irish Catholics, she could use tough moral arguments that hit hard to a people steeped in ideas of religious respect and responsibility. It was very difficult work, and she was berated, mocked, and reviled many times by bitter Irish contemporaries. Priests threw her out of rectories after subjecting her to tirades that she listened to with patient attention. People dodged her on the street. Others harangued her furiously when they met her. She bore all this with humor and modest resignation, and she did not relent.

McGarry's relations with higher Catholic church officials were always tenuous. They could not reject her principles or her work, but the vigor of her advancement of black rights made them highly uncomfortable. Dennis Cardinal Dougherty and John Cardinal O'Hara, his successor, were conservative men in a city known for its conservatism. Disturbances of the status quo were unwelcome. Cardinal O'Hara had no real grasp of the racial transformation underway in his archdiocese and would simply state that it was good that blacks would inherit the Catholic facilities the Irish had built. The turmoil and bitterness, the expanding segregation, and the impatience of blacks with "go slow" rhetoric seemed beyond understanding to the frail archbishop who had been born and raised in the small-town Midwest. McGarry's work, however, was usually far beyond the control of most higher church figures. She found supporters among others. Monsignor John Keogh, a lively old waterfront priest from South Philadelphia who preached total abstinence from alcohol even in the 1950s, was eager to support housing reform for blacks. Brother Augustine of LaSalle College, son of a hard coal miner, was a fine teacher and activist for social justice. Younger priests like Michael Jordan, a Jesuit, and Jack Mc-Namee were very able co-workers.[70]

In performing her duties for the Commission on Human Relations, McGarry was always alert to bring younger people into her field of interest. She was fortunate in finding two young men of enormous energy and conscientiousness who shared her zeal for interracial justice. One was John A. McDermott, a solidly built, ruddy-faced field representative with an enormous capacity for work. McDermott had a bulldog quality that fixed responsibility on people in difficult situations despite their reluctance to get

involved in meetings or talk to their neighbors. In racially changing neighborhoods, the tactics of pacification called for getting
clergy, police, youth workers, and local notables to work for calm
and support nonviolence. McDermott worked full days and frequent weekends in addition to attending an extraordinary number
of evening meetings in areas where agitation often reached fever
pitch. He worked under McGarry, and she kept the same kind of
schedule.

Another very resourceful aide was Myles Mahoney, a young
man with a degree in social work and one of the most engaging
smiles in the city. McGarry, McDermott, and Mahoney handled situations that involved threats, intimidation, attempts at suicide, and
the most morbid kind of psychology. They all knew the immense
city almost street by street and retained in their heads the patterns
of racial division that lay across the urban landscape.

In working with the police, who were often Irish, they had
many problems. The police did not take vandalism very seriously,
yet vandalism was the most common tactic used to frighten blacks
who crossed racial lines. The police also were not very pleased
with having to perform riot duty and endure long cordon or sur-
veillance duties at sites where blacks were surrounded by hostile
white neighbors. In this problem, ethnic affinity between commission staff and the police was an asset, but the police often shared
the racial attitudes of those in the local areas they patrolled. The
commission staff of blacks, Jews, and Hispanics often envied the
way McGarry and her team utilized the wide range of contracts
they had at various city levels.[71]

Outside of her strenuous work for the commission, McGarry
was not at all content to pursue a relaxing personal life. With her
earnings, she helped other people and paid for the expenses of the
Catholic Interracial Council, and she used her house, within the
shadow of the Church of the Gesu, to stimulate all kinds of discussions and planning. She advised contractor Matthew McCloskey in
selecting students to receive scholarships from his Martin de
Porres Foundation. In the 1960s, she began to work in a more struc-
tured way toward improvement in her own neighborhood. With the
support of sympathetic priests from the Jesuit parish like pastor
William Michelman and the cheery elderly priest, Horace Mc-
Kenna, a whole range of activities were launched to aid families in
the area. Weekly classes for new members of the parish; a Mothers
club dealing with budgeting, child care, and family problems; more
sports for the youth; teenage leadership groups; a credit union; a

health program; an employment service; and a neighbors association were all set in motion. Jane O'Donnell, formerly with the Catholic Worker movement, moved into the parish, and young women from the Grail movement, a Catholic feminist group, aided the work. This white cadre worked diligently for the black community surrounding the Gesu church. It was the kind of no-nonsense, grass-roots grappling with ghetto problems that McGarry like best. By the time the civil rights movement emerged in the 1960s, Anna McGarry was one white woman who had been working at it for thirty years.[72]

The situation of Spanish-speaking families in the city did not escape McGarry's attention either. In 1953, she and her colleagues, some Spanish-speaking, campaigned for a facility to deal with the city's Puerto Rican population. Racially mixed, discriminated against like blacks, and with even worse income and housing problems than blacks, Puerto Ricans needed all kinds of social services. After a conference with McGarry and her allies, John Cardinal O'Hara did agree to support a facility, Casa del Carmen, in the heart of the main run-down Puerto Rican area where educational, health, and social services would be available.[73]

The great increase in the black population from 378,000 in 1950 to 535,000 in 1960 changed the ethnic geography of the city.[74] The slum and mill districts that had first been the homes of the Irish and that had then mingled Irish, Jews, Italians, and others beginning in the 1890s, were now dominated by blacks. The grievous social problems that were part of black history in the city were made even worse for thousands of families by the deterioration of social life in a changing industrial setting. The old areas that had been decent working-class neighborhoods and the institutionalized slums became spectacularly dilapidated. The buildings had been used and abused for a century, and there were no family funds to renovate them. They crumbled and were bulldozed, and much of North Philadelphia became a wasteland of cleared lots and abandoned wreckage inhabited by the crippled, the hunted, and the haunted. In the outlying areas of the city, big new Irish parishes had arisen, and their residents were largely contemptuous of the blacks who had taken over the "old neighborhoods." In her speaking engagements, McGarry faced down the hostility of such suburbanites in dozens of parish and community sessions. With a forceful conviction, she insisted on the human link between the whites in their newfound security in better housing areas and the blacks caught in the ghetto.

Philadelphia had now become segregated on a new and massive basis. Nevertheless, the civil rights surge of the 1960s, and all of the difficult changes McGarry had worked for, had created channels of influence and social improvement for great numbers of blacks. Further, McGarry's work had created several models for social reform activists. She had created a prototype for grass-roots work in the ghetto, before the federal "War on Poverty" plans of the Lyndon Johnson administration. She created, as well, a profile of civic responsibility for Irish Catholics in the city's mainstream of government and social welfare activity, a sphere from which the group had long absented itself in favor of working within its own Catholic network of charitable agencies. She developed techniques of interracial pacification that were spread to other areas through the various Catholic interracial councils across the country. By the time of her death on January 3, 1978, McGarry was known and respected in social action circles far beyond Philadelphia. Toward the end of her life, she did achieve local recognition for her work, yet there were many people of her own background who recoiled from her association with blacks at any level of community life.

In what ways were the Catholic ideology and ethnic background of Anna McGarry interactive? The church had actually had a weak record in confronting racism in her lifetime.[75] The Irish Catholics specifically had, for the most part, an unenviable record of conflict with blacks. McGarry was able to surpass the limitations imposed by these facts and develop a personal drive and organizational base that stimulated her contemporaries. Although she held no offices in Irish organizations, she knew the officeholders and their constituents. Although not a labor official, she knew and worked with union leaders. A common background and common ethnic style abetted her. She was able to advance her own commitment among ethnic conservatives because she could command their respect. Her appeals to practical-minded people about the interest they themselves had in relieving black disability were hard to counter. She was sufficiently challenging in her address to issues, notwithstanding her genial personal ways, to face down the often vitriolic racism of her ethnic fellows in a way that demonstrated the kind of tough persistence and radical Irish spirit that animated other Irish-American reformers such as Mary Kenny O'Sullivan and Mary Harris (Mother Jones) of the labor movement and Daniel and Philip Berrigan of the peace movement.

Anna McGarry's career had taken her from a world of Irish Catholic pieties into a larger urban arena of fiercely antagonistic ethnic groups and a lifelong confrontation with frightening social problems. Aside from her deep religious commitment, two things sustained and propelled her as a personality—an unflagging persistence and a confident ethnic style—and both of these qualities were integral to her Irish identity. As others in the city's Irish community worked for labor organizations, Irish nationalist goals, education, and professional careers, she worked for interracial harmony. Her activities demonstrated to blacks the resources for good among her kind of people. Her career provided lifelong evidence of that Irish Catholic idealism that had spread through an international ethnic network of religious endeavor and had built in America a monumental urban system of social service and educational leadership.

3 Communication
Passing the Word

Communication is the essence of group life. It embodies the consciousness, common values, and social memory with which the group is invested. A whole world of assumptions, attitudes, and references is contained in this stream of discourse in which members of the group participate. There are deeply important symbolic and emotional implications involved with certain names, expressions, and rhetorical images. For the Irish, a people with a rich linguistic heritage, the process of communication in America presented peculiar problems. Although they shared the English language with the host society, they usually spoke it with a dialect and pronunciation difference deriving from their Gaelic language background. Because the Irish were a minority group, the mainstream media did not adequately accommodate their cultural, historical, and religious views.[1] It was necessary, therefore, for them to cultivate their own subcultural media, and this they did while participating in the mainstream media as democratic opportunity gradually expanded.

Language and communication are forms of action, not merely reflections of ideas or processes transcending the individual. Group life confirms much of its identity through the special use of accepted language that signifies group identity and status; this confirmation is an ongoing experience and an exercise of group bonding. A great deal of this bonding occurs almost unconsciously in daily contacts within the group. Greetings and phrases, inflections and clichés are all part of it. Some are venerable: "Keep the faith," "It's a fine soft day," "As sweet as the flowers of May," "I'm sorry for your trouble." These are the hackneyed, yet still common terms of Irish-American colloquialism.[2]

But there are high points of communication experience as well, and these are equally influential in binding ethnicity. They may consist of words from a song redolent with emotion or the stirring of an audience by a speaker putting Ireland's historic case for liberty, or they may emanate from attending productions of the plays of Sean O'Casey. Whatever the setting for such ethnically enriching climaxes of expression, they are a form of communion for the group that has deep significance. With the invention of modern media of communication, it has become possible for such experiences to be widely transmitted, and this, in turn, has facilitated the process by which people who have become marginal in their ethnic identity can with facility engage themselves again, perhaps only temporarily, but with emotional resonance, with the group and its modes of discourse and feeling.[3]

The section that follows gives examples of how this group developed communication media in Philadelphia. The tradition of ethnic journalism in America is vast and varied, and the publication of Irish newspapers in Philadelphia for over 150 years shows how extensive in time the tradition has been. The invention of radio presented subcultural groups with an entirely new vehicle for sustaining ethnic contacts and interactions, and Patrick Stanton's fifty-year career of broadcasting his weekly "Irish Hour" is probably the longest individual ethnic radio presentation on record.

The task of affirming the Irish intellectual tradition and teaching about the group's history and culture could not be easily accomplished for a variety of reasons. Irish-American communities long suffered educational disabilities complicated by poverty and cultural dislocation. The curricula of universities treated subcultural concerns as negligibly marginal, if at all, and Catholic institutions tended to be preoccupied with a non-Irish Latinized Catholicism that undervalued Irish cultural assets. Hence, the propagation of Irish learning among the Irish-Americans was problematical, and how the group responded to this difficulty is recounted in the section titled "Lines of Learning."

"A man's community is, quite simply, the set of people, roles and places with whom he communicates," Seymour Mandelbaum has written. The Irish have often been accused of being "clannish," and the loquacity and fellow feeling in Irish groups suggests the accuracy of the view of another scholar that "perceived similarity" itself stimulates communication.[4] Their sense of community, strong in Ireland, had to be reestablished in the American setting, and that meant they had to adapt and extend their old traditions of oratory, verbal enjoyment, and political discourse and use the new inventions of newspapers, radio, and other media to penetrate a new environment. The result was a distinctive adventure in cultural exploration for this ethnic group.

News from the Old Country

A central difficulty for studies of ethnic groups is that such groups were frequently segregated partially from the broader society and were often immersed in a poverty that did not permit the easy cultivation of elaborate means for cultural expression. While the commentary of the general society upon ethnic minorities is valuable as a testimony to contemporary attitudes and conditions, such commentary usually reflects a strong bias. Even if it is fairly objective, it is no substitute for evidence derived from within the minority group itself. The use of ethnic newspapers has enabled social historians to illuminate areas of minority experience for which other documentary sources are often nonexistent. Ethnic newspapers help to reveal the interests and way of life of countless people who left no personal archives or marks of the encounters in the communities in which they lived. Such newspapers chronicle events in both the old country and the new and provide clues to otherwise unrecorded subjects that were of great importance to minority readers.

The ethnic newspaper can be a source of biographical information and of material on business, education, and religion. Such material is of keen importance in gaining knowledge of populations that seem all but inarticulate because of the paucity of written sources of indigenous origin.[5] The sponsorship and editorship of the newspapers can reflect the leadership of an ethnic community. The editorials and news coverage reveal social and patriotic activities, exile politics, and intrigues; announcements of gatherings and festivals indicate organizational and church strength; classified advertisements tell of employment conditions, housing opportunities, and the efforts of families to reunite; business advertisements testify to economic advancement and success; and obituary notices give details of long-forgotten figures who may have been widely influential in minority communities but relatively unknown in the broader community.[6]

L.M. Cullen explains that literacy and journalism in Ireland grew up under peculiar conditions that endowed both spheres with a keen political sense. The scribes and poets of the old Gaelic order became schoolmasters in the seventeenth century after the defeat of their Gaelic clan patrons. They were powerful advocates of political agitation. Literacy was identified with their views. They both created and served the new literacy in English that was seen as a key to political influence and economic participation. Hence, the Irish reading audience was politicized early. Grievances and dissenting views repressed in Ireland were expressible in America.[7]

Despite the fact that the Irish spoke English and developed with alacrity the literacy that went with that language, in the world of pluralist America, they needed their own newspapers. The general press could not do for them what they required. Specifically, Irish papers did more than bring them news of the "old country." They provided vehicles for sharing and reshaping a group heritage and for promoting group affiliation in a much more effective way than the general press could. As informational media, they helped develop a coherent rhetoric of immigrant life, giving expression to nationalist and ethnic goals.

In his classic study of the history of American journalism, Frank Luther Mott devotes little attention to ethnic and immigrant newspapers. Nor does William Leonard Joyce in his study of Irish editors and newspapers provide more than a passing mention of Philadelphia Irish publications, despite the fact that they were numerous.[8] Generally, the Irish press is barely alluded to in newspaper history, and this is strange, for the Irish were for generations one of the largest immigrant groups in the nation and one whose newspapers were printed in English. Although not nearly so prolific in founding papers as the Germans were, they not only moved into mainstream journalism with vigor, but also contributed heavily to the development of the Roman Catholic religious press and several Protestant publishing streams as well. They also maintained an array of nationalist and fraternal publications over a long period of time. The existence of this long tradition of Irish journalism has occasioned surprisingly little study, although the value of the tradition as a source of insight into Irish-American affairs is amply demonstrated by an important work such as that of Thomas N. Brown on Irish nationalism, which relies heavily on newspaper sources.[9] Philadelphia is an appropriate locus to pursue study of this evolution, for it was for a good portion of the nineteenth century, one of the nation's major publishing centers. The city developed publishing enterprises early and eventually spawned a wide array of ethnic publications in various languages.

In the eighteenth century, largely Protestant emigration from the north of Ireland provided a cadre of politically conscious, activist Irishmen to the city. Service in the American Revolution distinguished a number of Philadelphia Irishmen and endowed the group with a patriotic image. In the 1830s, a surge of economic growth and the development of outlying areas began to alter the city's social structure and outlook. Religious conflict, immigrant poverty, and inadequate municipal services all contributed to social stress, manifested in working-class and interreligious riots, especially in the serious disorders of 1844. After the Irish famine of

1846–1847, the Irish-born population in the city grew and stabilized at about 10 percent of the total, remaining at this proportion from 1860 to 1910 when a gradual decline set in. This meant that throughout this period the Irish-born population never fell below one hundred thousand, a significant newspaper sales pool. Social mobility dispersed the Irish throughout the city beginning in the mid-nineteenth century, and for generations more Irish immigrants arrived to inhabit the old ghetto areas, replacing those who moved out. After the 1930s, the Irish community was no longer focused around residential considerations but sustained a network of organizational and church ties that maintained group affiliation and identity and could be linked by newspapers. Since the Irish community contained a literate and activist element that was able to express the outlook of the group through newspapers, there was, during this long immigrant experience, a market, albeit selective, for newspaper sales.[10]

Several features of Irish newspaper publications in Philadelphia are significant to any student examining their role in the city. The Irish papers did not stabilize as long-term local institutions. Despite the fact that they represent persistent attempts of minority journalism, appearing and disappearing over a 150-year period, they did not attain the strength and position of general-circulation newspapers. Although Irishmen ran some of the city's largest general circulation papers, no Irish-American papers in Philadelphia can match the hundred-year longevity of the *Irish World* published in New York.[11]

Another significant feature of the publications is that very few copies of them have survived. The fact that papers printed in five-figure runs, some of them for more than a decade, have all but vanished from the libraries, archives, and collections of the city is a demonstration of the effects that time, cheap newspaper stock, and lack of interest can have on sources for minority group history. This scarcity of copies explains to some extent the lack of citation of these papers in historical works dealing with the city, although the overall neglect of social and minority history is a more patent explanation.[12] Fortunately, the Balch Institute for Ethnic Studies in Philadelphia, an endowed research and library facility dedicated to ethnic studies, is now an example of what can be done by private philanthropy to help protect the records of ethnic groups.

The record of Irishmen in journalism in the city begins early. In all, there have been eighteen Irish papers in the city since the first decades of the nineteenth century. The most notable of the early Irish editors and publishers was Mathew Carey, a spirited Dublin man, exiled because of his protestations against English rule in Ireland. Carey arrived in America, in 1784 and the next year began the *Pennsylvania Herald*.[13] His magazines, the *Columbian Magazine* and the *American Museum*, were pioneering ventures in distinctly American content and orientation. Carey's publishing activities continued until his death in 1839. His own writings on economics and the condition of the poor and immigrants in Philadelphia, as well as his vivid description of yellow fever epidemics, are essential materials of social documentation. Carey maintained a keen interest in Irish emigration and in the Irish nationalist movement. Although his paper and magazines were not specifically Irish, Carey himself was indelibly Irish and was taunted as "Paddy" Carey for his compassionate writing in behalf of immigrants from the old country. Carey also played a prodigious role in developing American publishing through his production of books, pamphlets, and guides and through importing foreign publications. His work has two marks that would characterize Irish-American journalism in the future: it would be a journalism of controversies, and it would be allied to the small business and commercial activity that brought it advertising.[14]

It should be kept in mind that the Irish-American journalists of the city were part of a broader literary tradition of the Irish abroad which produced scholars and writers in England, France, and Spain, as well as in America. In Philadelphia, this tradition included Robert Walsh, publisher of the *American Review of History and Politics*, a strong intellectual voice in the new America of the 1820s. It included playwright and novelist Dr. James McHenry in the same period. Philadelphia Gaelic scholars Mathias O'Conway and Francis O'Kane were linked with the Gaelic-speaking refugees of the 1840s. While Daniel Kane O'Donell and Maurice Francis Egan were Victorian journalists, they were also poets and novelists, as was John T. McIntire in the twentieth century, and all wrote of the problems of Irish adjustment to America. Priest scholars like historian Father Peter Keenan Guilday and classicist Father Luke McCabe were part of this tradition that maintained strong cultural links with Ireland and sustained coteries in Philadelphia from the eighteenth century through the twentieth.[15]

The first newspaper published primarily for Irishmen in Philadelphia was the *Erin*, a well-edited biweekly launched by W.B. Hart in 1823. The paper was printed to correct the "imperfect and incomplete accounts received in this country of the state of

Ireland" and to expose "the machinations of those who have degraded the name and trampled the liberties of Ireland."[16] The paper gave news of the arrest of rebellious Irishmen in Dublin and agrarian violence against English landlords in Cork. It flayed the sectarian bigotry of Protestant Orange Lodges and gave publicity to the local Catholic schism in Philadelphia at St. Mary's church involving Reverend William Hogan. Philadelphians who affected British accents and ways were excoriated as "bastard lordlings." News of Joseph Riley's Second Brigade, Pennsylvania Militia, was mixed with columns on ladies' fashions and reports of the fall of Bernard O'Higgins, supreme director of the new Republic of Chile. The four-page paper, of which two pages were given over to advertising, had a fairly wide range of subject matter considering the limits of its size and its express dedication to Irish affairs.[17] It bespoke the libertarian French Revolution sentiments that had animated Irish rebel leaders in the rebellion of 1789, and it proclaimed them fiercely.

The years of the 1820s were lively ones for the Irish in the city, for two other papers were launched, the *Catholic Advocate and Irishman's Journal* and the *Irishman and Weekly Review*. These papers were contestants in a roaring religious dispute involving an attempt by Catholic trustees to take property from a bishop.[18] Contrasted with the *Erin*, these papers were narrow and intensely Catholic and foretold an era of Irish-Catholic apologetics that would last into our own day.

The social fabric of the city continued to be unsettled in the following decades. As the dislocations of the Industrial Revolution began to change the city's pattern of work life from apprenticeships and small shops to proletariat and factories, Irish-Catholic immigration increased. In these times of distress, the people found in Andrew Jackson a leader who promised reform and better treatment. It was in these years that the Irish-Catholic Democratic following was first formed. One of the Democratic papers was the *Irish Republican Shield and Literary Observer*, published between 1827 and 1833. Only a single issue of the paper survives, but, judging from its fiery content, Jacksonian Democracy never had a more partisan and vitriolic champion.[19] The paper was edited by George Pepper, later an editor in Boston. Pepper's pen was a veritable scourge. His paragraphs, mixing news with flaming editorial comment, lauded such local Jacksonians as Mathew Carey, John Binns, Patrick Keogh, John Maitland, and William Haley and reviled such members of the Orange Order as James Gowen. Advertisements offered land for immigrant purchase in upstate Pennsylvania, an endorsement of "Mr. Donnelly's Academy" by the Catholic bishop, and a variety of legal and medical services. The paper's heated political style no doubt gave it a strong appeal to those Irish workers who could read, for they had deep grievances. Unfortunately for its editor, the poverty of the readers soon overtook the publication itself.

In the 1840s, the Irish leader Daniel O'Connell mounted a drive to break the legislative union of England and Ireland, and his efforts prompted a good deal of support in the United States. In Philadelphia, this "Repeal of the Union" drive spawned a Repeal Association and a newspaper, the *Philadelphia Irish Citizen*, in 1843. Thomas Dunn English, a friend of Edgar Allan Poe, was one of those associated with it. Either Poe wrote for the paper or one of his friends published material under Poe's name. This paper did not outlive the Repeal Association's furious disruption when it was diverted by a bitter debate of Daniel O'Connell's anti-slavery views.[20] The clarion O'Connell ushered in the age of Irish political mobilization, and, for that, newspapers were vital.

The Irish newspapers at times engaged in controversies with powerful figures in the local community. Bishop James Wood became disenchanted with *Catholic Herald* editor James Spellissey early in 1864 because of an article on "Secret Societies." Spellissey was a partisan of the underground revolutionary group the Fenian Brotherhood, which had been organized in Ireland but which spread rapidly and widely in the United States. Pledged by a secret oath to overthrow English rule in Ireland, the organization concocted an array of plots and insurrection plans through the years of the American Civil War to injure English interests wherever possible. When the Pope at the behest of English diplomats issued a circular condemning the Fenian Brotherhood, Spellissey pointed out that the Catholic church had various secret organizations within itself that acted in secret proceedings. Bishop Wood, of English background, condemned the Fenians in a pastoral letter and withdrew his support of the *Universe*, Spellissey's paper. Spellissey changed his paper from a vehicle for Catholic views to a more distinctly Irish publication and continued to support the Fenians. Bishop Wood went on to plan a rival and ultimately successful paper with his endorsement, the *Catholic Standard*. These kinds of controversies indicate the strains in an Irish population that had differences of class, goals, and interests that reflected varying attachments to Ireland and varying interpretations of its affairs.[21]

One of the most successful papers established by an Irishman was founded in 1847, the year in which the Irish population began to grow rapidly. The *Philadelphia Item* was not a specifically Irish journal, though it always had a large Irish following. Thomas Fitzgerald founded the *Item*, which continued for fifty years under the founder and his sons. Beginning as a penny paper, it gradually expanded, as did Fitzgerald's wealth. It embraced a wide readership and in the 1880s had a circulation of over 180,000.[22] It also signalized the Irish entry into business in the city and was an important vehicle of business information as the group prospered.

Papers appealing to the Irish as such, however, never fared as well as the *Philadelphia Item*. In the period after the Great Famine immigration of the 1840s, there were still many Irish who could not read and write, and it is not unusual to find in payrolls of the time well over 50 percent of the Irish laborers signing for their pay with a simple "X." The Irish were also a group with a strong folk tradition of oral storytelling and discourse. It was probably much more enjoyable to hear news from one of the local raconteurs with all the embellishment and humorous comment that could be supplied by such persons than to read the cold print. But readership was a serious habit among those seeking learning and status, and reading rooms and clubs abounded.

Some of the Philadelphia Irish papers published for so short a time that we have no surviving copies by which to evaluate them. One was the *Irish Standard*, a short-lived venture launched in 1879.[23] Another, the *Sunday Leader*, was set up in 1878 by Colonel James O'Reilly to propagate Irish revolutionary aims. O'Reilly, who had a brilliant record in the Civil War, was a member of the Fenian Brotherhood. Despite his commitment, he was unable to make his paper last long enough to serve the cause. The repeated efforts and failures in the field of nationalist publication can be partly explained by the adversary views of the Irish writers and editors toward the stifling of free opinion in Ireland. Prosecutions for "seditious libel" were common there, and control of the press in Ireland through bribery and patronage was ubiquitous. America offered freedom from such coercion.[24]

A paper that succeeded in promoting the rebel cause in later years had a longer life. The *Clan na Gael* (Children of the Gael) was published weekly between 1882 and 1896.[25] The Clan na Gael was a secret society dedicated to militant physical force operations against the British Empire, and this organization gave the paper its name. Judging from surviving issues dating from 1888, the paper carried on steady propaganda for the Irish cause. One article refers to Joseph Chamberlain, a parliamentary foe of Irish Home Rule, as "Judas Chamberlain." Others castigate British terms for international treaties with the United States. One issue tells of a gift of five thousand dollars to fund the fight against British coercion legislation in Ireland. One of the leaders noted in its pages was "Dynamite" Luke Dillon, a protagonist of dynamiting campaigns against England. Dillon, a Philadelphian, spent years in Canadian prisons after being caught on a dynamiting mission there, a foray directed against British Empire installations.

Philadelphia after the Civil War was a major publishing center, and mass circulation papers were coming into their own. There was probably little difficulty in finding editors, reporters, and printers for the Irish papers in the second half of the nineteenth century. General community papers line the *Philadelphia Times* (1876–1902) and the enduring *Taggart's Sunday Times* (1863–1901) had Irish editors like Tyrone-born Frank McLaughlin and John Taggart. For years, Israel Sheppard, a Tipperary man, was an editor of the *Public Ledger*, and Stephen Farrelly was manager of the Central News Company, a distribution network.[26] Such men, along with reporters, cartoonists, and a host of politicians and mid-city characters, could be found nightly at Harry Connolly's famous saloon at Seventh and Chestnut streets talking the news of the morning editions.

Intermittently, some man with money or some organization would get the idea of setting up a newspaper to promote Irish interests. Thus, in the 1880s, the agitation of the Irish Land League, led by the charismatic Charles Stewart Parnell, generated enormous interest in America's drive to finance the purchase of holdings from the landlord class by small Irish farmers. One network for its fund-raising and publicity in America was the Irish National League. A paper published from 1889 to 1891, the *Free Man and Irish American Review*, promoted Parnell's campaign and the league and reported on boycotts and agrarian unrest in Ireland along with news of the Irish activity in the U.S. designed to support Parnell.[27]

Some Irish papers were strongly colored by local politics. One was the *Irish-American News*, which came and went in 1892. It championed local politicians like William McAleer, perennial congressman and Democratic stalwart. The bankroll behind the paper, which mixed Irish news with Democratic party doings, was probably that of William F. Harrity, a man of considerable wealth and chairman of the Democratic National Committee that helped put Grover Cleveland in the White House.[28]

During the second half of the nineteenth century, one of the ornaments of the newspaper world was the scholar-intellectual who was also a working newsman. Before the age of yellow journalism, there was room in the closely printed columns of newspapers for long disquisitions on subjects of scholarly and literary interest. Literary columns were often presented daily. One of the writers with strong ties to the Irish press who represented this talent-rich journalism was James Shelton Mackenzie, born in Cork of Scots-Gaelic parents and full of the lore of Irish literary traditions. Mackenzie was a classical scholar and a tower of literary information and criticism of ponderous capacity. For years after coming to America, his writings were carried in the *Press*, one of the daily papers of the city with a heavily Irish staff and readership. He was also the Philadelphia correspondent for the *Irish World* of New York. In addition to newspaper copy, Mackenzie turned out Irish historical novels, translations, books of literary criticism, and ephemera in copious amounts.[29]

Another such journalist was Robert Malachi McWade, whose love for the orations of Demosthenes led him to edit a book of Greek compositions. Antrim-born McWade was close to the revolutionary Fenian Brotherhood and tried to aid the short-lived publications such as the *Sunday Leader*, which failed in the 1870s. He had contacts with most of the powerful figures in Irish and Irish-American circles. He wrote two books in the 1890s dealing with Parnell's campaign for land reform. In addition to being an editor for several daily newspapers, he was a tireless fund-raiser for contributions to disasters, floods, and war victims.[30]

The Irish newspapers throughout the country depended on one another a good deal for swapping of coverage. The New York *Irish American* and the *Irish World* each carried local news pages on which appeared items of interest from the Irish communities across the nation. Stories, letters, and reports from Philadelphia appeared in the New York papers regularly. The larger Irish nationalist and fraternal organizations were nationwide in their structure, and news of their policies, conventions, and disputes frequently appeared in Irish papers. Such coverage was compressed and used in the Philadelphia Irish publications.

A standard feature of the Irish papers was a column listing inquiries by those remaining in Ireland about missing family members: "Peter Phillips, left Cork over thirty years ago, last known to

have resided in Philadelphia. Any information will be greatly ap-
preciated by his brother, Patrick Phillips, Macroom, County Cork."
Such appeals got results often enough. Somebody from the same
townland or some acquaintance in America would respond, and
the information would be placed in a companion column reflecting
sometimes good tidings and sometimes tragic reports of death and
distress.

Large fraternal organizations such as the Ancient Order of Hibernians also generated newspaper projects. Philadelphian Maurice Wilhere, a president of the AOH, launched the *Philadelphia
Hibernian* in 1893.[31] The fifty-five divisions of the Hibernian organization in the city provided a ready means of distribution, but this
was not enough of an economic base, so the paper folded a year
later. A somewhat similar project was the *Irish-American Review
and Celtic Literary Advocate*, edited by P.J. McManus and published first in 1898.[32] It provided news from Ireland under county
headings, coverage of local Hibernian affairs, and anti-British articles that reached a crescendo during the Boer War. The pages of
these papers feature effusive biographies of local Irishmen and
lithograph scenes of Hibernian balls with the dancers decked out
in high Victorian finery.

The advent of mass circulation metropolitan papers in the second half of the nineteenth century was accompanied by a gradual
increase in crime news, illustration, and want ads, while politics,
editorials, and letters to the editor decreased. For Irish-American
readers, this shifting of the equation in contents made more desirable the patronage of a subcultural press in which the latter three
kinds of writing were given fuller play. Not only did the leaders
seek out and utilize journalism, but the political meetings, nationalist celebrations, dances, and athletic and social events of the
Irish community were all dependent on information disseminated
through the group's newspapers. The readership responded to this
information in scores of ways, among them contributions to various
causes, patronage of Irish businesses, and commentary within the
community about the Irish news carried in the pages of the Irish
papers.[33]

These nineteenth-century papers competed with the great Philadelphia dailies such as the *Evening Bulletin*, the *Philadelphia
Inquirer*, the *Public Ledger* and the *Philadelphia North American*. These papers could be relied upon for reports of visits of
Irish leaders to the city. While the Irish coverage of the dailies
was scanty compared with that of the Irish-American papers, the

coverage of crime, politics, and entertainment in the dailies was far superior. In addition, there were Catholic papers such as *Griffin's Journal*, published by Martin I.J. Griffin. This paper, later the organ of the Irish Catholic Benevolent Union, specialized in reprinting accounts of American Catholic history and benevolent association affairs. It was published from 1873 until 1900. The weekly paper of the Catholic Archdiocese, the *Catholic Standard and Times*, replacing the earlier *Catholic Herald* in 1866, was a strong mass-circulation vehicle for religious news, but it also featured steady Irish coverage, often on a county by county basis.[35] While not as fiery as the Irish nationalist papers, the archdiocesan weekly was highly partisan to Irish interests and, indeed, was often almost completely dominated by material on Irish affairs.

With such competition, the Irish papers had to serve specialized groups and capitalize on special Irish political and nationalist causes, such as the Land League drive or the "dynamite" crusade of the physical force revolutionaries. At times, such special coverage was highly important, as in the case of the *Irish Press*. In 1918, the U.S. government yielded to British pressure and banned from the mails the *Irish World* and the *Gaelic American*, the two leading Irish-American nationalist papers in the country, both published in New York. The 1916 insurrection in Dublin had set in motion a train of events that led to a guerrilla war against British power in Ireland. In 1918, stories of British repression and growing Irish hostilities were not good propaganda with England in the midst of World War I. In order to stifle news of the Irish freedom movement, England pressed successfully for suppression of the Irish-American papers. Joseph McGarrity, a Tyrone-born Philadelphian, began the *Irish Press*, often hastily composed and edited, and kept the American support groups informed and in touch with the day-to-day battles in Ireland. The paper served a strategic purpose at the climactic period of modern Irish nationalist effort.[35]

After the 1920s, when the Irish-born population began to decrease, the prospects for local Irish papers declined sharply. Still, there were occasional efforts to provide the city's Irish with their own news medium. Robert V. Clarke, a native of County Mayo and a prominent figure in Philadelphia Irish organizations, and David Roche, a Cork-born activist, attempted to promote the *Irish American* in 1952 and 1953, but were unable to keep it alive. The paper reflected a modernized interest in Irish development, opposition to the partition of Ireland, and dissent from the tide of wild anti-Communism propounded by Senator Joseph McCarthy at the time.

Robert Clarke later edited the *Irish American Herald* from 1968 to 1970, a photo-offset monthly news round-up of Irish affairs.[36] The audience was limited by the diminished Irish population, however, and the publication terminated. The city's two Irish radio programs, conducted for decades by Patrick Stanton and Will Regan over local stations, then provided the only broad means of communication for the city's Irish population. Later, Charles Murray, sheriff of Philadelphia County, did publish his short-lived *Shamrock* tabloid from 1976 to 1977.

Analysis of the editing of the older Irish papers indicates that copy was almost invariably assembled in pragmatic fashion without much quality control. The range of interest extended only to Irish subject matter and American topics bearing on such material. At times, local political or Catholic issues became matter for coverage. There was usually little discrimination between reportage and editorial comment, the two being mingled in a thoroughly didactic journalism. Reprinting from papers in Ireland and such larger American papers as the *New York Herald* and the *Irish World* was frequent, and occasionally a correspondent's report on some event in Ireland or in the British Parliament was featured. Speeches were often reprinted or generously excerpted, especially on those subjects of high interest to Irish nationalists, such as English coercion acts or speeches of American churchmen or politicians condemning English rule. Patriotic poetry was a standard element in the papers, with issues of papers carrying one or two poems a page, a use of verse in keeping with the interests of a people with a rich tradition of ballad and folk poetry. Most of the topic sentences and headlines were almost ritualistic in their stereotyped nationalism. Thus, the *Clan na Gael* was filled with such leaders as "Every tyrannical effort and artifice had been made and will be made by the Tory government to delay it, but the unity of the Irish people . . . and the sympathy and material support of America will win in the end," or "Generation after generation of English statesmen have exhausted their ingenuity in fruitless endeavor to discover an absolutely certain method of stamping out the Irish Nation."[37] Biographical sketches, especially in fraternal papers, were ordinarily fulsome to the point of adulation. Lithograph portraits, emblems, and scenes of social and athletic events were illustrative fare, but the standards of printing were seldom high.

The chief characteristics of these minority publications were notably consistent over the long period of their successive appearance and demise. They were largely vehicles for nationalist exhortation

and propaganda. Their intellectual level was awkwardly pretentious in the nineteenth century and sharply expedient in the twentieth, appealing directly to an audience that was literate but not
extensively educated. Their pervasive nationalist and ethnic consciousness was heavily reinforced by religious solidarity and a
homely interest in old-country news and local accounts of meetings, arrivals, deaths, births, and social trivia. The papers paral-
leled mass-circulation dailies in featuring coverage of gruesome
and sensational events, but only when these involved Irish prison
sufferings, agrarian violence, or English military repression. Ex-
plicitly or implicitly, the local names appearing in the papers had
political significance. The very fact that some of the publications
existed is attributable to the political motives of members of a
group whose political proclivities were powerful. The publications
were inspired also by the constant need of the Irish to raise money
to support their long tradition of agitation against English rule in
the homeland.

In March 1981, a new chapter in the annals of Irish publication
was begun in Philadelphia. Anthony Byrne, a former U.S. Marine
Corps officer; Jane Duffin, a teacher and sociologist; and Nancy
Mortimer, a former employee of one of the local daily papers,
started a monthly newspaper called the *Irish Edition*. The original
intention was to provide a vehicle for the cultural life of the Irish
community, which had been experiencing a considerable revival of
interest in traditional music, books, lectures, and organizational activity since 1970. The issues, ranging from sixteen to thirty-two
pages, were well-printed and had good layout with modest advertising support. The lead articles dealt with activities and gatherings of the Irish community, visits by notable lecturers and
performing groups, and events related to Northern Ireland and the
reaction of the local community to the violence, hunger strikes,
and tension there. The political dimension of the problem was in-
escapable, and the editors felt compelled to present news about it
even though it went beyond their original cultural emphasis. One
reason for this was the paucity of information about the situation
in the American press, a condition found by researchers to be attributable to British news management at the source.[38]

The *Irish Edition* printed a number of short stories, book and
play reviews, historical articles about the Irish and Irish-American
tradition, and original poetry. One column called "The Greenhorn"
by Maureen Benzing, a regular feature for some time, recounted the

experiences of immigrants from Ireland. Pictures of local Irish people and events added visual interest. Stories about musicians, politicians, writers, hard coal miners in upstate Pennsylvania, priests visiting Northern Ireland, and distinctive events made the paper unusual. Most Irish-American papers, such as the *Irish World* and the *Irish Echo* published in New York, stuck to the old formula of presenting news from Ireland along with chatty local gossip columns and announcements. There was a column on local political news and coverage by correspondents in Ireland. The *Irish People*, also published in New York, was circulated in Philadelphia, but it was focused entirely on Northern Ireland and the work of Irish Northern Aid in opposing British and unionist presence there. The *Irish Edition* was more moderate, diverse, and thoughtful in its coverage of Ulster's tragedy. It was probably the best Irish newspaper that Philadelphia had ever had since the *Erin* in the early nineteenth century.

Editors Byrne and Duffin, both American-born, had no previous newspaper experience upon entering into the venture. There were no subsidies other than their own free time and ample energy. Yet, they were perceptive enough to gather a wide range of contributors and put out a very interesting newspaper that gave voice to an Irish community that was more than a museum of immigrant memory. The *Irish Edition* represented the Irish-Americans with advanced educations and lively interests who viewed Ireland as a rich cultural treasury. Such readers and contributors got their news of Ireland from personal visits, television, and the general press. They relied on the *Irish Edition* to interpret that news. They fashioned their views of Ireland from reading and measuring the old country from an American perspective, and that measuring process gave them a modernized, much less sentimental, and more seasoned view of Ireland's life and its Irish-American echoes. Thus, to the long chronicle of journalism in the city was added a further vehicle that affirmed the identity of the Irish community and provided expression for its current opinion and social adaptation.

Because of the scarcity of copies of the nineteenth-century papers, extended analysis of their contents is not possible. Some things can be concluded about their sponsorship, however. Obviously, some were the projects of nationalist revolutionaries, such as W.B. Hart of the *Erin*, Luke Dillon of the *Clan na Gael*, and Joseph McGarrity of the *Irish Press*. Papers like the *Irish-American News* were narrowly local political vehicles with politician sponsors. The

Irish Edition has been primarily a cultural publication. Clearly, the inspiration of the papers has been as varied as the Irish community's disposition over time.

The role of the papers has included not only the giving of information, but also the provocation of controversy, as was the case in the 1830s at the time of the Catholic religious schism and throughout the years with nationalist agitation. "Advocacy journalism" has dominated. Because of this ideological orientation, the business history of these publications has been one of small returns and short lives, for they were not able to meet the broader needs of the Irish population.

The papers do reflect change among the Irish in that the organized groups they represented follow the sequence of Irish organizational evolution since 1820. The longer-lived official Catholic papers show the stabilization of the church in the city after 1860, while the creation of the *Irish Edition*, with its material on books, theater, and traditional music and its modernized view of Ireland, reveals the change of the local Irish community to a post-immigrant ethnic group posture.

The question of just how these publications held their readers, even for a time, is of interest. Michael Schudson provides an insight derived from his study of the social history of journalism. Such newspapers gave a stimulus to the social and political roles that people played. They had arisen as journals of politics and opinion in the nineteenth century, and they continued at least partly as such as time went on. They also were part of the democratic market society that permits and extols free choice and cultural freedom. They were egalitarian in their creation and orientation, and they developed among their readership the capacity for sustained awareness that was part of the exercise of literacy in a free society. For the Irish-Americans, they were subsidiary pleasures in the exciting world of the city.[39]

The Irish Hour

Although newspapers were an expedient vehicle for ethnic communication, the pace of events in the American environment was so rapid that a medium even more swift was required to inform people of the meetings and affairs that brought the Irish together and reinforced their cultural bonds. In the period after World War I, the old residential configurations of the Irish in Philadelphia began to undergo extensive changes that would continue for a generation. The large areas of Irish concentration dating from the heavy immigration of the 1800s were breaking up as automobiles, better public transportation, and suburban attractions lured more and more people away from the inner city. The Irish organizations remained very active through the war for Irish independence from 1919 to 1922, but then a decline set in. Some new influence was needed to keep the Irish in touch with one another in their new dispersion across the expanding urban landscape. Although nobody could foresee it at the time, a young actor was thinking in the 1920s of the prospects for a local radio program that would be a very strong influence indeed in maintaining communication with the Irish community and in serving as a vehicle linking the Irish to the broader urban community. The young actor was Patrick Stanton, and his radio program, "The Irish Hour," would become the longest running ethnic radio show under one man's auspices in the history of American broadcasting.

The novelty of radio in the 1920s was very appealing, even glamorous, and it was not less so for people born and raised in the isolation of villages in remote rural areas in County Donegal and County Mayo. Ireland began its first radio broadcasting from Dublin in 1926, but the low-power transmission did not reach very far abroad in the country. When Patrick Stanton began his radio program in 1926, it could be said that, because the Philadelphia community probably had more radio sets than all of Ireland, he reached more Irish listeners and reached them before any other radio service. He was the first radio voice of the Irish.[40]

Patrick Stanton was born in Charlesville, County Cork in 1907. He was the seventh of sixteen children in a poor working family. His father had a hard time supporting the large family. Partly to ease the burden, Patrick was sent to America in company with an aunt in 1912. He grew to be a handsome and clever boy, and he also had a very fine voice and excellent diction. For a time, he studied for the priesthood in his teens, but he changed his mind about becoming a priest and developed an increasing interest in the theater in the 1920s in and around New York. He took part in little theater companies and summer stock and worked with actors such as Clifton Webb. In some productions, he went on the road with touring companies, and, for a time, he got bit parts in early films made in New York and Philadelphia.[41]

In 1926, the city of Philadelphia was celebrating the sesquicentennial of the founding of the American nation. There were many extravagant schemes for the celebration, and Pat Stanton was drawn into some of them that involved radio broadcasts of ceremonies and local events. One of the early radio stations in the city was Station WELK. Stanton obtained a job as an announcer with the station and was soon petitioning the management to begin an Irish radio program. Since program material of any kind was scarce at that time, he received a favorable reception. On St. Patrick's Day in 1926, he went on the air with his first program, "The Irish Hour."[42]

It is difficult to imagine the emotional effect of his program in today's world of communications saturation. One woman recounted that she could not believe what she heard in 1926 and thought that her employers were playing a trick on her when they bade her listen to the voices coming from a box in their home. She heard the soft Cork accent of Stanton providing news from Ireland and promising a rendition of "She is Far from the Land" by a local tenor. She was amazed and so were thousands like her. To hear the speech of the old country, to hear recent news directly from Ireland, to hear the songs and melodies of traditional Irish music was for such people a delightful, exciting experience. Stanton read poetry to the audience, interviewed guests, and told of local dances, sporting contests, and religious events.[43] His program soon developed a following that was to be extremely faithful. It filled a void of loneliness for thousands of immigrants and provided swift communication for the Irish organizations and businesses in the city.

Stanton's program became a weekly ritual in Irish households. It was, above all, musical, and musicians like John McGettigan and his orchestra were broadcast live. The Four Provinces Irish Orchestra with Jack Coll as its leader tore through many a jig and reel on the air. In the kitchens of Irish homes, and in the kitchens of the great houses where the Irish were still commonly employed as servants, the music would set feet tapping and frequently sent listeners off into impromptu set dances with the sheer exhuberant pleasure of it. Stanton became more and more knowledgeable about Irish music as week after week he presented local talent on the show. The musicians themselves were often fine folk artists, part of a tradition full of vitality, and their appearance on the program brought people out to the Irish dances at which they played in halls across the city.[44]

Station WELK eventually became Station WDAS, and Pat Stanton became vice-president of the broadcasting corporation using those call letters. With more experience in administration and general programming available to him, Stanton set his sights on owning and operating his own station. Through the 1930s, when it was difficult to obtain sponsors because of the economic depression, he lived with the bad times but kept as his goal the development of his own station.

In addition to his radio work, Stanton involved himself in a wide variety of activities in the Irish community. He organized entertainment troupes of singers, dancers, and instrumentalists for the Feis Ceoil, an annual music festival. He wrote a weekly column for the *Irish World* about Irish activities in Philadelphia. He continued as toastmaster, master of ceremonies, and producer of Irish events for years. Commenting on these activities in 1961, he said,

> Perhaps I shouldn't refer to advancing age, but after the week I have just put in, I know it's here. Monday last I had a tour with the Right Honorable Mayor of Dublin, Robert Briscoe, and had the privilege of presenting him to a filled dining room at the Poor Richard Club as well as presenting the distinguished guests who came to do him honor. On Wednesday evening I addressed the Parent Teachers Association, and on Thursday evening I attended the Horse Breeders Association banquet at the Plaza Hotel in New York—and I don't even own a pair of riding boots. I did six full hours of Irish programs during the week and a regular week's work schedule of some ten hours to boot . . . and you know, it's amazing how many people think that all I do any time is The Irish Hour. If they happen to call right after the program they invariably say, "Pat, I'm glad I got you before you went home." And sure, why should I disillusion them? I actually think a great many of them envy my short work day.[45]

The radio broadcasting business was not all smooth by any means, although economically it was a growth area. In the late 1930s, Stanton and Station WDAS where he was employed were picketed by backers of Father Charles E. Coughlin because the station refused to carry Coughlin's fiery broadcasts. Coughlin's appeal was fading at the time, and he was having trouble getting air time after his anti-Semitic and anti-Roosevelt outbursts. Stanton received a furious round of anti-Semitic mail from some of his Irish constituency, and Reverend Thomas J. Higgins, president of St. Joseph's College, wrote him protesting his refusal to allot Coughlin broadcast time. Within the Irish community there was bitter disagreement over Coughlin's radio crusade against the New Deal, and Stanton was strongly opposed to the radio priest's rhetoric.[46]

In the early 1940s, he finally got the opportunity to file with the Federal Communications Commission for the use of a frequency with the call letters WJMJ, but there was competition from a Cincinnati group seeking the same frequency. A long litigation ensued, but, by June 1948, Stanton had been accorded a limited license to broadcast as Station WJMJ. By this time, he had married and had three children, but he managed to keep a schedule of long hours at his young station.

Over the years, Stanton had built up a list of sponsors whose names became bywords in the Irish community because of the publicity he designed for them. The betrothed bought their wedding rings at Farnan Jewelers or Haggerty's Jewelry Store. They bought furniture from the Dunhill Craft Company, painted their new homes with Finnaren and Haley paints, and celebrated their anniversaries at Cavanaugh's Restaurant on Market Street. When air travel to Ireland became feasible, Aer Lingus advertised on "The Irish Hour," as did a whole network of travel agents.[47]

Pat Stanton had a gift of getting people to work with him. He knew hundreds of musicians and entertainers, many of whom had been weaned on Irish music but who had gone on into the mainstream entertainment world where jazz, musical comedy, operettas, and all kinds of music increased their earning possibilities. Billy Donahue was an organist and pianist who had played in theaters during silent films. He put together variety shows and, with announcer Charles Shannon, broadcast them nightly over radio station WPEN in Philadelphia prior to World War II. He was every inch an entertainer in the energetic American style, and he was one type of broadcasting talent that Pat Stanton knew well as competitor and friend.[49] Ed Reavey was another kind of musician, a folk musician and fiddler from "Corktown" in West Philadelphia who played his fiddle on Stanton's show. Reavey had a head full of hundreds of Irish tunes, and could compose more on demand. The music Stanton encouraged through "The Irish Hour" was Reavey's kind of music for the most part.[49]

With his program director at WJMJ, Mike Deagan, Stanton was well aware of the technical changes that kept broadcasting in a constant state of evolution. It was a lively business with steadily expanding possibilities. The growth of the recording industry transformed broadcasting in the 1930s, and several companies specialized in producing Irish records. Smaller radio stations were not given the records for promotion as became the practice later. Pat Stanton had to buy the records he broadcast, and he did so, purchasing records in the United States, England, and Ireland until he had built up a huge collection of recorded Irish music.[50]

The introduction of recording on tape greatly extended programming possibilities in yet another innovation. It became possible to tape-record all kinds of Irish events, sermons, speeches, special concerts, messages from Ireland, and interviews with visiting dignitaries. These could all now be recorded independent of the time "The Irish Hour" was scheduled for broadcast. The flexibility was a boon, and programming became much more diverse. In the 1950s, Stanton was able to find sufficient sponsorship to increase "The Irish Hour" presentations to three a week, one at midday on Sunday and two evening shows.

Through his connection with travel agents and the nascent efforts of the Dublin government to stimulate tourism, Stanton became interested in making films to encourage visits to Ireland. He made and narrated three films giving panoramic views of the country. His showings of his color films *Ireland Today* and *Here Is Ireland* were popular features at parish and organization gatherings. The films were typical of his habit of enterprise: he could take an idea from concept to design and execution to completion, gathering sponsors, managing production, and arranging for broadcast and distribution.[51]

As "The Irish Hour" became a local institution, it developed a capacity to generate its own patronage and programming. Young Irish musicians and singers vied to perform on it. People constantly wrote to Stanton asking that announcements of dances and gatherings be made, and birthdays, anniversaries, and bon voyage wishes were always part of the commentary that was built into the program. Every year around Christmas, Stanton would pick some charity and promote it actively on the show and in his public appearances. One of his favorite charities was an orphanage conducted by nuns in Ballaghadereen in County Mayo. The Sisters of Charity benefited steadily from his promotional efforts devoted to an institution for the least fortunate in one of the poorest localities in Ireland. The show also gave airtime to short lectures and addresses by those interested in expounding on Irish history or campaigning to bring about the end of the partition of Ireland. Spokesmen such as Owen B. Hunt, a local orator and enthusiast, and John J. Reilly, a widely respected activist, pleaded their causes on WJMJ.[52]

A typical one-hour show consisted of eight or ten musical selections. These featured folk songs and traditional dance tunes, as well as recordings of artists like John McCormack and Father

Sidney MacEwan. Occasionally, Scots and English selections, especially music hall numbers by such old-time performers as Will Fyfe, would be used. By the mid-1960s, practically all the music would be on records or tape, as would the introduction and signature for the program. The show was regularly introduced by a wildly animated dance tune called "O'Sullivan Mor," a great favorite. There was some repetition of numbers on request from week to week, but this was kept to a minimum, for the repertory of available material was great and growing. A program schedule would include such selections as "Bendemeer Stream," sung by Michael O'Duffy; "God Save Ireland," sung by Teresa Duffy; "The Patriot Game," performed by the Glen Folk Four; "Jug Medley," performed by the Pride of Donegal (Richard Fitzgerald and his Bundoran Ceili Band); "Maire My Girl," sung by Kenneth McKellar; "Going Home," performed by the Johnstons; "Are You Right There, Michael?" sung by Brendan O'Dowda; and "Hornpipes," performed by McCusker Brothers Ceilidhe Band.[53]

It was the music more than any other feature that bound Stanton's audience to him. The selections consisted of everything from Irish folk and concert music to British music hall sing-along songs to Irish-American tunes, Hebrides love songs, Broadway music from George M. Cohan, the operettas of Victor Herbert, compositions by local players, traditional story ballads, Gaelic work songs, and an extraordinary range of jigs, reels, hornpipes, set dances, and instrumental medleys. Listeners became familiar with literally hundreds of tunes. In Irish families, it was a custom to teach children to sing along with the program. Families busy preparing Sunday dinner would have "The Irish Hour" tuned in and would hum and sing along with the music. Scores of local people developed a whole repertoire of songs for party presentations and group singing by learning the verses for the program.[54]

As the folk music revival took form in the 1960s, a whole new generation of listeners tuned in to the program to lilt through the lyrics of the weekly selections. Sheet music scores and songbooks permitted the memorization of all four verses of "The Felons of Our Land" or the six verses of "The Foggy Dew," and the records and tapes of favorite performers brought the music into greater currency. Records and tapes by the Clancy Brothers and Tommy Makem were enormously popular, replacing older groups like the McNulty Family. In this way, "The Irish Hour" sustained the rich musical tradition to which the Philadelphia Irish community was heir.

But Stanton was involved with more than the Irish community. For a time, he was the announcer for a Yiddish radio program, introducing musical selections in Yiddish himself. His station was host to a number of ethnic programs.[55] At the suggestion of Anna McGarry, he began a "Talent and Discussion Program" with the aid of the Catholic Interracial Council. The show was conducted by Jesse and Harriet Franklin, assisted by black entertainers and commentators.[56] A program on student affairs was conducted by local college students with Stanton's aid and the deft direction of Mike Deegan. What Stanton had accomplished was to compose programming that reflected the great diversity of the city. Unlike the larger network stations that appealed to a mainstream public, his station aimed at representing the ethnic cultural spectrum of the city, and it did this for Italians, Greeks, and Poles, as well as the Irish. This was an important feature of the station's operation, but it was not easy to organize. Representatives of various ethnic groups with good ties to those groups and some experience in or at least competence for, broadcasting had to be located and then persuaded to seek ethnic and other sponsors. Programs involved producing hard-to-find recordings, translating items from English to foreign languages and vice versa, and scheduling appropriately for particular ethnic calendars of events and observances. It was quite a polyglot task, but Stanton and Deegan accomplished it.[57]

In 1968, James H.J. Tate was sworn in as mayor of Philadelphia following the resignation of Richardson Dilworth. Tate had been head of the city council and active in a number of Irish organizations over the years. A Democrat and a veteran political figure, he was the first Irish-Catholic mayor in the history of Philadelphia. Pat Stanton was a lifelong Republican like many of the Irish who had made careers for themselves in a city that was renowned for its Republican domination prior to 1950. He had been largely oblivious to politics, however, not only because he was preoccupied with the radio business, but also because partisan political activity would have conflicted with the broad role he had to play in the development and management of his station. Ethnic affinity outstripped party loyalty when Mayor Tate chose Stanton to be his press secretary in 1968. The position involved directing the city's public information programs, stimulating tourism, and promoting the city's interest through publicity.[58]

Pat Stanton's career as press secretary required that he scale down his work with Station WJMJ. He had sold the station in 1965 for $650,000 and arranged a five-year consulting contract that kept him involved with it. The city post made this relationship more difficult to sustain, but Pat continued to broadcast "The Irish Hour" weekly. As press secretary, he was involved with tasks that were largely quite congenial: he greeted visiting dignitaries to the city, worked with the press and radio and television crews, and monitored city events and the publication and public contact activities of a wide range of city departments and institutions. Failing health eventually led to his decision to resign the position early in 1971.

During the last years of his life, Stanton continued his interest in the city's Irish community, especially in the Friendly Sons of St. Patrick, the St. Patrick's Day Observance Association, the annual visits of groups of Irish teachers, and the steady round of associations and events generated by the Irish groups. He also continued actively in professional associations in the communications field, an interest he had keenly maintained throughout his career.[59] It was "The Irish Hour" that was the focus of his most intent work, though, and he was determined to round out a full half-century of its production and presentation. Beginning in the 1960s, younger people became very interested in folk music, and Irish folk recordings and performers began to experience a considerable revival. "The Irish Hour" gained new listeners who were enthralled by Stanton's carefully assembled recordings of such great folk musicians as master fiddler, Michael Coleman, flute player extraordinaire Matt Molloy, and a whole archive of singers and instrumental groups. Newer groups like the Clancy Brothers, the Chieftains, the Wolfe Tones, and others added to the revival of old tunes and the delight of new ones. Stanton had seen the interest in Irish music decline notably in the 1930s and 1940s and was not too sure he liked some of the newer arrangements, but he could not help but be impressed by the revival of interest and talent.

Following Pat Stanton's death in 1976, Owen B. Hunt broadcast a special tribute to him. Hunt emphasized the cultural role that Stanton played, his sense of history of Ireland and of his people in America, and the charitable support he had encouraged for missions in the Third World, noting that Stanton had matched listener-donated dollars with equivalent amounts from his own resources.[60]

Stanton's career was a tribute to his own gifts and energy and also to the fact that he had the good fortune to enter the radio field when the industry was in a great period of expansion. Coming from a background with a strong oral and musical tradition, he was able to capitalize on these cultural factors in building his station.

His blend of entertainment and weekly commentary was distinctive and created a particularly loyal audience. His fine voice, diction, and discretion enabled him to present a dignified personality through "The Irish Hour" that conveyed an impression of avuncular friendliness and a quality of folk venerability that gave the entire show an especially appealing Irish character. This projection of Irish rural solidity, relaxed loquacity and familiar music was unique. There were other Irish radio programs in Philadelphia from time to time, notable that of Will Regan, who broadcast from various stations for over thirty years, and later of Joseph Gavin, who broadcast a show three evening a week over Station WIBF-FM. But none had the coherence and quality of continuity of "The Irish Hour." Stanton's resourcefulness and mellifluous assurance as a host and commentator made the difference. The Irish describe this verbal facility with the Gaelic word *blas*, that is, "taste." "He has the *blas* on it," they would say in admiration.

Stanton's achievement was part of the remarkable fusion of folk culture and modern technology that has been so widespread in our time. It was a blending of the time-honored and the time-scheduled through radio. This communications innovation in behalf of an Irish culture detached from its homeland has been a critical function for the preservation and continuation of an ethnic subcultural inheritance in the American environment. The swiftness and modernity of the radio medium was placed in the service of traditional values and usages by Pat Stanton, and, through the creative programming for which he was responsible, the bonds of community were preserved for his group in an increasingly impersonal urban world.

The way that Stanton was able to use his station as a medium for a spectrum of the city's ethnic groups was an illustration of the Irish faculty for serving as intermediaries for other immigrant and ethnic groups with American society. This role required not only a facility in English, but also a certain expansive disposition enabling the Irish to maintain understanding relations with a bewildering variety of groups. This faculty, of course, had a political dimension, and it was the recognition of this skill by Mayor Tate that led him to seek the services of a relatively nonpolitical specialist in Pat Stanton to serve as press secretary in a city rife with ethnic tensions in the 1960s.[61]

The question of why Stanton's program lasted for five decades while other shows vanished regularly can be answered with several observations. "The Irish Hour" lasted because Stanton lasted. That is, his interest and dedication to the program and what it represented had a fortunate longevity. For the Irish audience he cultivated, it was not only an entertainment, but it provided something other radio shows did not. It was a listening choice that signified ethnic distinctiveness. It was sufficiently varied in content so that, with the exception of the Father Coughlin episode, it transcended differences and conflicts within the Irish community, whether they were about local or national politics, Ireland's politics, the kinds of music to be enjoyed, or whether one's family was successful or unsuccessful economically. It was too, for a group with high verbal sensibility, a return to the old oral tradition through Stanton's friendly discourse. In the complex urban world, it was a weekly reservoir of speech, chat, and the kind of banter that echoed Irish life. Finally, it was, in its repetition of themes and music, a medium for instruction for young and old in the cult of Irish-American awareness. Stanton was the voice of the hedge schoolmaster of yesteryear, the village storyteller, the exponent of homely and reassuring knowledge about a half-make believe Ireland of song and legend to which his listeners had an incurable attachment. His program blended the Irish oral tradition with American communications technology, pioneering in a medium that would eventually have scores of Irish programs.[62]

For the Irish, Pat Stanton was more than an intermediary and a successful voice for their community. He was a breath of the old country, a reassurance that it and its values were still there no matter what wars and crises of American life intervened. For those born in Ireland, "The Irish Hour" was a tonic against loneliness, a weekly feast of musical delights, and an invitation to weekly dances, concerts, meetings, and festivities of ardent sociability. The depersonalization and disillusionments of the city might loom on every side, but at Sunday noon, after the racing melody of "O'Sullivan Mor" when Pat Stanton's familiar voice welcomed the Irish to commune with the spirit of their own tradition, the old feelings of warmth and Celtic vitality were renewed, and the Irish heard once again all of the echoing gaiety, melancholy, and drama of their past.

Lines of Learning

A transformation of Irish cultural outlook in the twentieth century ordained that the perception of what it meant to be Irish in America would in the future be manifest at a different level from that of minor ethnic newspapers or popular radio programs. Creation of an independent Irish state, the Irish literary renaissance, the Gaelic language revival, and a whole realm of music, theater, and historical development required that Ireland's culture be broadly addressed in terms of academic study.

The reflections of American ethnic life in higher education, always diffuse and peculiar, made the study of things Irish problematical. The American network of higher education grew in highly diverse profusion from a base of Anglo-Protestant imitations of English models, from a state-sponsored array of American gothic agricultural and normal schools, and from a bewildering variety of religiously inspired seminaries and colleges. The prestige of the older curriculum based on classical languages waned in the twentieth century, but it was only with the expansion of the social sciences, history, and broadened literature studies that the riches of ethnic and foreign cultures became widely accessible. The aversion of American students to intensive study of foreign languages kept them from delving deeply into such cultures, and the concern of many young people to be "American" and to put ethnic and immigrant subcultures behind them also tended to mask interest in their backgrounds.

Thus, amid the general vitality of American culture, most ethnic groups have had to assume responsibility for the retention and propagation of their own traditions while Anglo culture monopolized institutions of higher learning. Italian opera, French studies, and German classical music, and higher education techniques were patronized by the Anglo elite, but blacks, Hispanics, and American Indians, along with immigrants from various cultures, had to wait long for their traditions to be made available to the mainstream of education. In the case of the Irish, the expression of their tradition was delayed, while defective and mediocre presentations, often accompanied by a self-conscious grandiloquence, led to a devaluation of the cultural substance involved.

The Irish were less sequestered in American life than other ethnic groups. They moved actively into higher education through Catholic institutions. They already spoke English and their own past was accessible to them to a certain extent in that language. The nationalist upsurge in Ireland in the early part of the twentieth century was accompanied by a splendid burst of literary achievement that has continued through the century. But, in the United States, the achievements of writers such as Eugene O'Neill and James T. Farrell, though distinguished, were not linked in any definitive way to the broader Irish tradition. Irish-American literature, as distinguished from literature in Ireland, was on a different plane, and it did not readily relate to the splendor of the Irish literary renaissance. The Irish-Americans did not develop the same intellectual prestige as the old university Anglo-Protestants or the Jews of the new urban universities, and a strong Catholicism made the Irish suspect in intellectual life. In most centers of learning, Irish studies were regarded with indifference or intolerance, the same as would be studies related to most small nations or to immigrant traditions that did not have high prestige in American culture generally.

John V. Kelleher, for many years holder of a chair of Irish History and Literature at Harvard University, was a distinct exception in academic circles. There were few other permanent positions in the entire nation dealing with Irish studies. The University of Wisconsin made a special place for Myles Dillon. At the Catholic University of America there existed a chair of Celtic studies, but its contributions became obscure over the years. Ironically, the Catholic universities and colleges, frequently built with Irish money and led by those of Irish background, were rarely disposed to advance Irish studies. American Catholics were so conservative at the level of higher education that they retained curricula with a classical orientation long after such studies faded elsewhere. Latinity, philosophy, and theology dominated, and limited resources permitted little experimentation. The cultural diversity of the ethnic Catholics was seen as a pastoral problem by church leaders who controlled the colleges and as a regrettable anachronism by clerics who taught in colleges and by bourgeois Catholics who patronized them. Only after the 1950s did this attitude begin grudgingly to change. The simplistic universalism of the American clergy in Catholic institutions effectively forestalled any vigorous ethnic scholarship, except in some cases in which immigrant religious orders created small ethnically identified colleges.[63] Religious triumphalism of a self-assured Latinized Catholicism left little room for propagators of subcultural preservation.

In Philadelphia in the days before there were any noticeable protagonists of Irish interest at the college and university level, the learning of individuals, some academics and some not, served small circles of those interested in such studies. For instance, Professor Cornelius Weygandt at the University of Pennsylvania encouraged interest in Irish writing. Dr. Collins Healy, a librarian and bibliographer, gave occasional lectures, and Patrick Darcy taught Gaelic in union halls, the back rooms of Irish clubs, and anywhere else he could gather an audience. Tom Standevan, a virtuoso performer of the Uillean pipes, and Eugene O'Donnell, a gifted violinist, passionately taught Irish traditional music. Sister Mary Donatus of Immaculata College, a specialist in Irish medieval poetry, brought students together for discussions of Irish literature. Local bibliophiles like attorney Joseph Corcoran, Dr. Bernard Moss, and Seymour Adelman took a consistent interest in the acquisition of Irish books. Such involvement had little relation to the academic offerings of higher education before the 1960s, however.

In Philadelphia, the prestige colleges were those of Quaker foundation, such as Swarthmore, Haverford, and Bryn Mawr, that had been appropriated by the socialite and middle-class elite. Two major institutions, the University of Pennsylvania and later Temple University, dominated graduate studies. Catholic institutions such as Villanova University, St. Joseph's University, and La Salle University, enrolled Irish-Catholic males for decades, while girls of Irish-Catholic families until the mid-twentieth century attended a constellation of convent schools and colleges conducted by orders of nuns.

Specifically, Irish subject matter was generally treated in most institutions as part of broader courses in English literature or European or English history if it was dealt with at all.[64] The notorious rigidity of academic departmental lines and the difficulty of designing interdisciplinary courses, or courses that were more than massive segments of a given field of study, forestalled attempts to present specialized Irish studies until the late 1960s. In literature, this condition was altered by the sheer power of modern Irish writing, and courses on Joyce, Yeats, and Irish drama were included at the graduate level, while undergraduates found larger components of Irish writing in their literature courses. However, the relationship of the Irish literary renaissance to Irish-Americans and to the stream of emigration from which they historically derived remained unexplored. In the study of history, the broader categories held sway, and Irish history was almost always taught as a mere appendage to English history.[65]

The growth of interdisciplinary ethnic studies in the 1960s not only provided the first really extensive occasions for learning about black culture, but also gave Italians, Poles, and Spanish-speaking groups mention in course catalogs for the first time. The Irish figured with the other groups largely in courses that were social science and history electives. The gross classifications of American college and university course offerings could not really accommodate the diversity of the American social fabric and its subcultures, and there were strong academic complaints against the growth of ethnic studies. A more serious failing, though, was that the process of cultural differentiation and creativity that characterizes human learning was largely blotted out by the bulky blocs of subject matter invented for American academic convenience. This crude curriculum stacking could only add to further cultural shallowness and stereotypes in a country already too disposed toward oversimplification in its outlook.

The new movement of American ethnic studies developed in the wake of the book *Beyond the Melting Pot: The Negroes, Puerto Ricans, Jews, Italians and Irish of New York City.* written by Nathan Glazer and Daniel Patrick Moynihan and published in 1963. This book asserted that ethnic groups had not been dissolved by American life but had persisted in a surprising pluralist array into the 1960s. Michael Novak's *The Rise of the Unmeltable Ethnics* elaborated this theme. The popularity of the "new ethnicity" coincided with a rash of campus experimentation in the 1960s that gave rise to unusual and specialized courses in profusion. The University of Pennsylvania was host to a "Free University" of ad hoc courses. Temple University initiated black studies and courses for the Spanish-speaking. These changes were, in large part irregular and transitory, and by the mid-1970s they had receded. Courses on Irish subjects were not a significant part of the creative outburst, at any rate, and the Catholic institutions where most of those of Irish background were still enrolled were hardly touched by such course changes.[66]

Nevertheless, within most of the institutions of higher learning, there were scholars who pursued Irish studies despite the lack of accommodation with the general curriculum and in the face of the fact that in many cases their own careers would have been advanced more readily had they chosen some other subject for specialization. In the field of English literature, there was a real need for those learned about Irish writing. In the social sciences and history, however, there was little prestige and very little academic opportunity attached to research or teaching of Irish subject matter. The interest of those scholars who were prepared to teach, write and do research on Irish subjects was founded in a knowledgeable commitment to Irish interests and frequently in strong emotions and family ties to Irishry.

Lester Conner began teaching at Chestnut Hill College in Philadelphia after obtaining a doctorate in English literature from Columbia University. He had a deep interest in Irish authors. In the 1960s, he began his association with the Yeats Summer School held each year in the magnificent mountain scenery of County Sligo in the west of Ireland. As assistant director of that school, he developed broad contacts among Irish scholars. From the mid-1960s, during the academic year, he pioneered in teaching a highly sophisticated course in Anglo-Irish literature. He also found time after 1976 to begin work on a much-needed critical survey of twentieth-century Irish drama and to complete a study of the dramatization of Brendan Behan's *Borstal Boy*. Conner believed that the continued success of new Irish plays, such as Hugh Leonard's *Da*, helped to build a consistent American interest in Irish drama that has been complemented by a growing interest in Irish music and fiction. As a protagonist of Irish studies, he frequently played host to Irish theater directors, poets, novelists, and critics.[67]

James Murphy obtained his doctorate in English from Temple University, where he cultivated an abiding fascination for the writings of James Joyce. As a faculty member at Villanova University, he sustained this interest until opportunities emerged to teach specific courses in Irish literature. In concert with other Joyce scholars, he formed the James Joyce Society, which met to dine, hear lectures, and lift a glass to the titan of modern Irish writing. In 1972, when the violence in Northern Ireland was at its height, Murphy responded to an interest expressed by students at Villanova and taught a course on the Northern Ireland problem drawing on his knowledge of the country and his visits to Northern Ireland. By 1977, he was able to add a graduate course in modern Irish literature to his undergraduate list. He saw the interest in modern Irish literature rise in recent years and broaden beyond the bigger names in the field to include a more widely representative array of Irish writers. With such colleagues as literature scholar Lucy McDiarmid, historian Tom Green, economist L.A. O'Donnell, and political scientist Joseph Thompson, he developed his interdisciplinary curriculum as a formal plan for Irish studies at Villanova. The program continues, but much larger resources needed for it to advance have been hard to find in tight school budgets.[68]

At La Salle University, founded by the Christian Brothers, historian Joseph O'Grady maintained an interest in the changes that had overtaken the Irish in the United States and despite a heavy teaching load, worked on a manuscript for several years investigating these changes. As O'Grady saw the process in his book, *How the Irish Became Americans,* published in 1973, the Irish-Americans by memory and involvement with Irish events gave themselves "the cohesiveness necessary for their role in politics, which, in turn, created the conditions necessary for their assimilation in American society. By remaining involved in Irish affairs they became Americans."[69] O'Grady and his colleague, Dr. John Rossi, kept a lively but informal interest in Irish studies active for students at their college, as did Patricia Haberstroh. Their own journal articles on Irish subjects and their intermittent courses in this field stimulated some of their students to study in Ireland.

Sometimes Irish studies do relate to active continuing areas of popular interest or to areas of academic enterprise that extend beyond the campus. Dr. Jack McCormick at Delaware County Community College has made the study of Irish military traditions his preoccupation. His lecture tours of the Gettysburg Battlefield where the Irish performed grim feats of valor in the Civil War are part of a rich knowledge of the Irish exploits in various American wars that he has taught and written about to the delight of both students and those with an interest in military history. McCormick uses visual aids, such as maps, portraits, prints, and cartoons as part of his classroom description of Irish military tradition from Bunker Hill to Bastogne. His teaching coincides with a continuing fascination of a segment of the public and a network of scholars who read and publish steadily about American military history. McCormick's writings on the Irish Brigade that came from France to aid George Washington, on the Irish Brigade of Thomas Francis Meagher in the Civil War, and on New York's Fighting 69th in World War I are both popular and respected. McCormick derives considerable satisfaction from the fact that a number of his students develop their interest based on his stimulation and have a strong affinity for such Irish studies.[70]

Mari Fielder Green returned to her native Philadelphia in the 1980s after obtaining a doctorate at the University of California. Her grandparents had been theater people and had a popular stock company in the city in the early 1900s, so she devoted her thesis to documenting their careers. She had pursued theater studies and written on the history of the Irish in the American theater. With an infectious enthusiasm for theatrical lore, she taught courses at Villanova University on Irish influence on the stage and screen. She was representative of the richly knowledgeable women ready in the 1980s to expand their role in academic life and in Irish studies.

Lucy MacDiarmid, whose writings on modern Irish poetry were widely praised, added to the Villanova Irish program, while Vicki Mahaffey at the University of Pennsylvania opened new areas in the study of James Joyce. Traveling to Ireland, rushing off to conferences, teaching, endlessly roving libraries, they still found time to raise children and keep household affairs in hand. The sophistication of their studies certainly placed them in the mainstream of academia, while their grasp of Irish influences in their fields made them great mentors for those concerned with such interests.[71]

An interest in George M. Cohan led William Lynch to pursue graduate studies at the University of Pennsylvania. His work for a doctorate involved completion of a thesis on the panoramic works of fiction writer James T. Farrell, the novelist who sought more vigorously than any other writer to portray the sweep of Irish-American life in the twentieth century. William Lynch earned a sabbatical from Montgomery Community College and packed up his family for a stay in County Cork. While in Ireland with his wife and four children, he developed an increasing interest in the poetry written about the struggle in Northern Ireland and produced several studies of the subject. He also edited the plays of George Kelly, uncle of the actress Grace Kelly.

"Young people are not so interested in Irish studies as they were during the time when ethnic roots and courses were in fashion in the 1960s," Lynch says. "Teachers will have to work harder to generate interest in Irish subjects in the future. They will have to collaborate and stimulate a youth population that is increasingly estranged from all history and literature."[72] Thus, in addition to the problem of arousing interest in a subject that students rarely see as earning vital credits toward their major fields of study, there is the added difficulty of maintaining focus on areas of liberal arts that are increasingly foreign to college populations.

Also stimulating interest in Irish Studies is County Mayo–born Michael Durkan, a tall man of easy grace and quiet manner. He is director of the wonderful library at Swarthmore College, where he also teaches. It is as a bibliographer, however, that he enjoys himself and indulges his passion for drama and poetry. In 1978, he and Ron Ayling of the University of Alberta published *Sean O'Casey: A Bibliography*, a definitive guide to the great dramatist's writings and studies about him. Durkan knows well that creative people are often driven souls of enormous energy, leaping from work to work without tracing their published production or even saving different versions of their output. Durkan says that bibliographic tracking and detective work go naturally with the library profession: "It gives tremendous satisfaction to bring order to literary splendor. You get to read all the versions and see the artist's gifts transform the objects of the creative struggle. Bibliography is, too, the basis of future scholarship. It has the power to shape that scholarship." For some years, Durkan has been compiling entries on the poetry of Seamus Heaney, and portions of this work have appeared in the *Irish University Review*. Thus, in patience and persistence, he gathers the threads of brilliant Irish literary tapestries.[73]

Robert Mulvihill pursued political science studies at the University of Pennsylvania for a doctorate when Northern Ireland was torn apart by violence after 1969. For his thesis, he chose to study the attitudes toward political violence of a sample of three hundred people in Ulster. At his own expense and at no little physical hazard, he conducted interviews among the bomb-shattered streets of Derry. He sought the views of Protestants and Catholics about their tolerance of violence for both social control and social change. He found those who approved of violence to be a minority in both communities, with some Protestants condoning violence to sustain social control and some Catholics approving it as a means to induce social change. He found that, although Catholics in Northern Ireland were more conscious of a historic sense of frustration, there are a multitude of social factors to be studied beyond that frustration to gain a real picture of Northern Ireland's peculiar views about violence. His work is one of a handful of direct empirical explorations of the social psychology of political violence in the Irish situation.[74]

Most of the academicians discussed thus far have been American-born, but Irish-born scholars have also worked in higher education in Philadelphia in recent years. For Mick Moloney, the rhythms of Irish music were bred in the bone in his Limerick birthplace, and it was only in adulthood that he began to examine folk music as an objective phenomenon. After completing college in Dublin, he worked on building sites in London and played in Irish musical groups at night. His interest in folk studies grew, and he spent time in Norway becoming familiar with Norwegian folk schools and collections. After coming to the United States, he entered the University of Pennsylvania in the Department of Folklore and Folklife to pursue his studies. Despite a very heavy schedule of playing guitar, banjo, and other instruments and singing at increasingly popular folk music festivals and concerts, he found time

to do research in an astonishing number of places. Collecting recordings, holding interviews with Irish musicians, and making his
findings available to the Smithsonian Institution, Moloney was
able to compile what constituted the first comprehensive professional study of the Irish folk music tradition across the country. It
was a mammoth task with delightful revelations of the persistence,
diversity, and musical vitality of the Irish in America stretching
back to colonial times.

Moloney was able to familiarize himself with a rich treasury of
vocal, instrumental, and dance music in numerous localities across
the United States. He was able to collect hundreds of previously
unrecorded performances and to evaluate them against a musico-
logical and folklore background. In his view, the Irish musical tradition in which he is interested has been and is a minority musical
culture. "But," he has said, "today it is stronger both in Ireland and
the United States than it has been for generations. The playing and
the dancing are better and the upsurge of interest in folk music has
aided it greatly. It has also benefited especially from the technical
achievements of recording. Records and tape cassettes now make it
possible for people to have available to them the best performances
even in the remotest places." It has been his judgment that the real
test will come not in faithful adherence to the musical legacy of the
past, but in the challenge of creative composition that is the heart
of any tradition.[75]

Another kind of scholar important to the area of Irish studies,
is the transient figure who comes to the area for a short time. Maurice Bric, a graduate of University College Cork, first came to the
United States to study at Johns Hopkins University in 1979 and
later arrived in Philadelphia. As a historian, he was able to obtain
a fellowship to aid him in completing his doctoral work studying
the impact of the Irish on the formation of American political activity in the early nineteenth century. He taught, lectured, and
wrote, much to the benefit of the local Irish community. His interest in the gifted émigrés who came to Philadelphia after the Irish
uprising of 1798 enabled him to make good use of the rich archives
in local institutions. He worked at the Philadelphia Center for
Early American Studies of the University of Pennsylvania. Teaching evening and summer sessions at the University of Pennsylvania and Chestnut Hill College, he also commuted to Washington to
teach there.[76]

Bric became involved in a research project gathering the biographies of Philadelphia Irish people. As a gregarious figure, a

Gaelic speaker raised in County Kerry, and a person committed to the extension of Irish cultural interests, he joined with others in the creation of a nonprofit corporation called the Center for Irish Studies. This was a collaborative group of people, most of whom were university faculty members, interested in the teaching of Irish subjects. Their interest was to foster studies in literature, social sciences, history, and art relating to Ireland and the Irish-Americans. Lectures by scholars from Irish and American universities were arranged. The Irish Consul General from New York helped launch the first year's activities in 1980. For the first time, the Philadelphia area had a forum for graduate-level Irish studies. The center was distinctive in that it did not represent simply immigrant interests and stereotyped extollment of the "island of saints and scholars." It represented a fully professional collaboration across various fields of discipline and was receptive to learned criticism of Irish life and society. It sought to foster interest in the latest currents of Irish learning as Ireland sought to modernize itself, change its own self-image and deepen its contemporary scholarly endeavors. Attorney Robert Hernan headed the center's efforts to make surveys of the local Irish and to present conferences of current Irish issues. A conference on the constitutional future of Northern Ireland brought key Irish figures from Belfast and Dublin to the city. With the aid of Dr. James Murphy of Villanova University, Dr. Lynn Lees of the University of Pennsylvania, Dr. Michael Durkan of Swarthmore College, and Dr. Lester Conner of Chestnut Hill College, a whole series of events were sponsored. As with many such enterprises, funds were always a problem; aside from one foundation grant, fund-raising was irregular, and despite its dedication, the corporation expired in 1988.

The growth of interest in the study and reading of poetry has been slow in America, so that a man who had grown up in the poet-haunted precincts of Dublin would be as much an evangelist as a writer in a place like Philadelphia. Thomas Kinsella was a poet who had the good fortune to be a native of poet-blessed Dublin. In 1946, he began his career as a civil servant in the finance department of the Irish government. By the mid-1950s, he was winning acclaim for poems that spoke penetratingly of the spent idealism and alienation from politics that affected the Irish generation that followed the old revolutionaries who had established an independent Irish state in the 1920s. Through the years, in addition to his full-time position at the finance department, he worked arduously at a huge project that blended poetry and literary scholarship, a translation and rendering into modern poetry in English of the great Gaelic epic the *Tain Bo Cuailinge*, the tale of the Cattle Riad of Cooley. This epic soars with the power of Celtic imagination, pitting warrior gods and violent kings and queens against one another in a vast war saga of pride and daring. With the aid of a Guggenheim Fellowship, Thomas Kinsella finished his translation and composition, and in 1969 a fine edition of the *Tain* was published by Dolmen Press in Dublin and Oxford University Press.[77]

In 1965, Kinsella left Ireland to teach at the University of Southern Illinois and, in 1973, was appointed poet-in-residence at Temple University in Philadelphia. He was able to continue a campus interest in Irish studies fostered previously by Howard Maloney and Mabel Worthington. He taught notable graduate courses on Ezra Pound and W.B. Yeats and continued to publish volumes of poetry that were darkly introspective and filled with a sense of life as a trembling struggle pursued at a cost of spiritual wounds and unrelenting anxiety. Critics lauded his *Nightwalker* and *Notes from the Land of the Dead* as searching descents into the troubled soul of man in the nuclear age.[78]

Traveling to Ireland frequently, Kinsella came to feel not only the necessity for a permanent home there, but also the need for continued association with the culture, inspiration, and learning of Dublin. He established a home there as well as one in Philadelphia and eventually devised a program of studies in Dublin for students of Temple University. Dividing his time between teaching in America and conducting the Temple Dublin program was strenuous, but he managed to keep to his rigorous writing schedule. Throughout, his wife, Eleanor, as vigorous a person as County Wexford ever produced, not only tended their children, but also strove mightily with the details of lodging and guiding the Temple students in Dublin.

As a teacher, Kinsella had long recognized that better anthologies of Irish poetry were needed. Existing anthologies were usually limited to the nineteenth and twentieth centuries. After consulting with dozens of specialists and working with translators, Kinsella was able to compile *An Duanaire* to partially meet this need. With Sean O'Tuama, a Gaelic scholar, he was able to publish this collection of vibrant translations from Irish poetry in 1981.[79] This anthology went part of the way toward what Kinsella felt was a crucial goal, the exposition of the fact that Irish poetry and literary tradition went far beyond the romantic and Victorian works that had become the common references to those with only a superficial grasp of the island's tradition. And the anthology served as an illustration of the riches teeming through Irish writing far, far back into the Celtic age before the birth of Christ. Intent upon confirming this view, Kinsella next assumed the formidable task of translating a huge corpus of poetry from Irish into English and relating it to the body of poetry written in Ireland in the English language. This great heritage was then compiled in *The New Oxford Book of Irish Verse* published in 1986. Reaching from pre-Christian times to the present, it is a monumental work of continuity and brilliance presenting in a sweeping range of centuries the towering Irish literary tradition.

Kinsella represented an Irish mind of strict and learned dignity, a mind that looked upon the political "patriot game" with a hard eye and saw the bourgeois leadership of contemporary Ireland as a plague upon the nation's ideals. This view was a far cry from the tourist tinsel and self-serving soft talk that was habitually fed to American visitors, and it was a far cry from the sentimentalized Mother Ireland of which the immigrants sang. Kinsella's Ireland had the grit of reality and the ache of disillusion in it. He portrayed it in the rigor and vigilant courage of his poetry, and this was not readily acceptable to many who found the Ireland of the thatched cottage and sweet, smiling colleens more compatible with their perceptions of Ireland than the scalpel words of the poet critic. His anthologies also spoke with a voice that sounded across the ages and placed the Anglo-Irish achievements of the last two centuries in a perspective that showed that they were, for all their radiance, merely an offshoot of the older, immense, and aeon-rooted tree of literature reaching back to ancient times. These views were not always popular, but Kinsella did not relent.

All of these scholars have been able to teach, write, and publish an abundant harvest of Irish studies. Individually, their attainments range from the interesting to the solid to the brilliant. In addition to the achievements that their personal careers represent, they have had a continuing impact upon students and academic colleagues. An evaluation of this impact is not easily made, for the mobility and cultural disparities surrounding these Irish intellectuals diffuse their contributions as teachers and cultural figures. Since, in most cases, their Irish studies have been pursued according to a highly personalized commitment, the relation of these studies to the institutional life of local colleges and universities is not readily calculable in any detail. The cultural perceptions of students and academic colleagues have undoubtedly been enriched. The boundaries of curricula have been extended to the profit of learning and research. The tradition of learning of one of the most culturally eminent small nations notably related to America has been upheld in another generation, but it is doubtful if this contribution is understood as such in the institutions themselves.

These protagonists of the Irish tradition, for whom their Irish studies have been the most important themes in their intellectual lives, had an essential relation to what could be called "the new Irish-Americans." The organizational patterns of the Irish community in the city had been changing markedly through the years spanned by their careers—the 1950s through the 1980s. The older immigrant societies, the county societies of Mayomen and Corkmen and Galwaymen, had been declining. New groups like the Philadelphia Ceili Society, the Irish-American Cultural Institute, and the American Conference for Irish Studies emerged in local chapters. Their membership was middle-class and educated. There was respect for the intellectuals in the broader Irish-American community, but, for the the most part, people did not steadily read poetry or attend lectures. For those who did, however, the bond of tradition was greatly intensified, knowledge of it was deepened, and the riches of its creativity were savored.

Evaluating the influence of these teaching scholars on their students is also difficult. All surely have a special impact on selected individuals. Indeed, many students from their classes have gone to Ireland to pursue their own studies. In the highly varied curricular setting of their institutions, though, it is difficult to determine if Irish studies have dominated the intellectual growth in the lives of those who cultivate them. They do seem to have produced a following that crowds the poetry reading appearances of Seamus Heaney, eagerly awaits the next volume of the work of Thomas Kinsella, and subscribes to a wide range of Irish literary and cultural concerns.

On campus, Irish clubs have emerged and dissolved along with a flurry of intermittent student organizations that are an unstable element of college life. St. Joseph's University, Chestnut Hill College, La Salle University, and the University of Pennsylvania have all had such groups. The interest of students in Irish musical events has been enthusiastic, judging from their attendance at local concerts at International House and the annual Irish Music Festival of the Philadelphia Ceili Society. Travel to Ireland has led many to be able to make informed contributions in class discussions and term papers. One Temple University student carried out a three-year videotaping project documenting the Irish community's activities. Students at Villanova University wrote critiques of the St. Patrick's Day coverage by the local television station that filmed the event in 1988. Younger writers contributing to the *Irish Edition* and other publications reveal a significant knowledge and attachment to Irish themes.

Establishing careers and forming families takes students away from their college-bred interests in most cases, so that it is not clear what retention of Irish attachments this generation of Irish-American students will experience. It does seem clear that there is a cultural core of intellectually oriented members of the community, however, that forms the chief audience for the transmission of the tradition. Martin Hurley, a journalist from County Cork living in Philadelphia for a time, carried out a survey for the Center for Irish Studies in 1988, and found that, of the more than three hundred people contacted, returns of questionnaires showed that over 95 percent reportedly read Irish books and avowed strong support for some system that would provide regular study courses in the Irish tradition for both children and adults.[80]

Beyond the work of the scholars themselves and the immediate responses of their students, there has been a steady renovation of library holdings and collections crucial to the continuation of knowledge about Ireland. Bernard Croke led in the establishment of a special Irish library at the Sisters of Mercy institution, Gwynned Mercy College outside of Philadelphia. Mick Moloney, musicologist as well as performer, collected a remarkable folk music archive for the folklore department of the University of Pennsylvania. Librarians were eager promoters of Irish scholarly events. The availability of books, journals, and music from Ireland has broadly expanded the means through which the Irish tradition can be cultivated in a city of long-standing Irish interests. A book distribution service begun in 1986 by Thomas Ruane met with steady success almost from the start. Through the work of Bernard Croke, head of the local Irish-American Cultural Institute, a whole range of Irish materials and experiences has been developed, and he and his colleagues have been generously hospitable to a variety of exhibits, lecture series, and projects for the local Irish community.

The effects of the university-based teachers of the Irish tradition on the Philadelphia Irish community have been gradual, but they have been a very significant influence for reorientation and change. Lawrence F. Fuchs has written about the reaction of the Irish community in New York City to the flowering of modern Irish literature: "The New York Irish ignored it, or if respectable enough, turned on the Irish authors, accusing them of using bad language."[81] This observation may be overdrawn, but there is sufficient truth in it to indicate the cultural deficits among the Irish-Americans in Philadelphia and elsewhere in the earlier part of this century. The Irish university scholars, despite their vocational tendency toward aloofness, did have an eventual impact, as did the popularization of Irish writing and drama through the mass media. They have developed a new cultural profile for the group and transcended the older immigrant, stereotyped, and childishly comic and combative images. They have constructed a strong cultural transmission line from Ireland to the United States. This was abetted by the rise in educational levels in both countries and the rise of ethnic studies in the 1960s.[82] In Philadelphia, the movement of the Irish scholars through the Irish community as they lectured to the Ceili Society, wrote for the local paper, the *Irish Edition*, and advised organizations and parents about Irish studies and projects has created a more culturally aware community.

This endeavor has not been an entirely positive experience. For those educators involved, there have been considerable difficulties aside from worrying about course enrollments in competitive campus situations. Some have had to travel back and forth to Ireland for years to develop their study programs. Others have been torn between the desire to teach and the need to publish. Some have postponed or yielded their personal specializations in favor of caring for Irish studies broadly. Few have had the kind of supports that accrue to those engaged in more popular courses of study that bring in heavy tuition payments to their institutions. Irish music still has not had adequate settings for presentation. Irish literary studies have been dominated by Yeats and Joyce. Teachers of the Irish language have been rarely available. Linguist Lois Kuter pointed out that in the listings provided by the American Conference for Irish Studies, 235 courses offered across the country are on Yeats and Joyce, but only 13 courses are given on the modern Irish language. In spite of the problems, the contributions of those cited in this account about Philadelphia Irish teaching are impressive.

The fostering of formal Irish studies represents an addition to the preexisting folk transmission of ethnic consciousness that informed Irish-American life in the past. Although academically vulnerable in the interplay of university politics, the work has created a cultural beachhead. The saturation of Catholic parochial, secondary, and higher education with Latinity and religiously permeated cultural forms that stifled the Irish tradition is fading. As secular universities make room for ethnic studies, there may be hope that financial support from various sources will be drawn to Irish subjects. The future of such studies is, however, so sufficiently surrounded by unknowns that no predictions can be set forth. If a people values its heritage, it will support it.

From time to time, the broader cultural community does advert to the Irish scholars. A museum lecture, an interview about a new book, or a well-advertised reading may bring them into the limelight on occasion. But they are rarely seen in such situations as more than accomplished individuals. They are not seen as part of an international Irish scholarly tradition that interacts with the old country to provide continual stimulation and to reflect Irish creativity. Indeed, each of these Irish scholars is linked intellectually and creatively more directly to the Irish than to Irish–Americans or to the mainstream American public. Ireland is both font and altar for their scholarly attainments. Yet, in spite of their keen ties to Ireland and their frequent trips to the island, they would readily admit the limitations of Irish life and their need for American interaction, openness and opportunity.

In Ireland, the university professors and scholars are very ambiguous about such figures as those whose interests have been outlined in this chapter. By and large, those in America live better, have more opportunity, and are more responsive to new influences than their Irish counterparts. There is a tincture of envy in the Irish view of the American academic scene: its scope and energy are a bit breathtaking. It may be superficially flattering to have scholars from America poring over Ireland's culture, but it is disconcerting also. The academics in Ireland are much too intent on their own struggle for places and prestige in a country of very limited resources to be too concerned about the dimensions of Irish studies abroad.

The Irish-American scholars, for their part, thrive on a self-possessed independence. They have taken an immigrant folk memory to the university. They have transmuted family traditions, sentiment, and personal interests into scholarship. The children and grandchildren of Irish workers and exiles, they have moved their interest in Ireland through the bureaucratic machinery of American graduate studies and polished it into a rich cultural ornament. For those born in Ireland, their American careers must ever be bittersweet with the regrets and rewards of exile. For those born in America, the sense of a transplanted cultural memory with all the limitations that this implies must suffuse their work. Still, all share in one of the most ardent adventures of modern scholarship, the attempt to sustain and preserve wondrously fertile smaller cultures from the amnesia induced by technological mass culture.

4 Leadership
More Power To Them

Those with an interest in Irish-American history are by now aware of the three well-documented types of leadership that have come to be popularly recognized as part of this group's tradition. Political leaders, ethnic nationalist leaders, and church leaders figure notably in the record.[1] Indeed, the Irish urban political boss has become one of the archetypal figures of American life. There are, however, differences and distinctions among such leaders, and more intent study shows that the reality cannot be fully understood by reliance on simple and popularized portraits.

Leaders are men or women of many aspects, and their gifts and roles embrace many facets of the social groups with which they are involved. They are information bearers both within the group and in relations with the broader society. They are also evaluators and interpreters of information, sometimes as priests, sometimes as political advocates, and sometimes simply as wise and respected figures. Leaders are, perhaps most notably, communicators who express the views of their constituents.[2] Considering the prominence and durability of Irish-Americans as leaders in their own ethnic group's life and in the general American society, it is surprising that a more elaborate portraiture of their leadership styles and variations has not been produced.

This chapter presents profiles of leaders that reveal dimensions not usually perceived in popular presentations. The first personality dealt with is Mike McGinn, more of a folk figure than a community leader, and yet a man in a significant role for his Irish followers, a man with widespread contacts and influence as a nationalist activist. Another figure, Michael J. Ryan, was both a nationalist organizer and a representative community leader, and the chapter about him gives a picture of how an Irish-American leader functioned when the group had extensive power in Philadelphia and across the nation. The third figure, James Finnegan, was certainly a politician in the accepted sense, but he was also a skillful reform leader, and the profile of him illustrates his distinctive gifts and orientation.

John Higham wrote that the tasks of ethnic group leadership included providing security and services, and security included a sense of psychological belonging in what was often an unstable and unfamiliar milieu. In addition, leaders had to encourage group solidarity and ethnic concern for the homeland, as well as caring for the image of the group that was projected to the broader American community.[3] The three men whose careers are reviewed here are clear examples of that process. They each sought the interests of their people according to their respective political views. They each encouraged group solidarity and advancement by strengthening organizational ties and enhancing ethnic consciousness. None were "professional" Irishmen in the sense of being paid to perform their roles for the group. Their service and fidelity to the group's needs arose from their own identity and participation in the Irish-American tradition. Leonard Doob has pointed out the way in which tradition provides authority figures with a certain stability and a mold for expectations that tend to be fulfilled. Robert Cross has described the very long record of Irish-American leadership evolution and the achievement of "psychological autonomy" through leadership roles and symbolism.[4] The careers of the three men treated here provide examples of how these forces worked in their times. It is of interest to note that, contrary to the observations of Arnold Rose, the voluntary associations of the Irish community in which these leaders functioned had strong "lower-class" adherents and were actively political. The orator and attorney Michael Ryan may have had many businessmen as followers, but he could also turn out thousands of admirers for torchlight parades and major addresses. Michael McGinn worked almost entirely among working-class people, and James Finnegan represented a political constituency that was definitely of the working and "lower" classes, to use Rose's designation.[5]

Leaders must be able to command followers, and each of these men did that. They aroused responses from their contemporaries. They gathered men into meetings, often very large ones. They had colleagues who worked with them on committees and in coalitions. They were able to state issues to the public repeatedly and to promote actions on the basis of their arguments. Finally, they were able to raise money for the causes in which they were interested. They had qualities that others admired and did things that others envied.

In his study of American ethnic leadership, Victor Greene has examined the ways in which leaders of immigrant communities created an ideological ethos for ethnic life, blending their values with those of American society. This positive conception of group life fostered an American pluralism that permitted the pursuit of goals such as Irish nationalism or Irish succession to urban political power within the framework of a democratic polity that was distinctively inventive. It allowed the persistence of ethnic difference and a durable subcultural identity along with the thriving of the mainstream culture. The three leaders described in this chapter were all part of this process.[6]

The Clan Man

The Irish nationalist in America has long been the subject of derogatory judgment. He has been called an unreasonable animal, a demagogue and swindler, an advocate of assassination, dynamite, bloodthirsty bluster and delirious lying, a man animated by savage hatred of England. Even in the 1970s, when some Irish-Americans supported nationalists in Northern Ireland, officials of the government in Dublin rebuked them as misguided, romantic, and living in the past, and British Prime Minister Margaret Thatcher had even harsher things to say of them.[7] Such estimates often reflect conservative attitudes and, at times, reactionary viewpoints. Those who have prospered in Ireland and in America have traditionally decried hard-line nationalist agitation, especially since the consolidation of an independent Irish state has created a whole civil service and bureaucracy intent upon the defense of a status quo containing certain privileges. Yet, the Irish nation owed a great debt to those nationalists in America who gave of themselves over the generations to press Ireland's case for liberty. They could have turned their backs on the injustice and repression that was Ireland's historic burden like many another, but they did not. In far-off America it would not have been difficult to put the condition of distant Ireland out of mind. They could have avoided self-discipline and sacrifice in the service of nationalist ends. They chose instead to defy distance and derogation and to contribute to the development of their people and their people's political future. In doing so, they had to transcend bombasts, informers, political opportunists, and those bent upon feverish self-aggrandizement. They did that also.

To dedicate oneself to a remote goal in spite of setbacks and continuous difficulties requires something adamant in the personality. Those familiar with the Irish people can recognize that solidity that is borne within the committed Irishman. Whether he is a tough Cavan farmer, an Antrim stone cutter, a Galway fisherman, a teacher in Roscommon, or a docker on the Dublin quays, there is an inner force there that is present in him in a certain Irish way.

The man may be garrulous or taciturn, educated or unlettered, but there is a stubborn intensity inside that is both the essence and the expression of the ideals of Irish peoplehood. It predates nationalism and is a kind of primitive belief in oneself and one's social roots, and it has a vivid life within the course of Irish idealism. Mike McGinn had this quality, as everybody who knew him could confirm. He was an exile nationalist, a committed zealot in behalf of the cause of Irish independence, and he choked on compromise.

Mike McGinn was born in County Cavan in 1877. Small farms amid lakes and rambling hills were the scenes of his boyhood. The land in the valleys between the hills was arable but thin, and the hills themselves were rock-strewn and segmented into tiny fields by whitethorn hedges. Boggy hollows alternated with fields of oats. Cattle in meadows mused hungrily beside villages of thatched poverty. Only in the big houses, the comfortable homes of the Anglo landlord class that were usually reached through stately tree-lined roads, was there sufficiency and relief from the staring poverty that gave the county one of Ireland's highest rates of emigration. In the ditches and fields, the men struggled to drain the eternally drenched soil and coax food for their families from holdings too small by far. In this world of arduous farming, Mike McGinn began to know his Ireland.

There was a story told about the boy Mike McGinn. His father was a member of the Fenian Brotherhood, the failed revolutionary underground that had fomented plots and uprisings in the 1860s. The Fenians in the generation after Ireland's Great Famine had sheltered the guttering flame of the country's nationalist hopes against almost insurmountable political adversity. One night there was a meeting in the McGinn house, and the boy Michael hid himself under the table to listen curiously to the men in their meeting. He was only five years old at the time. During the evening, he was discovered and hauled from beneath the deal-board table. Since only oath-bound Fenians could overhear the brotherhood's secrets, the decision was made to swear in the child on the spot. The oath was duly administered, the record of the local Fenians was kept clean, and a nationalist career was set in motion that would not end until Irishmen had won the right to conduct their own government.[8]

There were few books in the houses of the farmers in those days, and the books that were present were not accidental. They were chosen with the same calculation that governed the choice of spades or churns or haying forks. The books had to be used for something. Hence, it was that one of the first books that the boy Michael McGinn became acquainted with was an extraordinary compilation of political polemic and historical argumentation, *A Catechism of the History of Ireland: Ancient and Modern, a New and Revised Edition with an Account of the Land Agitation,* published in Dublin in 1884 by W.J. O'Neill-Daunt, an energetic agitator and eloquent nationalist of County Cork.[9] This book was a vessel for the holy creed of nationalism as the penny catechism of Catholic usage was for the holy truths of religion. The book had a clear purpose, the presentation of Irish nationalism in formulas for memorization. Once indoctrinated in childhood with O'Neill-Daunt's questions and answers, the young nationalist would find it impossible to forget the material learned by rote. From the ages of the pre-Christian Gaels forward to the invasion of Strogbow in 1171 A.D., then to Edwards First to Fifth, to Richard the Third, Henry the Eighth and "Black Bess, the Bastard Queen," Elizabeth, the Penal laws, the Rising of 1798, and the Famine, a huge catalog of wrongs and rebellions, wars, exactions, and persecutions were set forth to discredit utterly any English claim to Ireland or Irish fealty. In the 1880s, this book was the distillation in which Michael McGinn was steeped. It was packed with quotes, bits of speeches, accounts of English duplicity, and economic arguments in behalf of Irish liberation. From this eclectic little volume, the McGinn boy, coached by his elders, committed to memory the documentation of his country's misfortunes beside the turf fires of Cavan.

The boy who was sworn as a juvenile revolutionary, growing to manhood in the rural setting of impoverished Ulster, found, like many others in his young adult years, that opportunities were severely limited. He resolved to take the route that hundreds of thousands of his compatriots had taken in the nineteenth century. At the age of twenty, he left his homeland for America and came to Philadelphia in 1897. His adjustment to the new world of an industrial city was according to a formula that had become traditional over generations of immigration. When you came to America you sought out relatives, friends, and references from the old country. They helped to get you a job. On the job or in the boarding house where you rented a room, you met lads like yourself. They invited you to join an organization to which they belonged, a group like the Cavan Men's Catholic Social and Beneficial Association.[10] At meetings of such groups, you could extend friendships, learn of dances held jointly with the Cavan Ladies' Society, or arrange to go on picnics to the city's parks. Such contacts reduced the loneliness of the newly emigrated, led them to better jobs, and kept people in touch with news from Ireland. For strong nationalists, there were also groups like the Clan na Gael, a successor organization to the Fenian Brotherhood.

Mike McGinn joined the local Clan na Gael by having his references in Ireland verified. The Clan was a secret society, founded in New York in 1867 by Jerome J. Collins. In order to insure against infiltration by British agents or American police, the organization checked on the credentials of those who transferred from one country to another. All kinds of people belonged to the Clan—physicians, professors, politicians, businessmen, and plain day laborers—although only a selected few of those enrolled were identified in any public way as members. The Clan was sworn to use all means to subvert English rule in Ireland, and its activities of a violent nature included some sensational bombing and assassination episodes in Ireland, England, and the United States.[11] Men were drawn to the secret organization because of the long record of rebellious activity of such groups, because of the frustration of political activity in Ireland, and because of the aura of adventure that surrounded the group's shadowy undertakings.

The Philadelphia branch of the Clan was a vigorous network. It had survived the betrayal and revelations about the Irish underground that had been made public by Major Henri Le Caron, a British agent who had for some years infiltrated the Clan in Chicago. Le Caron, whose real name was Thomas Beach, had testified in 1889 in London about Clan plots and bombing missions at a Parliamentary hearing that sought to implicate Charles Stewart Parnell and other Irish leaders in violent activities. Philadelphia's branch had remained untouched by the scandal in Chicago and by later revelations of an internal murder within the ranks of the Illinois group. Le Caron considered Philadelphia the key information center and the major focus of Clan conspiracies in the 1880s. John J. Bradley, Dr. Peter McCahey, Luke Dillon, and Roger O'Neil, all of whom had been involved in a bombing mission in England, Bernard McCready, a textile manufacturer, Miles Carr, James Maroney, a wine merchant, Maurice Wilhere, national head of the Ancient Order of Hibernians; and a long list of others all had extensive records of work with the secret organization. This network gathered funds, controlled other Irish organizations, maintained its own newspaper and propaganda system, plotted measures to undermine Britain's image and influence everywhere, and stimulated public functions to keep the Irish cause in the public eye. An interesting feature of the organization is that it included in its ranks a number of men who were believed to be moderates and opposed to violent methods in behalf of Irish liberation, such as Maurice Wilhere and the prominent political figure Michael J. Ryan.[12]

The Clan na Gael controlled the Irish American Club at 1421 Arch Street. On a Sunday morning after Mass, old men in front of the churches would hand out copies of the Clan newspaper. Notices of meetings at the club and elsewhere would be scanned, and on Sunday afternoons the members would gather. Speakers such as John Devoy, the implacable leader from New York, former prisoner of Fenian days, former French Foreign Legionnaire, and unrepentant rebel, would appear. Captain George S. Anthony, the master of the ship *Catalpa* that had sailed all the way to Australia to free Fenian prisoners from English prison camps, would address the meetings. The old minutes show that discussions could be furious: "We should be ready to sacrifice anything, even life, to free Ireland from the grasping hand of England," Brother Scullan said as there was murmuring against yet another assessment levied on members. "Dynamite was the medicine Ireland could give England," James Rooney declared when he tired of reports of propaganda and Parliamentary schemes. In 1897, when Mike McGinn joined the Philadelphia Clan, there was a drive to rebuild the secret bank accounts of what was called the Revolution Fund. Reports on conditions in Ireland, dynamite plots, Clan members seeking offices in the city, and the needs of unemployed members were all matters to be considered at the meetings McGinn would have attended.[13] There was probably more revolutionary activity under way in Philadelphia when young Mike McGinn began his Clan work than there was in his native Cavan where the local constabulary noted every move.

Young Irish immigrants had various job options open to them in the 1890s, none of which were connected to a life of ease. Pick and shovel work in construction gangs or on the railroads, labor in foundries and brickyards, hod carrying, wharf labor, or apprenticeship in some trade were the most common choices. For some, however, the recollection of village retail activity made the opening of a store or shop irresistible, and the opening of a saloon was one of the retail enterprises requiring the least capital, since the large breweries in those days helped to establish saloons with easy credit.[14] The Clan served as a network for Irishmen to obtain help with such endeavors as opening a saloon. Influential men with financial resources could be called on for help, men such as Patrick O'Neill, who had raised thousands of dollars for the Irish Land

League, or Hugh McCaffrey, a successful hardware merchant. With a loan, a limited inventory, and willingness to put in long hours, a man could make the saloon a steady business. Mike McGinn saw this and took his changes in opening a saloon on South Street. That was a hard choice, for South Street was a unlovely thoroughfare. At the turn of the century, it was shared by blacks and Irish who lived in the tiny streets that bordered its east-west axis. This street that ranged across the lower portion of the city's central business district led at both its ends to tough dockside neighborhoods. In between, it featured gin mills, pawn shops, cheap clothing stores, and shabby rooming houses. Mike McGinn had to run a hard saloon to deal with the clientele of South Street.[15]

The saloon was really a joint effort with other members of the Clan. There were a number of such enterprises in the city in which a number of Clan men would get together, pool their money, and try their luck as small-scale investors. These bars were located near railroad stations, ball parks, and major transit exchanges, locations which increased both their regular patronage and their utility as Clan centers of influence and communication. Such an operation depended on the key man in charge of the bar. Mike McGinn was a steady and trustworthy bar operator, both watchful and energetic. He had grown to be a tall, jut-jawed, sinewy-tough man with a shock of unruly hair and the muscular limbs of a farmer's son. He was usually full of banter and easy conversation. You could talk to him for hours, but you would never be able to get him to tell you what he did not think you ought to know, even though his conversation would be a stream of facts, stories, opinions, and jocular argument.

From the hard world of South Street, McGinn eventually moved to one of the heavily Irish neighborhoods, in North Philadelphia. He had married Katherine Kennedy in 1913 and begun a family that would at length include seven children. He had saved enough money to buy his own saloon at Somerset and Croskey Streets in St. Columba's parish, a heavily Irish neighborhood. The area was one of solid working people who lived in block after block of row houses. The men worked in construction trades or as mechanics or factory hands. Women worked in textile mills or shops or as waitresses, cooks, and servants. In many of the big families, though, the mothers were needed full-time at home to perform the household chores that kept the workers fed and presentable. In such an area, McGinn was "in his element." He could pursue his nationalist activities in combination with his business, avoiding any prominence that center-city location might have brought him.[16]

His position in the Clan had advanced considerably since his younger days. A decade of discreet service had earned him keen respect. He had performed all kinds of tasks involved with recruiting, organizing new branches, collecting funds, and making contacts with people whose aid the Clan required. He had met and worked steadily with the flint-hard Northern Ireland man named Joseph McGarrity, whose own flair for business was making him a millionaire. McGarrity was one of the three-man national directorate of the Clan; hence, McGinn was in touch with the organization's continuing plans in both Ireland and the United States.

One of McGinn's responsibilities was to gather and transmit to Ireland money collected by Clan branches in the United States. In Philadelphia, for instance, fund-raising proceeded on an uninterrupted basis. Each year on the anniversary of the death of Robert Emmet, the chief hero martyr of Irish nationalism, the Clan would hire one of the larger theaters in the city and present an evening of music and oratory. This event and an annual round of dances, raffles, picnics, sports competitions, and assessments of members kept money coming in. These funds permitted the Clan to take a secret part in electoral financing in Ireland, to organize demonstrations to embarrass England whenever an occasion arose, to conspire with England's enemies such as the Boers or the Russians, to conduct espionage, and to train its cadre of agents in agitation, sabotage, and the use of explosives.

Mike McGinn, who was affable by nature, could be intensely voluble in winning people to his purposes. His network of contacts was extraordinary. Sailors, musicians, actors, labor organizers, policemen, customs agents, chemists, gunsmiths, soldiers who had served with several armies, Chinese smugglers, German activists, priests, professors, and travel agents were all part of his huge array of acquaintances. He knew them and in dozens of ways helped them, and they felt obligated to help him. It was a simple system of attachments, and it was all based upon McGinn's own ardent personality and trusted bonds of friendship.

One character McGinn had befriended in his days on South Street was a big black West Indian, some of whose forebeares were Irish, who had a vigorous detestation of all things British. The black man knew enough of the Irish language so that he could exchange salutations and the time of day with Irish speakers who were McGinn's clientele, so McGinn employed him as a bartender.

He was huge, tough, and able, but he had one failing: he could not resist going to the Orangemen's parade each July 12. The Irish Protestants in the city had a parade up Broad Street on that date every year. The big black man would position himself at Broad and Spring Garden streets, and, as the drummers and pipers marched by, he would begin throwing stones or whatever was handy at the paraders. At this same intersection were two foundries that employed largely Irish labor. When the black man began his assault, they would be encouraged to start tossing nuts and bolts at the Orange marchers. Soon a real riot would be under way. This went on for years—each year the West Indian would be arrested, and each year McGinn would bail him out, remonstrate with him, and the whole thing would blow over until the next July 12.[17]

The period prior to World War I brought the Clan to a higher pitch of activity. In 1913, Joseph McGarrity was in correspondence with old Tom Clarke, a Fenian who had spent years in prison, about the ferment in the secret organization in Ireland. The long period of political bickering that followed the death of Charles Stewart Parnell in 1890 had made Irish people cynical about parliamentary activity. England kept promising Home Rule to Ireland but failed to bring it about. Young people under the spell of a rising Gaelic cultural movement sought some new ideal for Ireland, and the conspirators of the Clan were ready to provide it. The ideal would be not a limited Home Rule for the country within the British Empire but an independent Irish republic that would be renewed in spirit and free of centuries of British dominance.[18]

In 1913, Luke Dillon was released from a Canadian prison where he had served fourteen years for a bombing escapade designed to hamper England's war against the South African Boers. The plot had been a Clan project. Dillon returned to Philadelphia and immediately took up his Clan activities again.[19] As McGarrity's aide, he was in constant touch with McGinn and the other Clan organizers in the city and beyond. In the summer of 1914, Roger Casement arrived in the United States. The renowned humanitarian, explorer, and champion of oppressed peoples had joined the revolutionary network, and he visited Philadelphia in time to hear that the Clan-financed importation of arms for a projected uprising had been successfully carried out at Howth near Dublin. In a demonstration in Dublin, three people had been shot and killed by British troops in the landing of the arms. The Clan organized a parade of protest about the killings, and Casement addressed a meeting at a center-city theater where an additional two thousand dollars was raised to buy more arms for the growing ranks of the Irish Volunteer force in Ireland.[20]

Casement and others conspired with German officials against Britain as World War I began, and the pace of underground preparation quickened. McGinn redoubled his efforts, organizing, publicizing, and tending a honeycomb of Irish agitation at the local community level in Philadelphia. At his saloon, he would at times be so carried away in his evangelical expositions to some customers that he would forget to serve others. "Ah, well," he would say when they left, "They'll be back if they're thirsty." With friends such as Tom McGuigan, he was able to procure various kinds of guns and ammunition, which were hidden in the cellar of his saloon. The task of getting guns to Ireland was carried out by sympathetic sailors. Each sailor was paid for the perils of smuggling when the guns in his care were delivered to Ireland. McGinn's contacts were especially active in this work.[21]

This kind of commitment exacted a toll on McGinn's family. Though his business was very good, he often used income from it for Clan purposes. He did so open-handedly, and, as a result, the family did not live as well as those of other saloonkeepers. It was during this period that McGinn began making quick turnaround trips to Ireland. Whether he escorted smuggled arms on the ships he took or whether he conveyed funds and messages to the Irish underground is not clear, but after the Easter Rising of 1916 the tempo of activity became frantic. McGinn and others worked in a euphoria of effort. They had the first opportunity in generations to put arms into the hands of Irish rebels with some chance of success, and they were unsparing of themselves in the campaign to support the independence movement.[22]

Between such courier trips, McGinn furiously worked at keeping Clan financial and organizational records, organizing solicitation campaigns, setting up newspaper delivery routes for McGarrity's *Irish Press*, and promoting attendance at rallies and protest meetings. The prettiest Irish girls were recruited to beg for donations at the doors of downtown department stores, churches, and railroad stations. The canisters they carried bore slogans such as "Help the victims of English Terror," "Fight the Black and Tans," and "Ireland Begs for Your Mercy."

McGarrity was a major figure in the Irish-American network, strenuously involved with the national politics and propaganda of the cause, dealing with the irascible John Devoy, devious politicians like Judge Daniel Cohalan of New York, and a steady stream of emissaries from Ireland seeking aid, recognition, and contacts throughout the country. He was far above the level at which men like McGinn worked, but he was very dependent upon them. The Irish in the city neighborhoods had to be mobilized to support the fight for freedom. They were not, for the most part, used to making heavy contributions from their wages for anything but special church collections. The wealthy Irish of the city were even less disposed to part with money for a revolutionary campaign. The Clan members were used to contributing. Others had to be placed in situations in which they could not avoid the obligation. McGinn was an artist at devising such situations. At one point, he demanded that saloonkeepers contribute cash to the cause from every third round of drinks. At factories where there was heavy Irish employment, he had men stationed on payday to collect on the spot. He had people patrol the entrances to savings banks to importune thrifty old ladies who were making deposits to forgo saving in favor of contributing to the Irish was chest.[23]

By 1920, McGinn's saloon and cellar at home resembled an arsenal. He had Thompson submachine guns, some of the first ever produced, stacked in crates. Pistols, ammunition, bayonets, sword canes, and all kinds of weapons manuals were sequestered on the premises. People in the neighborhood knew about this, and they favored it. The police and federal agents were none the wiser. Discussions and rapid negotiations took place at all hours of the day and night. McGinn's family never knew who could be on the doorstep at any time to see him or to be fed or given money for train fare for some mission. Men on the run, sailors, shady arms dealers, politicians, and printers were all part of the underground cavalcade as the intensity of the fighting in Ireland increased.

There was a factional split in 1920 between the adherents of the new Irish Republic leadership headed by Eamon De Valera and the powerful New York cadre of Judge Daniel Cohalen and old John Devoy. The split was occasioned by a disagreement about how money raised for the revolution would be handled, for Cohalen, who had presidential ambitions, wanted much of it to be spent in the United States. McGinn and his colleagues went with the De Valera group. It was imperative to reorganize the underground network after the split, and McGinn with others pledged to support five full-time organizers to strengthen the Clan districts across the country. The reputation of men like McGinn helped to heal the disunity and maintain the revolutionary network at this crucial time.

In August of 1921, Luke Dillon sent a telegram to McGinn urgently ordering a special meeting of McGinn's Clan section, known as District 12, to make an emergency levy of contributions. The war in Ireland trembled between further death and tragedy and a possible truce at that point. Dillon reported that "the British government threatens to resume and intensify [its] campaign of murder and pillage and every man must be ready to answer this eventuality." McGinn, as ever, vigorously solicited his network of contributors. In September, Dillon thanked him in a fraternal letter that brimmed with optimism that "the hour is at hand" when the "glory of freedom" was dawning for Ireland.[24] Finally, in 1921 the British agreed to a treaty that conceded many of the Irish demands, and the guerrilla warfare subsided.[25]

Still, the state for which these men had sacrificed so much was stalked by misfortunes. Hard-line nationalists opposed the treaty, and in 1922 a civil war broke out pitting former comrades against one another. Men like McGarrity, Dillon, and McGinn cast their lot with the hard-liners but were unable to maintain support amid the confused and bitterly disillusioning strife. Events in Ireland gradually led to a defeat of the foes of the treaty, and the killing finally ended. The old network, much reduced, was kept in being. McGinn continued to look after its finances, and, as it shrank through years of peace and indifference, it became a collection of older men, intent upon their memories, nursing the hope that fulfillment of their larger hopes would somehow, someday emerge. Unable to hold the support of the increasingly diffused Irish population, they came together, now in smaller and smaller halls, to commemorate the Easter Week martyrs of 1916.[26]

Luke Dillon died in 1930. Joe McGarrity died in 1940. Mike McGinn lived on in his little house in St. Columba's parish. When friends called, he was fond of reading aloud with them from a small book that had been published in 1916 with an introduction by Padraic Colum. The book, *Poems of the Irish Revolutionary Brotherhood*, contained compositions by Thomas MacDonough, Padraic Pearse, Joseph Mary Plunkett, Roger Casement, and W.B. Yeats. A poem written in Irish by Pearse was a favorite:

> I have not gathered gold;
> The fame I won perished;
> In love I found but sorrow
> That withered my life.
>
> Of wealth or of glory
> I shall leave nothing behind me
> (I think it, O God, enough!)
> But my name in the heart of a child.[27]

The old men gathered at the Irish American Club on Broad Street where they played cards, watched the news on television, and told their stories to one another. McGinn brought to the club a scarred old tin trunk, which he had brought with him as a young fellow when he came to America. He cut a slot into the top of it, and, when the men lost at cards, they had to put money into the slot. McGinn sent the money to their headquarters in Dublin or used it for Clan expenses.[28]

Toward the end of his life, McGinn was bedridden and without much money. He worried about his files and his trove of Clan papers. He had been unable to retrieve a diary that Roger Casement had kept in America before his journeys to Europe and Ireland that ended with his execution. Old friends would visit McGinn and read to him, sometimes from the book of poems that Joe McGarrity had himself composed and had printed:

> For days that now are distant
> I'm often thinking long,
> For Irish hills that echo
> The skylark's sweetest song.

> But Irish hills and Irish larks
> Are far off from me now,
> And far from me the little wren
> And the blossomed blackthorn bough.[29]

What were the sources of the kind of Irish-American militancy that McGinn and his companions represented? Critics of the Irish frequently attributed it to some genetic or psychological affliction that left the group prey to unpredictable and incorrigible behavior. A view more grounded in the realities of the Irish political and social situation in the nineteenth century could provide a different interpretation. Basic to the position of Ireland's predicament was English intransigence in the face of a nascent nationalism. The world's largest empire could not tolerate rebellious nationalism within a few hours of its seat of imperial power. On the part of the Irish, the lack of a natively controlled state that could command full loyalty and restrain aberrant tendencies created a vacuum in popular political tradition that was filled by nationalist legendry. Immigrants to America were even freer of constraints in their protests in the face of this condition. The romantic revolutionary tradition in Europe, of course, contributed to the Irish agitation by providing models and conspiratorial contacts. In an age of rising nationalism, and after a long history of avoiding extinction, the Irish rebels believed fiercely in ultimate victory, and this belief off- set the price they had to pay. As members of an Irish tradition that had little real opportunity for popular political participation or en- gagement with the formalism of a free civic culture, the men of the underground were forced to rely on their own communal and per- sonal instincts. Thus, their historical ideas were based on the views of their families and immediate social worlds from which English dominance had exacted an embittering toll. The conscious- ness of their own ethnic ties provided them with the ambit for their revolutionary designs.[30]

Why was Mike McGinn successful in his role as underground organizer? His own character traits of personal idealism, persis- tence, and democratic approachability provide part of the answer. His early attachment and devotion to the Clan na Gael and the net- work of contacts it afforded gave him the social support he needed for his long career. The coincidence of his adult years with the ris- ing tide of militant nationalism in Ireland made his personal efforts much more fruitful than they would have been in other periods when Irish nationalism was frustrated and suppressed. There were negative features to his career, such as the almost total preoccupa- tion with in-group matters that truncated a broader vision and the personal concentration on a single theme of endeavor that undercut prospects for a more rounded life, but these were limitations that were fully accepted.

The kind of leadership that McGinn represented was that of an esteemed folk figure. For centuries, the Irish had not had their own free political leaders, and, during those generations, aside from priests, leadership was largely a responsibility of local community figures whose personal qualities impressed their neighbors. Through poverty and adversity, such men guided opinion and or- ganized local responses to hunger, evictions, English tithes and rack-renting, and the work of collaboration in sowing, cutting turf, and harvesting. This kind of leader met his community face to face every day. Specialists in political analysis have termed this kind of leader the "political middleman." He is a figure who relies on per- suasion to exert influence. That McGinn developed his role in an American urban environment did not diminish his significance as a traditional folk figure, a category of resistance fighter long famil- iar in Irish tradition.[31] HIs lifelong commitment to Irish national- ism was both highly personalized and communally expressed. He gained no prominence beyond the circles of friends and associates who knew him. Many of his activities were kept secret, his work remaining largely unsung even when the goal of Irish independence was achieved. Whole echelons of other men arose to claim the victory. But, if Ireland's democracy was to have its full meaning, it would have to find a place in its memory for ardent, indomitable, and little-known men like Mike McGinn, who reached back from their havens of immigration to plant and defend the blossoming arbors of freedom in their native Irish soil.

The Orator

Beyond the world of working-class fraternity where Mike McGinn tended the fires of Irish-American nationalism, there was a broader dimension of Irish activity that gave scope to leaders who were educated, ambitious, and skilled at the manipulation of the affairs of large-scale organizations. Their careers were involved with issues of both American development and Irish nationalist agitation. Events in the United States and Ireland propelled one campaign after another into the headlines of the nation's newspapers as these Irish-American leaders grappled with the problem of how to project Irish issues to American opinion and to the Irish constituencies that were the bases of power of the leaders themselves. Victor Walsh in studying Irish nationalist activities in Pittsburgh concluded that the dynamic behind the Irish organizational campaigns was not simply that of ethnic solidarity in search of assimilation, nor was it only an ethnic radicalism at work, but rather what was played out in one campaign after another was an interaction of Irish issues and a range of American social influences.[32] This interaction was complex and full of vitality, and the evaluation of Irish-American political and nationalist organization when seen in this framework could perhaps provide us with a model that could be used to interpret ethnic organizational life much more accurately and informatively than has been the case in the past. Indeed, the image of Irish-American nationalists as bombasts and mad bombers is still very much with us and is very misleading in view of the real stature of the leaders involved, the complexity of the conditions they faced, and the huge fund drives and organizing campaigns that they promoted. A review of the life of one Irish-American leader, Michael J. Ryan of Philadelphia, provides an opportunity to consider the progress and problems of a whole generation of powerful figures who expressed the goals and yearnings of Irish constituencies.

Ryan's career is significant because it spanned three major phases of Irish-American nationalism, a whole lifetime of organizational leadership when the Irish were not only a powerful force in American life but also a critical influence in the animation of political drives of nationalism in Ireland. First, Ryan was deeply involved as a young man in the Land League activities that sought to redeem landholdings in Ireland from the grip of the English landlord-class. Second, in his middle years he was the national head of the United Irish League, the chief American supporting group for the Irish Parliamentary Party, which sought Home Rule for Ireland within a British constitutional framework. Third, when the Rising of 1916 in Dublin ignited the drive for an independent Irish state, Ryan was a mature and experienced figure, widely known in Ireland and America, and able to participate in efforts to secure a solution to the Irish guerrilla campaign and political agitation after World War I.

The city of Philadelphia during Ryan's youth had 100,000 Irish-born residents and a thriving network of Irish organizations. The Irish Catholics of the city were in a period of extensive institutional growth. Catholic schools, hospitals, and orphanages were being built with remarkable energy. Though unable to attain dominance in the political and social life of the city, the Irish could and did construct an extraordinary complex of institutions and constituencies out of their own resources. Their parish steeples dominated the working-class neighborhoods throughout the city, and their organizational endeavors outflanked prejudice and discrimination by providing media for education, economic cooperation, and social mobility.[33]

In 1884, at the age of twenty-two, Ryan was admitted to the Philadelphia Bar after reading for the law in the office of George H. Earle. He was tall, highly articulate, and robust. He made his first foray into local politics by working for the Democrats in the mayoral campaign of 1884. In Philadelphia, the Democrats were a party foredoomed to go down in defeat before the all-powerful Republican machine that reigned over the city's politics from one generation to the next. Still, the Irish Democrats conducted intermittent wars of harrassment and electoral challenge for individual offices whenever the Republicans made a miscalculation or put up a vulnerable candidate in the Irish wards in North and South Philadelphia. In 1881, the city had elected a Democrat, a reformer, Samuel King, to the mayor's office in a rare spasm of public protest under a bipartisan "Committee of One Hundred." He was driven from office in the 1884 campaign in which Ryan worked partly because he had appointed the first blacks to the police force. Ryan continued his political activities, running for a congressional nomination in the heavily Irish First District in 1886, and won a surprisingly heavy vote while losing the nomination.[34]

It was not possible for a man to be in politics in the Irish neighborhoods of the city in the 1880s without making known his views on a wide range of Irish issues. One of the time-honored campaign circuits involved the meeting halls of Irish county societies, the Ancient Order of Hibernians and other groups. Ireland's affairs extended right into the wards of Philadelphia, and candidates were expected to know and discuss tenant rights, no-rent mainifestos, boycotts, Parliamentary participation, and other concerns about life in Ireland debated in the Irish newspapers of America. The militant Irish nationalist organizations were adept at setting up candidates to be grilled on such matters. In addition, the rights of labor, problems of anti-Catholic discrimination, and relations of the United States with England were keen political topics. Michael Ryan tutored himself in such issues and developed an increasing facility to discuss them. He became a lecturer for the Irish National League and gave addresses in the meetings that were held by the twenty-four branches of the Land League in Philadelphia. The Land League activities gradually merged with those of the Irish National League, and Ryan became a state delegate from Pennsylvania in the latter organization, making his first entry into the shifting currents of the national Irish American leadership stream.[35]

As a young orator, Ryan was not only an exponent of a long Irish tradition of oratorical facility with such legendary precursors as Henry Grattan, Daniel O'Connell, and the Irish Parliamentarians who followed Charles Stewart Parnell, he was also part of a Philadelphia succession of orators who arose from the Irish community. These orator-advocates included Father Patrick Moriarty, a fiery Augustinian priest who defended the Irish in the turbulent period following the famine influx from 1846 to 1860, and Daniel Dougherty, a lawyer famous for his speeches in defense of the cause of the Union.[36] Audiences of thousands gathered to hear such rhetoricians in a time when oratory was a major influence in shaping opinion, encouraging public debate, and providing diversion. Speeches were often reprinted in pamphlets as well, providing material for debating clubs and schoolroom recitation. Ryan was part of this tradition whose devotees studied Cicero and Edmund Burke, competed keenly in the local debating societies, and advanced their careers by extensive public speaking.

Ryan's profile was sharpening in 1886 when Charles Stewart Parnell and William E. Gladstone's Liberal Party launched a campaign for Home Rule in Ireland, a bid for limited Irish self-government under the British Crown. As a sequel to the continuing agitation to secure land for the Irish people, Home Rule had a strong appeal for the American Irish. Ryan could enter into support for Home Rule with fully developed talents as an orator, as a man of political promise, and as a man with extensive local connections and growing national ties. His constituents in the area where he was politically active included the population around the Church of the Gesu, a huge Jesuit edifice that was the focus of a big Catholic district where successful Irish businessmen had spacious brownstone homes on Girard Avenue, and where windows framed in white marble looked out from ornate Victorian parlors in the houses of adjacent streets. In this area, Ryan courted the support of one of the city's most upwardly mobile groups, for the "lace curtian" Irish were intent upon gaining respectability, creating an image of competence, and expressing their ethos through work on behalf of Irish undertakings and Catholic growth. The constituency Ryan sought to represent was conservative and even bourgeois. Dale Light has shown that more than two-thirds of the members of the Irish National League were in the white-collar and proprietary classes, and these were Ryan's following. The Irish leader William O'Brien, who had extensive firsthand contacts with the Irish-American network, recalled that the group as a whole, supposed by the British to be implacable foes, was moderate and had to be patiently persuaded to more aggressive viewpoints.[37]

By 1890, there were twenty-three councils of the Irish National League in the city. At a single meeting, they voted to forward $2,150 to Ireland to relieve hunger among families evicted by landlords.[38] Ryan was engaged with the foremost Irish-American endeavor of the day, the enthusiastic support for the cause of Parnell. The attempts of the British to turn back Home Rule agitation by coercion and to frame Parnell with forged documents implicating him in violence merely spurred further Irish-American commitment. When Parnell's colleagues William A. O'Brien and John Dillion visited America in November 1890, Ryan organized a spectacular center-city rally for them. Fifteen hundred people welcomed the Parliamentary leaders at city hall. They were escorted that night from the Bellevue Stratford Hotel through files of an honor guard holding torches aloft as bands played Irish martial music. At the Academy of Music, Ryan chaired a meeting at which O'Brien told the packed audience, "We come from a country that has had five thousand political prisoners last few years." To resounding cheers he and Dillon were given a check for thirteen thousand dollars to aid the Home Rule drive. The next night at another rally in Ryan's home area, another three thousand dollars was contributed.[39]

The great drama of the Parnell years ended in 1890 in the tragedy of the O'Shea-Parnell divorce case scandal that caused religious support to fall, and, as English Liberal Party allies abandoned the Irish leader, his career was smashed. It left his followers bitterly divided as they fought for command of the wrecked Irish party. Opinion in Ireland and America was either alienated or deeply confused. A rump organization, the Irish National Federation, was set up in December 1890 to rival the Irish National League. A year later the League was dead. Michael Davitt, perhaps the most popular Irish leader after Parnell, said in 1896, "I am convinced that unless there is reunion [of the Irish Parliamentary party] no future of the constitutional movement here in Ireland will obtain sanction or support from the Irish race abroad."[40]

After years of disillusionment, the Irish Parliamentary nationalists did pull themselves together, and in 1898 William O'Brien formed the United Irish League. Its branches spread swiftly in Ireland. The goal remained what it had been in 1886, Home Rule for Ireland, but the UIL branches also became involved in local boycotts and pressure campaigns against landlords. Ryan was to be a key figure in the UIL. He threw himself into the work of reorganizing Irish-Americans to follow the lead of John Redmond, who had assumed direction of the Irish Parliamentary party with the backing of John Dillon and William O'Brien. By 1904, the UIL convention in New York drew delegates from thirty-three states that were part of the league's network.[41]

In 1908, Michael Ryan was elected president of the UIL. The organization was directed by the Parliamentary executive committee in Ireland, but there was still great scope for American leadership. Effecting collaboration among Irish-American groups was a continuous process. Large organizations like the Ancient Order of Hibernians, headed by Ryan's fellow-Philadelphian Maurice Wilhere, were not always easy to maneuver behind the Parliamentary strategy. The Home Rule goal was still there, however, a familiar grail to be sought by sheer persistence against the intransigence of the reactionaries of the British political parties. In the kind of patronizing statement that infuriated the Irish, Sir Edward Grey said, "Ireland may still redeem her past by providing the excuse for Imperial Federation."[42] Indeed, much of the problem of Home Rule was that it would provide a model for imperial devolution, a thing feared by imperialists. Nevertheless, it was a familiar and peaceful goal and one that most Irish-Americans thought reasonable.

Under Ryan, the UIL steeped up organizing work, especially among the white-collar, shopkeeper, and business class that he knew well. by 1910, John Redmond would write him of his gratitude after a visit to America, saying, "What struck me more than it ever did before was the widespread interest taken in the present phase of the Irish movement by business and professional men." Redmond expressed his conviction that "the Irish in America will not allow the Irish Party to be beaten."[43] This had to be Redmond's hope, for the Irish Parliamentary party had that year contested seats in eighty-two constituencies in Ireland at an estimated cost of $100,000. Ryan's aide in the UIL, Secretary John O'Callaghan, had sent a fifth installment of fifty thousand dollars to the Irish political leaders in November 1910.[44] American money was fueling Irish Parliamentary pressure in a continuation of that extraordinary transatlantic influence on Irish affairs that had become traditional for the Irish-Americans.

In the *Philadelphia Public Ledger*, Ryan explained in a long article why American aid was needed to propel the Home Rule movement. The poverty of Ireland, the extra expenses of Irish members of Parliament who had to travel to and live in London, the enormous resources of the English ruling class working against Home Rule were all cited as reasons. Ryan noted that the goal of a republic advocated by Irish militants would be rejected completely and bitterly opposed by Irish Protestants, but he dismissed the threat of secession by Ulster Protestants loyal to the Crown if Home Rule were granted.[45] In 1911, following a national meeting of the UIL, Ryan issued a statement saying that, thanks to the overseas Irish, "the UIL is the only national organization since the Act of Union (in 1800) which can boast of having brought the cause of Irish self-government to the threshhold of assured and final success."[46]

The drive for Home Rule was to encounter increasingly bitter resistance from the Anglo-Irish ascendancy class and from the Protestants who were settled most densely in the counties in the northeastern corner of Ireland. In 1910, a liberal government under

Herbert Asquith forced through Parliament an act limiting the veto power of the house of Lords, a governing body which was a major obstacle to the granting of Home Rule, The Ulster loyalist group most opposed to Home Rule chose Sir Edward Carson to lead a resistance against any change in Ireland's status. After reviewing a parade of fifty thousand Orange Lodge members in 1911, Carson threatened to set up an independent Ulster state if Home Rule were granted. Aristocratic and military factions reinforced Carson's agitation. An Ulster Volunteer Force was organized to oppose the Crown and began arming and drilling. Catholic nationalists in other areas of Ireland formed their own militia. In 1914, Parliament did at last pass a Home Rule bill with a clause permitting Ulster's exclusion from the limited Irish self-government scheme. The confrontation with Ulster, however, was postponed by the outbreak of World War I. Up to this time, Ryan's chief, John Redmond, had held his political supporters together, but the prospect of military conscription that would compel Irish nationalists to fight a war at England's side split the Irish Volunteer militia leaders. Redmond had promised Irish collaboration in the war effort, but the more militant nationalists refused to follow his lead.

The tension in Ireland had its reflection in America. Militant nationalists led by wealthy Philadelphian Joseph McGarrity repudiated any Home Rule arrangement that would permit Ulster to exclude itself. McGarrity headed efforts to gather funds to arm the Irish Volunteers, the nationalist paramilitary units that were imitating the Ulster Volunteer Force in preparing to fight for their point of view, and he was a key figure in the Clan. In 1914, McGarrity called on Redmond to renounce any Home Rule and to insist that the nationalists be allowed to import arms to Ireland just as the Ulster loyalists were doing. McGarrity's group assailed Ryan and the United Irish League for refusing to help raise funds for arms. Ryan had previously attacked McGarrity's fund-raising activity. As a constitutionalist and a moderate, Ryan could not countenance the commitment of McGarrity and his adherents to physical force and revolution in behalf of an independent Irish republic that he knew would be fiercely fought by England. McGarrity, General Dennis Collins, Denis Spellissy, and Patrick Griffin headed a network that had cells in major eastern cities and in distant centers like San Francisco, Butte, Montana, New Orleans, and St. Louis.[47]

In July, Ryan launched a major effort to support Redmond's militia, which was pledged to collaborate with Britain in the battles of World War I. Ten thousand dollars was raised immediately toward a one million dollar goal, which McGarrity claimed would not buy arms for eventual Irish liberty but would be used for Parliamentary party election funds. Ryan's increasingly antagonistic break with McGarrity's adherents was a step that would have notable effects on Ryan's career and leadership, for the militants were winning over Irish public opinion. But, as he was fond of repeating, he believed that England could delay but could not defeat the drive for the moderate formula of Home Rule.[48]

It is pertinent to note that Ryan's moderate nationalist outlook emerged gradually. As a young man, he had been president of the Irish-American Club in Philadelphia for three years. This club was controlled by the Clan na Gael, and Ryan was an active member of its secret network. Whatever his earlier sentiments, by World War I, Ryan had for years been a backer of solutions to Ireland's problems sought through the British Parliament. The old revolutionary agitator, Dr. William Carroll, wrote to the archrebel John Devoy in 1910 that Ryan and Redmond betrayed the nationalist cause. Ryan's political aspirations would not permit him to identify with the physical force advocates as his career advanced. He condemned those who, as he saw it, talked of revolution and did little else. He was to find that the underground conspirators were doing much more than talking, however.

In addition to his very active role in Irish-American affairs, Ryan did not neglect his local political involvements. in 1914, he ran for the Democratic nomination for governor of Pennsylvania, opposed by Congressman A. Mitchell Palmer, and lost his bid. In 1915, he campaigned against Philadelphia Mayor Rudolph Blankenberg. Ryan went to the core of the problem of Philadelphia's servile political status under the Republicans and called for a new Pennsylvania Constitution that would break the fetters that controlled the city from the state level.[49] These candidacies were made possible in part because in 1911 Ryan had been elected president of the oldest Irish organization in the city, the Society of the Friendly Sons of St. Patrick, which gave access to a wide range of connections. With his increasingly reinforced ties, he was able to mount a strong campaign for public service commissioner of Pennsylvania, and in 1916 he was chosen for that position.

But the armed rebellion in Dublin in 1916 that declared an Irish Republic amid conflagration and shellfire changed Ryan's status irrevocably. The 1916 uprising had been aided by his enemy, Joe McGarrity. The incredible daring of the rebellion and the execution of its leaders in what was seen as heroic sacrifice drew youthful opinion in Ireland to the cause of the newborn republic. In October 1914, Ryan had already believed that the United Irish League was dead when Home Rule was placed on the British statute books. John Redmond's support for Britain's war effort gave Ryan the excuse he needed to break with his longtime allies of the Irish Parliamentary party as the extreme nationalists arose in glory. Home Rule was forgotten as a new grail, the Irish Republic, was exalted. Ryan had to alter his orientation or be cast aside as militant nationalism took control of Irish politics. The Sinn Fein (Ourselves Alone) movement that took the stage in the wake of the rebellion swept aside the old Irish Parliamentary party. Ireland moved toward a guerrilla war of independence in 1918. Ryan's attachment to constitutionalism became a liability after decades of work. The successors of the 1916 rebels were a dynamic new cadre, driving Ireland toward a turbulent future. Ryan understood this, and he made numerous pro-German statements at Irish meetings, urging Americans not to aid England in a European war. In 1918, he successfully maneuvered himself into the role of giving the major address at the Irish Race Convention in New York that had been organized by the physical-force contingents.[50]

Ryan's experience in Irish-American affairs, his great power as an orator, and even his image as a moderate made him useful to the militants. Ryan could serve as an intermediary in various situations. The fact that there was rancor between him and the other leaders was neither extraordinary nor a bar to joint efforts. In the United Irish League, he had always been a proponent of surmounting factionalism, and his political skill held together coalitions of vigorously dissenting personalities. His adroitness and conservative reputation made him uniquely valuable in 1919 during the crisis period of the Irish independence movement when the battle against England involved not only guerrilla war in Ireland but also a struggle to win world opinion and American sympathy for the emerging Irish state. The opportunity for Ryan to exercise his talents on a larger stage than ever before arose in 1919 when Irish-American leaders sought to induce Woodrow Wilson to press for Irish independence at the Paris Peace Conference.

By 1917, the Sinn Fein rebels had begun active efforts to mobilize American opinion in behalf of an Irish Republic, and their representative, Dr. Patrick McCartan, conferred with Ryan and other leaders. McCartan and Dr. W.J. Moloney of Boston took a more moderate position than the fiery one of John Devoy, Judge Daniel Cohalen, and Joseph McGarrity, heads of the underground movement, who had wholeheartedly supported the rebellion. As World War I ended, President Woodrow Wilson's peace plans and his doctrine of "self-determination" for small nations became matters of intense interest to the Irish as the Paris Peace Conference was planned. Devoy said, "If Wilson leaves Ireland out [of peace conference consideration], I'm afraid he will not live long enough to live it down." In the winter of 1919, it was decided by the Irish-American leaders that a delegation should be sent to Paris to urge Wilson to include Ireland's case in the postwar discussions of the status of European nations. The delegation was to represent the American Committee for Irish Independence, a broadly representative organization. The commissioners chosen were Frank P. Walsh, a prominent labor lawyer; Edward F. Dunne, former mayor of Chicago; and Michael J. Ryan. Although Ryan was believed to be close to the militant wing at this time, he assured Senator David Walsh, a powerful Democratic party leader, that he believed the delegation should accommodate itself to President Wilson's position at Versailles.[51]

None of the delegates had been associated with anti-Wilson elements in the Democratic party, but Wilson knew of Ryan's pro-German statements prior to American entry into World War I. At a political rally in New York's Metropolitan Opera House, Wilson's aide, Joseph Tumulty, urged him to meet the Irish delegates. Wilson was reported to have responded that Tumulty should "tell them to go to hell."[52] Wilson's antipathy toward the Irish and his Anglophilia were well known. On March 31, 1919, before leaving for Ireland on the journey to Paris for the peace conference, Ryan expressed the hope that the delegation would pose against Wilson's truculent attitude toward discussion of the Irish issue: "America is our home and we proceed with the hope that the blessings of civil and religious liberty under which our Republic has grown great will be extended to Ireland. . . . Our President has declared in favor of the freedom of small nationalities and for the right of the governed to determine the form under which they should live. The claim which we shall urge on behalf of Ireland in cooperation with Ireland's representatives is just this."[53]

Prior to going to France, the delegation sought permission from the British government to visit Ireland, and, after much haggling, permission was reluctantly granted. Enthusiastic crowds in Dublin and elsewhere hailed the Americans, and the British alleged that the delegates made statements that were inflammatory and highly partisan. The British press fulminated in outrage and demanded that the delegates be barred from proceeding to Paris. In the highly charged atmosphere of Ireland in the midst of guerrilla war, and with British repression reaching new heights of terror, the statements of the delegates were bound to reflect the conflict. Indeed, they were no stronger in their comments on British violence than the dispatches of journalist George Creel, President Wilson's own appointed observer in Ireland. Wilson, however, used the British outcry against the delegation as an excuse to avoid meeting it, despite strong pressure from U.S. Senate leaders urging that he confer with the Irish-American group. Wilson was furious at this Irish-American imposition on his cherished peace strategy: "I don't know how long I shall be able to resist telling them what I think of their miserable mischief making."[54]

Frustrated by Wilson's rejection, the delegates themselves fell out. Ryan believed that Walsh and Dunne were too extreme in their views, and he returned to the United States in May 1919. Wilson finally told Walsh that Ireland's case for self-determination was a "great metaphysical tragedy." This was sore comfort for the Irish, and John B. Duff has written, "Wilson's attitude alienated all of Irish America."[55] Alan Ward, a student of Anglo-American relations, indicates that the Irish-American commissioners were stigmatized by such things as Ryan's role as vice-chairman of a pro-German "Friends of Peace" group in 1915, and Wilson doubted their patriotism.[56] Joseph P. O'Grady, reviewing the whole episode, concludes that both Ireland and Wilson lost severely in the tangled standoff of wills and intentions.[57]

Ryan's speeches on the conditions in Ireland were a major influence in mobilizing still further support for the Irish cause. As an orator, he was truly gifted in dealing with such emotional material. Early training in the classics and constant practice in rhetoric, long platform experience, and an atmosphere of drama touching Irish issues gave his speeches notable power. On March 13, 1919, at the Philadelphia Academy of Music, Ryan addressed the traditional "Martyrs Celebration" in memory of Robert Emmet and other fallen Irish heroes. England sought a "super sovereignty," he told the audience. "England's overlordship means that her ships continue to carry our goods and her merchant marine shall dominate the seas," he said. He recited England's exploitations of Ireland and decried those who contended Ulster was opposed to Irish independence: "For thirty years prior to this year the majority of the elected representatives from Ulster were nationalists. . . . Ulster is part of Ireland's heart, and while Ireland lives can never be torn from her." The speech [attacked the League of Nations proposals of

Woodrow Wilson "savagely," as the *Evening Bulletin* said, with Ryan characterizing the peace conference as "a gathering of birds of prey."[58]

At an overflow meeting of the Philadelphia Irish at the city's Metropolitan Opera House on June 8, 1919, Ryan thundered forth the determination of the Irish to win their liberty: "There is a unanimity of opinion in Ireland that is past all understanding. The desire for freedom permeates the very thought and atmosphere of Ireland. Those men over there are determined to win their freedom even if they have to go—more and more and more of them—to the dungeon and the scaffold. The same spirit exists among the women of Ireland, too, and even from the children comes the inevitable cry, "Up the Republic!"

Referring to Lloyd George and the hope of Ireland for "a degree of self-government unparalleled by any past offers made," Ryan said "abominable censorship" was keeping the truth about the Paris peace sessions secret: "Danger is menacing the world, and instead of making a peace of justice and peace that will stop forever the death and destruction of wars, our President, M. Clemenceau and Lloyd George, speaking for Robert Cecil, are merely allotting the earth, parcelling out this section and that of one country and another." So great was the audience for this speech, that overflow crowds had to be accommodated in street meetings near the Opera House. The wildly cheering crowds roared approval of Ryan's report of Ireland's struggle and his attacks on England and Wilson.[59] During these hectic months, Ryan worked strenuously to obtain funds for the Irish independence campaign, setting a goal of $150,000 for Philadelphia. He addressed audiences repeatedly as part of this effort.

After the peace treaty of 1921 between England and an Irish Free State granted a measure of Irish independence, the mass enthusiasm he had helped generate faded, along with Ryan's own national prominence. He continued to give ceremonial addresses through the 1920s, but advancing age and the growth of mass media and more commercial diversion reduced the appeal of the kinds of speeches for which he was noted. During the Depression of the 1930s, Ryan organized a soup kitchen to help feed the unemployed. He continued to associate with churchmen and Irish leaders, but his political career declined as did the bank he had founded, the Girard Avenue title and Trust company.

The career of Michael J. Ryan is a prototype of numerous Irish-American careers of the period from the Civil War to the 1920s.

The Irish-American network provided a vehicle for personal development and also an opportunity to reach national prominence. Michael Ryan's abilities exemplify the gifts involved with mobility in such a network: His intelligence, political aptitude, and oratorical skill combined to promote his ambitions. Sean T. O'Kelly, later president of the Republic of Ireland, who met Ryan in Paris in 1919, considered him one of the most able of the Irish-Americans of his generation but "tremendously vain."[60] For a bootmaker's son to be in a position to pressure the heads of nations at Versailles was occasion for some ego-satisfaction, and Ryan may have inflated himself for the occasion. His career had taken him from local politics to the heights of climactic struggle for Irish freedom, and this was fulfillment of a long-delayed aspiration for Irish-Americans, the group that he represented through an active lifetime.

Such a man as Ryan was especially adapted to the role of mobilizer and mediator in behalf of Irish nationalism in his time. The elaborate Irish organizational network of the United States required men with sufficient breadth of ambition and understanding to assume national positions and to manage the often acrimonious personal and regional interests involved. His tutelage among Philadelphia's Irish groups prepared him for this role. The orator's adeptness led leaders in both Ireland and America to recognize his estimable qualities, among which was his gift for large scale fundraising that funneled hundreds of thousands of dollars into nationalist organizations over the years.[61]

In various respects, Michael J. Ryan represented the values of the Irish-American business and middle class of his time. He had the ambition that was appropriate in a hopeful America, but he also had the moderation of outlook that would not threaten this ambition with radicalism or reproachable activities. The one exception to this was his tactical mistake of speaking favorably of England's enemy, Germany, before 1918. Such remarks may have pleased Irish listeners, but they horrified American Anglophiles. Although he had strong organizational bonds, he was not beyond very American pragmatic changes of orientation, as was shown by his redirection of efforts after Parnell's party floundered and also by his movement toward the militant nationalists as the Sinn Fein revolution grew in strength. There was in his career, as in others, an abiding ambiguity about the attraction of serving the Irish cause. Espousing that cause was good local politics, but it was a limited trajectory simply because the Irish-American was all but excluded from the main arena of endeavor, Ireland itself. The Irish-American leaders had to settle for that, substituting idealism or local advantages for the status of full partisans on Ireland's field of battle. This revealed the ambiguity of ethnic identity in American life, the countervailing forces of ethnicity and the rampant Americanization of the day. Ryan was, too, an exponent of that attempt to resolve this ambiguity by a strident commitment to Americanism and proclamations of loyalty to the land that had given the Irish haven.

As a personality, Ryan did have a flaw remarked upon by many who knew him—his vanity. As a man of humble origins, perhaps he overcompensated for the climate of mockery and derogation that so often surrounded the Irish during his lifetime. His success as an orator may have induced him to yield early to the blandishments of appreciative audiences and see himself as a young Pericles, larger than life. There was about him the egotism of the bourgeois careerist and the heightened individualism so widely present in the late nineteenth century. John J. Reilly verified a story that betrays a histrionic streak in Ryan. When the news of the 1916 rebellion in Dublin reached him, he came to Reilly and others, enraged and distraught. "My whole life's work! Smashed! Ruined!" he proclaimed, seeing the rebellion only as a death blow to constitutional moderation.[62] Others were concerned for the heroes of the uprising, trapped and fighting desperately in the flames of the General Post Office in Dublin. Ryan's sudden break with his fellow peace delegates in Paris also shows an almost willful concern for his own position and reputation. In this respect, his personality is in sharp contrast to that of such a man as the old revolutionary, the self-effacing Mike McGinn.

In both his national and his local role, this man's activities show the implications of the links that the Philadelphia Irish community maintained with the broader Irish subculture in America and with affairs in Ireland. Ryan's speeches and work made him a tribune of the Irish-American tradition, pronouncing its history and its significance for his contemporaries. The presence of such men, blending their personal ambitions and organizational attachments, exhibited the cultural and political identification that the group was able to project. In his long and energetic life from 1862 to 1943, Michael J. Ryan saw an amazing revolution in Irish life from the postfamine period of national exhaustion to the creation of an independent national state. He also saw the emergence of the Irish from the status of a subservient caste to a vital and achieving group in American society. Men like Ryan made the changes in both countries possible.

Finnegan's Finesse

The orbit of urban leadership embraced far more than Irish organizations and causes. Daily engagement with the public affairs of the city demanded that the Irish contend with others in local government and politics, and their leaders often represented a shrewd mixture of ethnic style and pragmatic talents. Before the age of John F. Kennedy and his brothers, the presence of the Irish was traditionally accompanied by a popular historical portrait that depicted them as ugly practitioners of the blackest arts of urban corruption. Mayor Richard Daley of Chicago symbolized this tough, persistent, and pugnacious leadership that was assumed to be typical of Irish-American political behavior. Senator Joseph McCarthy, in a grotesque enactment of the caricature in the 1950s, produced a national trauma with his manifestation of malignant demagoguery. For millions of Americans, his rhetorical excesses and irresponsibility typified all they wanted to know about Irish politicians. There were, however, at all levels of political life throughout the country Irish-American officeholders and political figures who represented far different styles of leadership and standards of public commitment. Men like Senator Brien McMahon of Connecticut, House Speaker John McCormack of Massachusetts, and Senator Thomas Walsh of Montana would be impressive in any assembly.[63]

But the real pulse of Irish politics was in the big cities of the nation where Irish politicians had for most of the nation's history been engaged in the feverish pursuit of electoral victories and governmental power. It was in the municipal affairs of cities with budgets and populations larger than those of some of the new nations in the Third World that Irish politicians displayed their skill, and their leadership styles varied remarkably. Mayor Frank Hague of Jersey City, who declared, "I am the law!" was strikingly different from civil liberties champion Paul O'Dwyer of New York City. Wealthy, conservative Senator James Buckley of New York was a chilly contrast to eccentric and histrionic Congressman Dan Flood of Scranton. Irish leadership in both style and substance varied remarkably, reflecting the diversisty of Irish-American evolution in the country. In Philadelphia, where the Irish came to power very late in the city's history, one politician, James Finnegan, played a crucial role in the reform of the 1950s that greatly altered the structure and reputation of America's most historic city, a city that had been renowned for its unrestrained political corruption for generations.

In 1946, the post–World War II era dawned upon a Philadelphia that was still sunk in Victorian attitudes, platitudes, and solitudes. The city was still largely a warren of old crenellated architecture. Its huge Broad Street Station across from city hall was a red brick mausoleum of dignity in which dwelt the barons of the Pennsylvania Railroad. Its financial district was still housed in ornate nineteenth-century buildings with marble columns and entablatures. Politically, the city had been notorious for generations. Local political life ws the same as it had been in the 1870s, dominated by a Republican political machine that had become legendary for its predations. That machine, in turn, had for generations been a satrap of the railroad, mining, and business powers of the state, the Mellon Bank in Western Pennsylvania, the Scotch-Irish businessmen in Pittsburgh, and wealthy old archconservative Joe Grundy of Bristol and his counterparts across the commonwealth. Philadelphia's Republican body politic was not only corrupt and contented, it was stuffed and cemented—stuffed with booty and cemented in privilege.

It was not that reformers had not challenged the Republican machine, which had begun its reign in 1876 under "Jimmy the First" McManes, a tough Northern Ireland Protestant immigrant. Over the decades, Republican party factionalism prompted brief reform sallies, such as that of Samuel G. King, who was elected mayor in the 1880s. The reforms never really imperiled the machine's adamant foundations. The long and sordid record still has not been studied in any scholarly way, but it would surely yield some important lessons in the shortcomings of American urban government. It is sufficient to note in this chapter that the Philadelphia Republican machine was one corrupt political construction that definitely could not be blamed on the Irish. Lord James Bryce, E.L. Godkin (editor of the *Nation*), leading Anglo preachers, cartoonist Thomas Nast, and a host of commentators laid the evils of city politics to Irish-Catholic immigration. The Philadelphia machine was built, bossed, and made brazen before most of the city's Irish ever had much of a part in it. Gradually, however, some of the Irish did enter into its crooked realm, while another portion of the group remained steadfast political followers of the city's hapless Democratic party. Notable among these was Billy McMullen, a South Philadelphia political leader who was a precocious model for dozens of others in his career of half a century of manipulation and dealing in behalf of his agitated constituency of street fighters, unemployed, hostlers, hustlers, and dockside laborers. By the 1880s, popular Irishmen like Cork-born lawyer Michael J. O'Callaghan had moved to the fringes of Republican machine power, and construction contractor "Sunny Jim" McNichol was a political figure who elsewhere would have been a good prospect for mayor because of his ability and electoral skills, but not in Philadelphia. By the 1930s, the Irish had at last moved up to key positions behind Mayor S. Davis Wilson, whose administration was so corrupt that it took a grand jury seventeen months just to draw up the indictments that were issued in 1939 against 365 persons. Mayor Wilson still had twenty-one bills of indictment against himself when he died that year. Wilson had been guided and abetted in his rule of rascality by Thomas W. Cunningham, John N. McGarvey, Judge Harry McDevitt, and Charles F. Kelly.[64]

The Irish Democrats had long been under the baneful leadership of John O'Donnell until his position was undermined in 1928. O'Donnell had been adept at obtaining crumbs from the all-powerful Republicans by selling out any other Democrats who showed any fight. It was O'Donnell who arranged to have the rent for the offices of the Democratic City Committee paid by the Republicans in return for his habitual sellouts. The campaign of Alfred E. Smith for the presidency in 1928 created new ranks of Democrats who could not be so easily bossed, and Smith got an astonishing 40 percent of the city's vote. Lewis Cassidy and Thomas Logue, with the aid of Democratic National Committee member John J. Raskob, went after O'Donnell and toppled him. What they won was a local party consisting of political wreckage.[65] Through the 1930s Franklin Roosevelt's New Deal brought more Democratic adherents into the ranks, and in 1935 when the handsome athlete and contractor John B. Kelly ran for mayor, a surge of Democratic voters brought him very close to winning the office.

The intervention of World War II postponed any serious move toward political change at the polls, but there were subterranean forces at work that would deeply move the city's political landscape at last. The return of millions of servicemen at the close of the war promised transformation in all areas of the country's life, and Philadelphia was ripe for change. A grand jury in 1948 again turned up widespread peculation. A city employee in the tax collection office killed himself but left a note implicating others. Other suicides followed. The scandal spread. The thievery of taxes was monumental. The Republican party was controlled by Sheriff

Austin Meehan and a group of ward leaders, and the exposure of
its plundering ways made it more vulnerable in the post-war years
of high expectations than ever before.[66]

A good deal has been written about how the reform administration of the Democrats arose in the city following this bout of post-
war political scandal. The accepted local wisdom is that a group of
young socialites gathered at the Racquet Club, discussed their wartime experiences and the condition of the city, and decided to get
into politics and "throw the rascals out." The socialite group,
which included Joseph Sill Clark, Walter Phillips, and Richardson
Dilworth, all attorneys, did become the symbolic leadership group
of the reform movement of the 1950s. The political movement that
sponsored what came to be known as "The Philadelphia Renaissance" is popularly seen as a demonstration of elite noblesse
oblige, a chivalric drama in which old family notables unselfishly
extended themselves to lift the mired city from its morass of lower-
class defilement and renew it according to the ideals of "the better
people." There should be room for at least one other interpretation
of how the reform of the 1950s arose and made its effects felt in the
affairs of the city.[67]

An alternative account of the political overthrow of the Republican machine and the promotion of changes in the city could begin with the key role played by Michael J. Bradley. Born in 1898,
Bradley was a stalwart New Deal Democrat from Port Richmond,
an industrial area adjacent to the Delaware River in the unlovely
cityscape of North Philadelphia. Port Richmond was one of the
city's neighborhoods where the Irish worked in the coalyards, railyards, and shipyards along the river banks. They lived in brick row
houses along with their Polish neighbors and strove to support the
earnest domesticity that was one of the secrets of Philadelphia's
stability. It was from this area that Mike Bradley went to World
War I with the U.S. Army Signal Corps. After the war, the keen-
minded soldier was placed in charge of telecommunications at the
Paris Peace Conference. Such a responsibility required a certain
verbal aptitude and sophistication, and in these Bradley was not
lacking. After the war, he returned to Philadelphia, took part in
ward politics, and in 1937 was elected to Congress from Port Richmond. For the next ten years in Congress, he fought for the Fair
Labor Standards Act and other New Deal measures to aid his
Depression-afflicted constituents. In 1947, Bradley nominated and
pressed the Democratic City Committee into accepting Richardson
Dilworth as candidate for mayor. It was his deciding vote that broke

the tie in the Democratic City Committee to nominate the former Marine officer.

The nomination of Dilworth was part of a stubborn effort on the part of Bradley to retain his position as chairman of the Democratic City Committee after severe defeats for the party in 1946. The Republicans were able to campaign locally against the national Democratic image, and voters at the moment identified the Democrats with wartime rationing and post-war shortages that were infuriating the public. John B. Kelly, trucker James Clark, contractor Matt McCloskey, real estate magnate Albert M. Greenfield, and other Democratic leaders wanted Bradley to resign after 1946. Bradley secured the post of U.S. Customs Collector for himself and fought to keep control of the uneasy forces of the local party. He knew in his bones that the Republicans were highly vulnerable, and he knew that Dilworth, a strident and energetic campaigner, would fight a good fight. Although he had secured Dilworth's nomination, his candidate lost the election to Republican ward heeler Barney Samuel. Even in its decline, the Republican machine was so rich in graft and resources that it could put up a stiff fight. Dilworth himself put on a great combative campaign of street-corner rallies and tough speeches, and the Democratic ward leaders had to admire him. In 1949, he nominated to run for city controller with patrician Joseph Clark picked to run for mayor on the same ticket.[69]

In 1948, prior to the presidential campaign of that year, Jim Finnegan, a former Bradley aide, took over and reorganized the Democratic City Committee. In the 1948 election, Harry Truman won Philadelphia by a slim eight thousand votes, but that was just the beginning of Finnegan's political achievement. Finnegan proved to be uniquely fitted for the role of steering the quarrelsome Democrats who were in many ways still their own worst enemies. He had grown up in the heavily Irish Most Blessed Sacrament parish in West Philadelphia. He had no base of power of his own among the ward leaders of the city. As secretary to Senator Francis J. Myers prior to World War II, he had learned well both the Washington scene and the Philadelphia political geography. During the war he rose to the rank of colonel in the army and after the war became Mike Bradley's secretary at the Democratic City Committee. At the committee headquarters, he was "his own man" and skillfully balanced the various factions in the party while strengthening his own leadership. Tall and handsome with wavy silver hair, he was heartily affable and had one of those swift and retentive minds that never rested in the calculation of political situations and possibilities. He was the kind of deft natural leader who did not feel compelled to be out front personally. His self-assurance was such that he did not need the limelight.[70] He esteemed power above prominence.

The candidate for mayor in 1949, Joseph Clark, was a Harvard lawyer from a wealthy family in the Arcadian Chestnut Hill area of the city. He was forthright, honest, and self-possessed, but never really at ease amid the tawdry turmoil of politics. He surrounded himself with men like Robert T. McCracken, a prominent attorney from one of the old-line law firms; Robert K. Sawyer, a good government campaigner; and Walter Phillips, the guiding strategist of the socialite and middle-class reform group. There were also top business leaders in the reform alliance, and they were gathered in the Greater Philadelphia Movement organization. Liberals and intellectuals from the Americans for Democratic Action added the protest sentiment and eager commitment needed for the reform cadre. Clark remained aloof from the ward bosses: he was a somewhat distant personality and even had trouble relating to his co-reformer Richardson Dilworth, who was a much more down-to-earth type. A politician of the old school, Herbert McGlinchey, who ran the Forty-Second Ward and was on the public payroll for thirty years, recalled his first encounter with Clark: "He came to me as a young fellow in 1928 and said, 'I want to get into politics.' I said, 'Get me some of the bluebloods in Chestnut Hill to vote for Al Smith.' Hell, that was it. He never got us one damned vote."[71] Whether the working politicians liked him or not, Clark had what the Democrats needed, and Jim Finnegan knew it. He had "prep school" good looks, connections with the bank and business heads who had always backed the Republicans, and a media image of debonair socialite style combined with high-principled commitment. In the first years of "media politics," Clark had the cachet needed for a different kind of political appeal, and, along with the feisty Dilworth, the duet could serve as singularly attractive figureheads, as the more cynical political operators saw it, for the shining vessel called "Philadelphia Reform."

It was necessary for Finnegan to build the links between the Clark-Dilworth group and the political warriors who knew how to work the wards for votes. The one without the other would be futile. This was a prodigious task. Trucking magnate Jim Clark had already challenged Finnegan and run his own candidate against Joseph Clark in the 1951 primary election, but Finnegan beat that scheme handily. Campaigning is different from electoral organization. Clark and Dilworth were good at speechmaking, making public appearances, and gathering enthusiastic supporters from the middle class. The people around Finnegan were electoral organizers. They included labor leaders from the AFL-CIO like Joe Schwartz and Joe McDonough, Congressman Bill Barrett of South Philadelphia, William Green from Kensington, public relations man Joe McLaughlin, and Charles Finley, a ward leader. These men had to be linked to Leon Shull and the fiery liberals of the Americans for Democratic Action like Emily Ehly and Ada Lewis.

The experienced major Democrats like John B. Kelly and Matt McCloskey were construction contractors whose businesses had done very well during World War II, and they could contribute and raise money for the Democratic drive. The same was true of real estate millionaire Albert M. Greenfield. Finnegan had to keep all these major figures in alignment and relate them to the civic worthies who believed in Clark and Dilworth. He did so largely by relying on Michael Byrne to carry through his contacts and his communication of strategy. Byrne, from the city's Nineteenth Ward, was an astute and highly skilled negotiator who had strong ties to the city's labor movement. Key men in the Council for Political Education were Ed Toohey of the heavily Irish building trades and Joe Kelley of the electrical workers union. Finnegan and Byrne cultivated the grass roots of the party and mapped out electoral work like generals moving military units.[72] It was Finnegan who, after hearing all the conflicting views and imprecations, would sit down and shape the framework for the Democratic efforts, often in meetings in which he was the only one remaining cool amid howling confrontations.

The good government forces realized that Philadelphia was subject to crippling influences from an incorrigibly Republican legislature and leaders at the state level. The legislature had blocked reform of the city charter in 1939 even though 70 percent of the city voters favored it. The city had to get the power to reform its own government and it could only do so through a new city charter giving it control of its own affairs. The primary champaign of 1951 was to be a vote not only on Joe Clark's candidacy, but on a Home Rule charter drafted largely by Robert T. McCracken, Abraham Freedman, and William Schnader, three really gifted examples of the species "Philadelphia Lawyer." The Citizens Charter Committee, including Republican mavericks like Judge Nochem S. Winnet, toured the city and the state speaking for the charter reform. Finnegan, Mike Bradley, and Mike Byrne worked hard to have the reluctant politicians at the state and city levels support a charter

that had strong civil service provisions and a modernized government design that threatened local traditions and prospects for patronage jobs. They succeeded in their persuasions. As Mike Byrne
was to recount, Clark and Dilworth were "the public relations,"
while Finnegan was "the real muscle of organization."[73] The charter referendum won by 119,000 votes in the primary, and Clark won
the mayor's office in a historic political overthrow. Philadelphia
was at last free to chart a new future for itself. The Irish politicians
had strong leverage in Kensington, Logan, Oak Lane, Northeast
Philadelphia, Bill Barrett's wards in South Philadelphia, and
Southwest Philadelphia, Finnegan's old neighborhood. In these areas, they outpolled the Republicans by about 25 percent, and this,
added to the other areas of the city where the reform appeal drew
support, gave the Democrats a winning mayoralty majority of
124,000 votes.[74]

Clark's cabinet was crucial in the making of his reform administration, as was the city council that was elected with him under
the new city charter. Mike Byrne was made assistant to the mayor
and was to be the channel for communication between the good
government forces and the city council. President of the council
was Jim Finnegan. The sweeping Democratic victory had brought
to the council Thomas Guerin of South Philadelphia, Charles Finley, John F. Byrne, Michael J. Towey, and James H.J. Tate, all Irish
politicians in the seventeen-member body. Tate had opposed the
city charter, but, because he was a friend of the powerful William
Green, he was in a strong position. In addition, he was a workhorse
with a remarkable knowledge of how the city departments functioned. Finnegan was concerned that the new council would have
no rational rule to govern its work since the old council had never
bothered about such niceties. The new charter had changed the
fromework for council business. Finnegan had Tate draw on his
knowledge of the state legislature of which he had been a member,
and, in one furious all-night typing session, Tate drew up the new
rules of council.[75]

Finnegan was so openly supportive of honesty for the members
that it was almost inconceivable to many of the ward bosses. When
he had his first meeting as council president he led off with an
extraordinary declaration: "Count me out of anything you have going," he said, meaning that he wanted no part of any of the illicit or
borderline arrangements that were the stock and trade of local politicians. The tentacles of vested interests were wound everywhere
in municipal affairs. Large law firms were always vying for insur-

ance and bond counsel work. One council member was a home-
builder, and zoning changes were a constant source of political
dealing. Other council members were engaged in a steady trading
of favors and jobs. Finnegan's declaration was highly uncharacter-
istic for one in his position, to say the least.

The statement was followed immediately in the meeting by an
even more shocking one. "Watch yourself," he told his fellow members. "Not only will I not cover up for you if you are caught at
something wrong, but I intend to actively expose wrongdoing."[76]
Such pronouncements were common enough as campaign rhetoric,
but for them to be asserted with a deadly sincerity in the closed
precincts of the council's private deliberations was astonishing.
Such was Finnegan's stature that he was able to make such statements, be taken seriously, and enforce them as well. It was this
kind of resolution and gritty address to reality that compelled other
council members to change their views of what was possible in
their relations with the new reform government. Finnegan simply
let them know where they stood, and, in affrays over the conduct
of such previously lucrative offices as the Department of Licenses
and Inspections or the use of council offices to conduct ward business on city time, he set tough standards.

The cabinet included a new commissioner of police, Thomas
Gibbons. Everybody agreed that Gibbons was an honest cop, and
this was extremely important in a city where police corruption had
been a byword for generations. Almost all the department heads
appointed by Clark were professionals with good backgrounds. Dilworth as city controller and a strong Civil Service Commission
worked to counter the old practices that had enshrined inefficiency
and made the city services a laughing stock. Another key appointment was that of George S. Forde, a graduate of the U.S. Naval
Academy, a tough professional, to be revenue commissioner, with
Romanus Buckley as his deputy. The revenue office had been a
center of wholesale thievery under the Republicans, and it had to
be watched very carefully if city funds were to be safeguarded.[77]

In a program of unprecedented renovation, the municipal machinery of the city was overhauled. Plans for rebuilding the city
rolled forth in profusion. A new food distribution center, a new
airport, a dramatic rebuilding of center city, urban renewal for
slum areas, and new sports complexes were all set underway. Each
new scheme seemed to inspire another as Edmund Bacon's planning commission mapped a remarkable transformation of the
downtown area. Mike Bradley worked in Congress to have federal

legislation passed that would make possible the creation of a huge
Independence Hall National Park, and he won this federal support
for the restoration of the city's historic district. In this enormously
complex process, Finnegan's hand carefully guided the enactments
needed from city council and the federal bureaucracy to make the
plans real with financial and political support. The city's "renaissance" was a dazzling effort, and national magazines and commentators extolled it. The publicity in national magazines and journals,
in the local newspapers, and at professional conferences saluted
Mayor Clark and Richardson Dilworth. The charisma of the upper-
class reformers dominated the imagery of the city's achievement.[78]
Behind the scenes, however, it was Jim Finnegan who was astutely
managing the political basis of the reform. The Irish Democratic
construction contractors were very much part of the rebuilding
picture, and they were making money from the projects. Similarly,
real estate moguls, architects, bankers, lawyers, and scores of participants in the energetic rebuilding activity were benefiting. In
this arena of contracts and profits, the political alignments had to
be shrewdly tended, and Finnegan directed the process.

The strains within the reform administration were ever-
present. Clark and Dilworth were bound together politically, but
they were not all that close personally. The good-government elements were deeply suspicious of the politicos. There were scram-
bles over big construction contracts. Matt McCloskey pressed hard
for corporate interests to preside over the center-city renewal, and
his firm won the lion's share of the reconstruction of the Pennsylvania Railroad site for the new Penn Center office towers. He also
built the Spectrum, a new sports stadium, but the roof blew off
when it was finished, symbolizing the many defects in the reconstruction activity. Architect Louis Kahn submitted a plan to put an
expressway through the downtown area that would wall off dé-
classé South Philadelphia, but the row house citizens there raised
the roof in their own way. Finnegan had to take the political flack
for such gaffes.

Three functions of leadership had to be carried out by Jim
Finnegan as the reform proceeded in the five years after 1951. First,
the leader had to assure that the political process would be more
representative than it had been in the past, for the city was now
more varied in population than it had been in the past, and those
groups previously excluded from party work and patronage had to
be recognized. The old Republican machine had paid scant attention to pluralism in any participatory sense. They had worked ac-

cording to a nineteenth-century formula of neighborhood ethnic tutelage at the lower levels and a pattern of exclusionist practices that had been perfected by the old Anglo-Protestant elite. After World War II, tokenism would no longer suffice. The reformers had promised a more open system and they had to deliver. Finnegan reached out through the city for ties to various subgroups besides the Irish. The Americans for Democratic Action was heavily Jewish, and its members had been in on the early crafting of the reform. They were highly important as a source of talent and ideas and were articulate advocates of liberal and professional input. Finnegan had to maintain close ties to this volatile and creatively active group.[79] He had to develop stronger ties with the swiftly growing black community. To see Finnegan listen attentively to Councilman Marshall Shepherd, respectfully attend to the orotund declamations of the lisping Reverend Luther Cunningham, or deal skillfully with the fiery Sadie T.M. Alexander and her flamboyant husband, Councilman Raymond Pace Alexander, was to see ethnic politics at work in the most proximate and artful fashion.

A second function involved the balancing of potent interests within the party. One of these interests was the judiciary. The Irish judges in the city alone represented a whole realm of influence, jobs, perquisites, and cleverly shielded emoluments that were nicely sequestered by longer terms of office for the judges and judicially contrived legalities that acted as shelters from the storms of the political cycles of the city. Among those involved were judges James Crumlish, Vincent Carroll, Gerald Gleeson, Francis X. McClanahan, Charles Guerin, Peter Hagen, and a whole fraternity of court officials, attorneys, and such hardy perennials as Sheriff William Lennox. The judges controlled most of the patronage of the school district and were linked to various city commissions, boards, and city hall oddities that were reserves of patronage. Finnegan was able to orchestrate them wonderfully in the interests of party harmony without violating either letter or spirit of the new city charter. As with the judges, so it was with labor, city employees, Democrats at the state and federal levels, and all the shifting elements of the party faithful.[80]

Third, Finnegan was an expert at conflict resolution that reduced the damage of inevitable challenges to reform policies and programs. Among many examples was the war about public housing sites. The federally financed program to build public housing required enabling legislation from city concil. The housing program was a showpiece of reform, but councilmen were under intense pressure to reject sites in their districts that meant change for old-line neighborhoods and that meant bringing blacks into white areas. Finnegan warned the liberals against the diffusion of sites into the explosively antagonistic white areas. Despite the pressure, he did maneuver the enabling ordinance through council in an all but magical example of his skill. The attempt to disperse public housing sites, as he predicted, created a firestorm of grass-roots opposition in white areas and went down to flaming defeat, however. Obstacles were encountered that forced the program back into the ghettos. The new zoning code, a new community college, correctional facilities, and a big expressway program brought repeated opposition. Finnegan had to sort out the central causes of conflict, choose a variety of appropriate bargaining assets, and patiently compose a solution for each.[81] Unlike other cities where federal renewal funds brought change, Philadelphia's program had to move into areas that had resisted intrusion for generations, and the opposition slowly grew.

The range of renewal had its limits, and by the mid-1950s the friction of opposition and the forces of exhaustion slowed the reform. Joseph Clark had from the outset wanted to be a senator and chafed under the indignities of being mayor in a contentious city. He left office, ran for the Senate, and won. Dilworth would succeed him. The reform coalition, faced with the steadily increasing responsibilities of running a renovated city, experienced splits and defections. Finnegan himself resigned from city council in 1955 to become secretary of the Commonwealth of Pennsylvania. His health was not good. The reform had been an exhausting commitment for him. There had been little time for him to assess his personal situation amid the constant battles and standoffs of the fractious Democratic party elements. Mayor Clark had tended to stand aloof from such conflicts, and the mercurial Dilworth usually added to the contention.

Richardson Dilworth succeeded Clark as mayor in 1956. Jim Tate became president of city council, succeeding Finnegan. Dilworth chose Joseph Gaffigan to be deputy mayor and to be his liaison with the Irish politicians. He made Richard McConnell, an excellent administrator, his director of finance. The glow of reform continued, but the fire burned lower. Dilworth's combative, opinionated style changed the atmosphere. As a lawyer, he knew the value of compromise, but one compromise deal he made almost blew up his reform image in 1956.[82]

In 1955, William Green, the most powerful figure among the Democratic political leaders, was in a difficult position. After years of rigorous Civil Service Commission administration, he had few disposable jobs for his political followers. As head of the Democratic party he had to have jobs to hold the electoral machinery together and to keep his leadership from being undermined. He had sufficient votes in city council to have amendments to the Home Rule Charter placed on the ballot exempting from civil service status the old offices that were part of the Philadelphia county government, such as sheriff and recorder of deeds. Mayor Dilworth agreed to let Green do this if Green would back his bid to run for governor. Leon Shull, a key figure in the Americans for Democratic Action, found out about the deal and excoriated it in the newspapers. Dilworth was furious. He needed Green's support for the nomination to run for the state's top office, and Shull had blown up his crucial arrangement. In a raving shouting match with Shull, he clearly revealed that he was not the reform purist that the media had come to extol and that the public had been led to esteem. The absence of Finnegan's finesse had produced a shattering division in the reform coalition.[83]

Dilworth's temperamental personality required the steadying hand of somebody like Finnegan. Other incidents caused difficulty. Revenue commissioner George Forde had confrontations with Dilworth because of the latter's desire to do political favors that would have been illegal and unethical, such as permitting underpayment of gate tax receipts at the municipal stadium or overlooking cheating on payments to the Water Department by big contributors to the Democratic party. Forde, a tough man, refused to accede to Dilworth's pressure. When Dilworth was elected mayor, he refused to reappoint Forde in a clear case of retaliation.[84]

The political framework that had been constructed under Finnegan soon came apart. Jim Tate, who became mayor after Dilworth resigned to run unsuccessfully for governor, shifted priority away from downtown rebuilding toward the neighborhoods he knew so well. The downtown business barons were not pleased. A gulf opened between city hall and business heads and also between Tate and the reform leaders. As Herbert Lipson, publisher of *Philadelphia Magazine*, put it, "The Establishment went back to the suburbs and pulled the crabgrass over its head."[85] Without Finnegan's ministrations, the old Anglo elite asserted itself again in its traditional negative fashion of sulking withdrawal. The

Clark-Dilworth aura faded. The tennis frolic in politics was over.[86] The other elements in the coalition became exhausted at the same time after a cycle of struggle with harsh urban realities.

Throughout this period, the Irish politicians fought among themselves. Mike Bradley fought Jim Clark. Jim Clark fought Jim Finnegan. Jim Tate fought the Democratic City Committee head Frank Smith. All of them, however, did share a certain cultural style. A number of them had been to school together. They were attached to their own Irish circuit and the constituency on which it was based, and this ethnic affinity made communication easier, even if it was communication in combat. Jim Finnegan had mastered the art of bulldozing and soft-talking the various cadres and had related them to the reformers. Without this linkage, the upper-class reformers would have remained a high-minded discussion group at the musty Racquet Club. Without Finnegan's deft skills, the politicians would have continued to spurn the reformers, for the Democrats in the city had for generations destroyed their own political opportunities. Finnegan's achievement is the more notable because it grew out of a career of what many would regard as pedestrian political work.

Beyond the political contributions they made, the Irish also brought to city government in these years a technical and administrative talent that helped transform the government. Revenue Commissioner Forde, Police Commissioner Gibbons, Ed Cummins in the Department of Licenses and Inspections, James Dillon in the Water Department, and scores of others gave notable service to the public. Few were from privileged backgrounds. The Irish city professionals were largely from the old neighborhoods. They had gotten to college and graduate school by sheer force of commitment in the 1930s or more recently on the G.I. Bill. Some had gotten scholarships to the Fels Institute for Local and State Government at the University of Pennsylvania, where Stephen Sweeney had tutored two whole generations of public administrators. Between these experts and the political decision makers, Finnegan and Mike Byrne played important liaison roles.

The connective and administrative contributions of the Irish in the Philadelphia reform grew out of a fundamental fact of American political life. There is no constitutionally sanctioned apparatus for party functioning in our system, yet the parties have for much of our history been the chief devices for democratic electoral participation. They have been conducted to relate to the special interests, ethnic, and localized pluralism of the country. Changes in government have depended upon party mobilizations, which in turn have depended upon patronage and "pork chop" benefits. This has led to corruption and to subversion of democratic ideals. Richardson Dilworth, putative idealistic reformer, trafficked in deals that were reminiscent of stereotypical bossism. Jim Finnegan, who was not seen as a reformist beau ideal by the publicists of reform, was more of a stalwart of good government than many of the "reformers." The role of congressional funding for projects pushed by Mike Bradley and Bill Barrett, funding often character- ized as "pork barrel" politics, was also highly important, yet would hardly be seen as "reformist."[87]

In his excellent comparative study of Irish-American political behavior, Steven P. Erie states that "in the twentieth century the classical Irish urban machines have served as engines of modern- ization, highly integrated into both the modern Democratic party and the national welfare state."[88] Despite its late arrival, the Phila- delphia Democratic apparatus served this purpose. It came to power under reform banners, but it was quickly transformed into a machine, largely because of the energy and methodical work of Finnegan, William Green, and Jim Tate. The machine arrived in time to be used to give one of the largest majority votes in any city for the candidacy of John F. Kennedy in 1960. It also arrived just in time to become the vehicle for the ascendancy to power of blacks in the years following the civil rights uproars of the 1960s. Al- though the old immigrant enclaves with their needs for elementary services were fading, the huge inner-city black population and its stricken underclass were a newly expanded machine constituency. Welfare services, neighborhood fix-ups, minority contract provi- sions, and access to the low-skill jobs that municipal employment afforded were all part of the machine's new lease on life. Without the Democratic groundwork of the 1950s, the transition to mass black political involvement would have been much more problem- atical and tumultuous.

The fact that much that was seen as progress in the years of the 1950s is now viewed as urban deformity, such as the highway, pub- lic housing, and slum clearance programs, is part of the revision- ism that always follows such bursts of change. Much of the city planning of the reform, led by the planning commission's Edmund Bacon, was flawed by racial assumptions, overblown pretentions, and devotion to downtown projects. The reformers for the most part remained oblivious to the flight of industry and the decline of jobs that attended their tenure. Jim Finnegan was part of these reform shortcomings as were all the leaders. They were all politicians trying to grapple with imponderables to which no urban group was equal and that in following decades would transform the major cities into vast centers of decay, social malaise, and administrative frustration.[89]

The emergence of the Irish into full political status in Philadelphia during the reform years was fulfillment of a long-delayed ethnic ambition. The flexibility of Irish leadership was able to accommodate the needs of reformers as well as the workers in the political trenches. Some of the Irish input was laced with liberal and labor ideology that derived from the 1930s, technical skills drawn from the Irish middle class, and the working-class solidarity of residents of the old neighborhoods. The Irish presence, however, was a prelude to their own ethnic displacement by burgeoning black power. Finnegan and his cohorts were part of a struggle to maintain a certain kind of urban order. Beneath his affable manner, the qualities he had of purposeful toughness, persistence, and hope were badly needed in that struggle. It is well for Philadelphia that he was far-sighted and committed enough to use those qualities for the benefit of the city and its people.

Conclusion

Consideration of the experience of the Irish-Americans presented in this book can lead to a broader understanding of the influences that have shaped our subcultural communities. Historically, much of the process of forming minority social networks in the American setting arose from the original predicament caused by emigration and dislocation, although the sources of ethnicity in other societies may have been different. Peter Marin has described the emigration situation well:

> Immigrants find themselves dislocated not only in terms of space but also in terms of meaning, time and value, caught between a past no longer fully accessible and a future not yet of use. . . . The subsequent drama is in some ways more profound, more decisive than the material struggle to survive. It involves the immigrant soul if by soul one simply means the deepest part of the self, the source of human connectedness and joy. The great tidal pulls of past and future, of one world and another, create a third and inner world, the condition of exile—one in which the sense of separatedness and loss, of in-betweenness, of suspension and even orphanhood, become more of a home for the immigrant, more of a homeland, than either the nation left behind or America newly entered.[1]

This is a moving description of a cultural condition, but it is notably negative. In addition to the awareness of loss, there is also a sense of retention, the consciousness of that which has been brought from the past. This portable inheritance, often fragmentary, distorted, and confused, is precious to the personality. It is the memory of an ethnic wholeness, or at least an aspiration toward some cultural unity and continuity. It is vital for the social well-being of people set adrift in strange circumstances. It was such an inheritance of legend, folklore, family memory, and social history that the Irish brought with them and molded into their new environment in America.

What cultural impedimenta did they transport to places like Philadelphia? Their legacy was a compound of both homely detail and historic experience pertinent to the group. From Ireland came an enormous fund of history and recollection embracing ancient Celtic language, art, and clan behavior, a later Christian heritage,

Gaelic folkways, plus Norman and Anglo-Irish infusions of social, political, and military experience. To this were added several centuries of modern nationalism and a literature of vast extent in Irish and English. Not all were conscious of the depth of this heritage, and, indeed, many were only selectively aware of it. But it *was* their treasury, their world of dream and drama rooted in the complex facts of the past. It was memorialized in ethnocentric tales and writings, extolled in speeches and recitations, and sung in ballads learned by heart for generations.

Particular examples of this tradition are contained in the material assembled in this book, and the process by which it was transmitted has been described. A more technical exposition of this process is provided in the Research Note at the end of the book. Family stories and daily interactions with people of the same background consolidate ethnic feeling. Formal associations give public recognition to Irish-American activity and identity. Community liaisons like the Brehon Society and the informational content of Irish radio programs and newspapers foster and confirm the ethnic affiliation. All of the mailings, meetings, petitions, picketing, and other techniques of expression contribute to the process. Studies of Irish history and literature take the ethnically conscious person into rich and highly intellectual areas of rapport with the broader tradition of the group. Representative of all these things, and symbolic of their cultivation, is the leadership that provides role models and significant communication styles for the group and that also takes its "cues" from the ethnic constituency to provide direction to its affairs.[2]

In Philadelphia, the dynamics of all this social experience have endowed the city with a significant Irish heritage that continues to be displayed in a number of ways. There is a consciousness of Irish identity that is focused on certain events and a continuous round of occasions. A survey of a sample to two hundred people associated with Irish groups and interests in the city in 1989 showed that this largely middle-aged, predominantly American-born sample had a strong commitment to Irish attachments and activities. One-fourth of the sample traced their Irish ties to generations beyond their grandparents. A parallel questioning of Irish organizations revealed a steady pattern of activity but a relative lack of innovation among the societies queried.[3] A review of the monthly calendar of Irish association meetings and events for 1989 showed more than four hundred gatherings that year for cultural and charitable purposes (and this was only a partial listing).[4]

The interest in ethnic identity within the group is confirmed by the persistent attention to family genealogy, often guided by specialists whose writings tutor those seeking to trace family roots.[5] Family surnames are regarded proudly, and Irish first names have a continued popularity. Recollections of local Irish childhoods appear intermittently in newspapers, and memoirs extend such reminiscences.[6] Participation by youngsters in festivals, dance classes, tours, and the Irish Way Program of the Irish American Cultural Institute that takes secondary school students to Ireland gives informal instruction in the tradition, while Sister Frances Kirk's youth exchange program with Northern Ireland and the nearby Ulster Project in Delaware for the same purpose offer other experiences.[7]

The organizational dimension of this interest is replete with groups that are part of the complex voluntary social life of the city. Although the older pattern of exclusively Irish work groups that prevailed among ironworkers, bricklayers, and transport workers has faded, construction unions often continue to be headed by men of Irish background, such as Ed Toohey and Patrick Gillespie. Cultural groups for music and lecture series flourish. The Donegal Association celebrated its centenary in 1988 with a year-long cycle of events and publication of a book on its history. Lacking the large memberships of earlier generations, the Irish groups appear to have settled into small but devoted circles of active, faithful adherents.[8]

The communications networks serving this subcultural community still include newspapers, magazines, and radio programs, but newsletters, computerized mailing lists, and electronic facsimile transmissions are now common in maintaining ties and spreading information from Ireland. The public meetings of yesteryear with their oratory and solicitations have been replaced by more personalized contacts stimulated by mail and telephone. Promotional material and book catalog distribution by mail provide a wide range of information about reading, music, travel, and special events. Direct telephone contact with Ireland is now an accustomed convenience for family news and social and business exchange.[9]

The leadership of the group has changed notably over the last generation. Many prominent business and civic figures today do not publicly emphasize their Irish background. Ecclesiastics are far less prominent than in the past. The elevation of a Polish-American and then an Italian-American to head the Archdiocese of Philadelphia in recent decades and the diminished religious consciousness of Catholics generally has moderated Irish-Catholic clerical status. Irish Protestants, while active in the Friendly Sons of

St. Patrick, have a low profile. The two most popular priests among the Irish in the 1980s were Father John McNamee of St. Malachy's parish in a ravaged black ghetto of North Philadelphia and Irish-born Father Michael Doyle of nearby Camden, whose parish is a much-praised experiment in inner-city social development.

Political leadership has similarly altered as the city's elections have become dominated by black candidates. Irish leaders preside in some of the remaining all-white wards, but suburbia is now their favored landscape. The election of Robert Casey in 1988 as governor of Pennsylvania and the talented Philadelphian Robert O'Donnell as the powerful Speaker of the Pennsylvania House of Representatives signifies the group's continuing political adeptness, but the old electoral underpinnings of its prowess in the city have diminished.

While Irish organizational leaders still play various civic and charitable roles, the leadership profiles in the community are more likely to be those of activists who rely on their own personal gifts rather than on broad organizational leverage. Cultural figures like musician and singer Mick Moloney, nationalist activists like lawyer Ann Gaughan, and educational advocates such as businessman Bernard Croke represent a new kind of competence in Irish affairs, less related to large organizations and more attuned to new communication skills.[10]

The cultivation of all these forms of interaction has created for this Irish-American community a social rhetoric through which it has transmitted its tradition. The rhetoric contains three orders or categories similar to those identified by Kenneth Burke.[11] The first is a memory of historical information and outlook. This provides the basis for the adherence to an ethnic identity and the conveyance of a tradition. The second order of rhetoric is a realm of analogies that refer back to Ireland and family or group experiences there. The third rhetorical dimension is particular, local, and pertinent to the ethnic group experience in Philadelphia. From these streams of discourse there have emerged an accepted vocabulary of ideas and terms and a catalog of memory enabling the Philadelphia Irish to enact their roles amid the general institutional fabric of the city.[12] This social rhetoric consisting of familial, organizational, and leadership communication is the essential medium of their ethnic tradition. It is both cause and effect.[13] It is the vital principle of their Irishry.

It is not only in Philadelphia, of course, that the Irish adaptation took place. Wherever the group was able to stabilize its community network, it expressed its identity and stimulated social interaction. There are now sufficient studies of Irish communities to illustrate this fact. Records and archives vary from place to place, but there is sufficient evidence to show the four social functions set forth in this book to have been activated in widely separate locations.

In smaller communities life Butte, Montana, and Worcester, Massachusetts, there is adequate documentation of such social interaction. In the larger cities, although there is ample documentation of the Irish presence, that presence is so extensive in time and numbers that enough research has not been done to permit full comparative study. The one study attempting such an approach is Stephen P. Erie's *Rainbow's End: Irish-Americans and the Dilemmas of Urban Machine Politics, 1840–1985,* and insightful analysis of the Irish political role in nine separate cities.[14] For the immediate purposes of this book, however, there are appropriate references to show the working of a community process similar to that in Philadelphia.

In the cultivation of identity, whether it was in the mining town of Butte or the milltown of Worcester, or in the great centers of Boston, Chicago, San Francisco, and New York, the Irish ethnic subculture rested on a sense of individual bonding with the Hibernian tradition. In a smaller locality, such as Butte, where 93 percent of the Irish married within their own group, the social and occupational solidarity of the group strongly informed the Irish population. David Emmons's book *The Butte Irish: class and Ethnicity in an American Mining Town,* perhaps the best single study of an Irish community, has a whole chapter devoted to community formation and organizational growth. In Massachusetts, whether in Boston or Worcester, the Irish presence was so pronounced that terms like "Irishtown" in Worcester and "Boston Irishman" became common parlance. Timothy Meagher organized his study of the Worcester Irish around the issue of the evolution of their identity. David Noel Doyle has evaluated the self-consciousness of the Chicago Irish that led to such a lively literary expression by Finley Peter Dunne and James T. Farrell. San Francisco's Irish population, distinctive in its social latitude, nevertheless maintained a notable sense of its own self-image. New York, of course, has been such a crucible of ethnic interaction that its pluralist definition of itself as a city practically ordained an ethnic identity for the components of its population, including the Irish.[15]

In these different cities, Irish social status and outlook varied over their long history in America. Their self-regard and community image altered in accordance with regional conditions. Thus, the ascent of the group from the excluded minority position in Boston detailed by Oscar Handlin to the drama of the years of the Kennedy family's "Camelot" is striking. In New York, the decline of the group from its heyday of Tammany political power in the early twentieth century to a subordinate role in contemporary times reveals very different perceptions among the Irish themselves and in their public position. The extraordinary feature of this transition is the persistence of the ethnic identity amid pluralist shifts and historical changes.

Organizationally, the record is even more diverse, yet marked by common themes of behavior. In Butte, labor union and nationalist activity predominated. In Worcester, the Catholic church and temperence societies were the poles around which much of the Irish community's energy revolved. In Boston, the struggle against poverty was the stimulant for much organizational innovation. San Francisco was the setting for pursuit of a broad roster of political, social, and educational endeavors. Chicago's Irish strongly supported religious institutional development but had a rich record of nationalist and political activity as well. In New York, the formation of church and mutual benefit societies began in the first half of the nineteenth century and proceeded apace until such organizations as the Ancient Order of Hibernians and heavily Irish labor unions were highly influential in the nation's largest city. The city gave rise to various elite Irish circles, one of which represented great wealth and another of which led intense Irish-American nationalist agitations.[16]

In all of these areas, communications about Ireland and its interests and about American-Irish affairs were maintained through various media. In Butte, labor publications and the correspondence and bulletins of nationalist and fraternal groups served this purpose. In Worcester, the Catholic newspapers were the Irish vehicle. In Boston, the influential *Boston Pilot* under such editors as John Boyle O'Reilly not only provided local news, but was also distributed far beyond Massachusetts. Dennis P. Ryan's book *Beyond the Ballot Box: A Social History of the Boston Irish, 1845–1917* lists a whole array of benevolent societies, institutions, and educational groups that formed a complex web of communications units. In San Francisco, R.A. Burchell has detailed the Irish labor and political network that maintained lecture circuits, meeting schedules, and public functions. Chicago's Irish nationalists are well documented in their correspondence and three newspapers. New York, the thriving center of the country's publishing and intellectual life, gave rise to a long series of Irish periodicals, most notably *The Irish World and Industrial Liberator*, printed for more than a century, and the fiery *Gaelic American* of archrebel John Devoy. This diffusion of organizational and news media supplied current Irish information as well as streams of poetry, speeches, debates, and controversies that fed the need for transmission of cultural consciousness and tradition. It was a key resource for the political and social orientation of the Irish in one community after another from the mid-nineteenth century forward.[17]

The leadership of smaller communities such as Butte and Worcester tended to arise from religious, political, and labor circles. In larger centers, the rise of an Irish middle class and of wealthy individuals complemented the exertions of social reformers and nationalists. Dennis P. Ryan's gallery Boston Irish charitable leaders in his *Beyond the Ballot Box: A Social History of the Boston Irish 1845–1917* and the leaders highlighted in James Walsh's *The San Francisco Irish, 1850–1976* demonstrate the influence of outstanding local figures who were also related to the affairs of nationwide Irish organizations. The highly constructive but quiet and rarely publicized leadership of nuns in health and education is indicated by Robert E. Sullivan and James M. O'Toole in their edited volume *Catholic Boston: Studies in Religion and Community, 1870–1970*. David Noel Doyle has suggested that Irish leaders in Chicago could be more accurately seen as imitations of American corporate style than as products of a transplanted folk culture. Whatever their character, these Chicago leaders have been a kaleidoscope of ethnic continuity. New York's Irish luminaries have ranged across the traditions of politics, theater, literature, exile nationalism, and immigrant organizations. The widely read critique by Nathan Glazer and Daniel Patrick Moynihan in *Beyond the Melting Pot* concerning the Irish devolution from power emphasizes the changing positions they have held amid the crosscurrents of pluralism in the metropolis. As the largest magnet of Irish immigration to America, the city has always been a stage for vivid leadership emergence. A succession of colorful figures from radical agitator Mike Walsh in the 1840s to labor leader Mike Quill in the mid-twentieth century has accented the prominence of one phalanx after another of Irish notables that have included mayors, senators, heads of national organizations, and successful exponents of a wide span of careers and professions.[18]

In a previous study, *Hibernia America: The Irish and Regional Cultures*, I traced the ways in which Irish-Americans became part of the history and lore of this country in all its far-ranging variety.[19] This adaptation was achieved in part through the process described in this book but also through other adjustments still unstudied. The early spread and later adumbration of the Irish-Protestant tradition and its relationship to the more numerous Irish-Catholic distribution is as yet unevaluated despite Rory Fitzpatrick's volume on *God's Frontiersmen*. The works of Hasia Diner and Janet Nolan on the role of Irish women in the panorama of immigrant stabilization beckon toward further research about the female role in Irish-American development. The necessity for more realistic and accurate religious history for the Irish-Americans has been shown by Jay Dolan of Notre Dame University.[20] Such study surpasses the simplifications of our previous views, and it is hoped that studies of the Irish presence in American life will provide instruction in the evolution of our democratic life.

The coexistence of the Irish-American subculture with a metropolitan and national mainstream culture of unprecedented social and communications potency places it in a vulnerable situation. John Edwards had pointed out that what is termed the "ethnic revival" of recent years has derived more from general societal considerations than from the vitality of the ethnic groups themselves.[21] However, there are significant influences in modern society that can also work to sustain ethnic networks. The rapid influx of immigrants resulting from changes in legislation and economic conditions, access to the "old country" through jet-age travel, the increasing ease of recording ethnic lore and materials and in maintaining communications, and rising levels of education and cultural perception all can activate ethnic awareness.

One notable consideration is that the older Irish-American tradition referred back to an Ireland that is now past, an Ireland of ruralism and folk culture. The folk memory, nationalist rhetoric, and ethnic affinity in the face of displacement and discrimination that shaped it are no longer current. Irish identity is being reshaped into a more pluralist, secular, confident, and self-critical form. It is not clear that the Irish-Americans are perceptive of these changes. They are still sympathetic to the many problems their kinsmen in the old country now face but less committed to actually aiding their complex resolution. The newer Irish identity of independent status, with more European ties and with mass media discourse replacing folk attachments, is not for the most part comprehended by those who have shared Irish-American ties.[22]

Conclusion

It seems clear that continued immigration from Ireland on some scale and the strengthening of Irish-American cultural ties are two necessities for the continuation of this group's ethnic presence. A tradition is only as viable as its adherents. Whatever the future holds, it is of great benefit to American life that the communal histories of subcultural groups be pondered. It is inevitable that Americans will be concerned about global issues and the direction of our larger society, but we will also be conscious of the fragility of smaller cultures besieged by novelties and technologies that threaten their survival. One of the tests of our freedom will be our ability to preserve the rich and precious patrimony that ethnic traditions and minority experiences represent. They have been and still are the atmosphere for the cultural breathing of most of mankind.

Research Note

Over the last two decades, studies dealing with the social and economic mobility of ethnic groups, the Irish-Americans among them, have been widely pursued.[1] These have shown that the penetration of the Irish into the labor and entrepreneurial systems of the country was at first halting and troubled. As immigration continued through the second half of the nineteenth century, however, greater opportunities arose. Yet, gains for the Irish-born remained minimal in many places, and the sons and daughters of Irish immigrants progressed at a rate behind that of the children of immigrant Germans, Scandinavians, and Jews until the twentieth century. The barriers of anti-Irish and anti-Catholic discrimination, limited cultural expectations, militant anti-labor practices, and other disabilities retarded mobility. When such mobility did occur, it was accompanied by various patterns of assimilative behavior but, among many Irish-Americans, also by a continued retention of ethnic attachments.

The twentieth-century fortunes of the Irish have received less study than the experience of the group in the nineteenth century. The decline of immigration after the restrictive legislation of the 1920s and the great transformations occasioned by two world wars, new mass media, and extensive shifts of population notably altered the role of the Irish in American life. Andrew Greeley in *That Most Distressful Nation: The Taming of the American Irish* and Lawrence McCaffrey in *The Irish Diaspora in America* have emphasized the decline of the Irish-Americans as an ethnic group, contrasting their contemporary social heterogeneity and broad adaptability with their previous history as a militant, cohesive, and hugely interconnected subculture. Greeley and McCaffrey emphasized the relation of the group to Catholicism and the influence that secularism and religious change have exerted. In 1963, Nathan Glazer and Daniel Patrick Moynihan saw Irish identity fading in their landmark book *Beyond the Melting Pot*. Their perspective was on a New York Irish community with powerful political and church dimensions.[2]

The changes that transformed the older Irish-American hegemony have certainly occurred, but what is less clearly perceived is that the Irish-Americans have shaped and reshaped their social posture numerous times, and communities based on mass immigration, urban voting blocs, and Catholic self-sufficiency have been only one form of ethnic configuration during a very long record of social experience. A group that created local and regional networks for itself for over two hundred years in America should not be assessed only on the basis of adherence to a late-nineteenth-century social contour characteristic of eastern cities. The citations provided in this Research Note are presented in an attempt to reorient studies of the group as well as to define key concepts in this book.

Fascinating though the diversity of Irish-American experience may be, and intriguing as the measurement of their social and economic progress is, even more fundamental is the ability of the group to maintain a distinct character over time and in various social contexts. I have tried in *Hibernia America: The Irish and Regional Cultures* to show the different patterns of adjustment that arose in different locales. The Philadelphia Irish community, which has been the subject of two previous studies by me and a number of works by others, affords the opportunity to examine the process by which the Irish perpetuated their identity and fostered the continuity of their development. Beyond the chronological and institutional analysis represented by my books *The Irish in Philadelphia: Ten Generations of Irish Experience* and *The Irish Relations: Trials of an Immigrant Tradition*, the ways in which the group preserved a subcultural tradition amid the swirling waves of social changes is of enduring concern. The compilation of three books on the same group in the same city may seem intensive to some observers, but the complexity and extent of the Irish social development in Philadelphia is actually much more elaborate and instructive than can be addressed in such books. For this group, for instance, I have omitted attempting to deal at length with demography, class structure, the role of religion, and other topics that would require replete volumes in themselves. The extent of the Philadelphia Irish-American record over two centuries involving hundreds of thousands of people clearly dictates intensive study of such social durability.

The continued existence of any ethnic group in a pluralist society demands the sustaining of group ties, resolution of internal and external conflicts, and the fashioning of an acceptable social alignment and position for the group.[3] These requirements take on a special importance in a complex society in which ethnic relations must be balanced in a fairly sophisticated manner. They can only be fulfilled when the processes promoting group vitality and loyalty, and ties of group association and communication, are operative. Such objectives and the processes that work toward them are an ineluctable outgrowth of ethnic consciousness. The historical material presented in this book shows in concrete examples how these dynamics function.

It is important to note that ethnic persistence often exists in parallel with assimilation, a process of change that represents an accommodation with the dominant culture and that results in a general degree of social homogeneity. While assimilation may reduce pluralism, it is seldom complete simply because it cannot erase historical memory. In a complex urban situation, it functions irregularly and frequently results in cultural patterns that are contradictory or are compounds of old and new ethnic typologies. Hence, the Philadelphia Irish have as part of their tradition an extensive legacy of interaction with the dominant culture and other groups, as well as elaborate social stratification within their group.

As has been asserted in the foregoing chapters, the specific means operating to sustain group ties include the cultivation of individual identity within the group, the social manifestation and reinforcement of identity through association, the fostering of distinctive group expression, and the exercise of group leadership. Integral to explanations of these social functions are the definitions and terms used to describe ethnicity. Though highly valuable, these definitions are not entirely congruent.[4] Most definitions of ethnicity focus on the boundaries of group life and how they are formed by social conflict or difference. In this book this is not the case, for the focus is on the historical and cultural content of group life and how the Irish have directed social behavior to share and pursue their cultural tradition.

The definition of tradition itself is important for this study. The Irish have a number of strains or themes within their tradition, including those emphasizing rural and urban backgrounds, religious difference, and class difference. The dominant strain represented in Philadelphia is definitely rural, Roman Catholic, and related to the Gaelic and nationalist themes and symbols long current in Irish society. There has also been an assumption into this Irish nationalist tradition of elements of Scots-Irish and Irish Protestant history as well as a panorama of Irish lore pertinent to American history, as is evident from the record of the Friendly Sons of St. Patrick.[5]

Changes in the definition of community are seen by Thomas Bender as one of the major issues in interpreting American social experience. He argues for a new definition of community based upon a historical notion of continual transformation, yet previous ideas of community based on locality and social networks remain viable concepts for social analysis. In this book, community means "a network of social relations marked by mutuality and emotional bonds."[6]

Clarification of the concept of identity is central to ethnic studies. Richard Alba says ethnic identity is a "subjective orientation" keyed to historical memory and cultural experience, while Morton Kaplan states: "Identity, more fully understood, involves the relationship of an individual to the social systems or subsystems that are relevant to his membership roles, his place in a hierarchy of being, and his responsibilities and prerequisites as a social actor."[7] We are indebted to both psychology and anthropology for an understanding of how the personality absorbs ethnic identity. Each person form infancy is subjected to a plethora of stimuli that give the personality a fund of models, aspirations, moods, motives, and constraints that are the subject matter of mental life. Timely reinforcement produces a rich accumulation of personal and social detail. The naming of persons and things, the association of places and events, and the meaning of rituals and recollections are all part of the pattern of designations that frame ethnic awareness. This awareness is the entry ticket to the ethnic tradition.[8] The individual compiles a persona not only through psychological self-appreciation, but indirectly, from the standpoints of other members of the same group or from the standpoint of the social group as a whole.[9] Such a complex process leads to a complex result. As Mary Black states, "Society establishes the means of categorizing persons and the complement of attributes felt to be ordinary and natural for members of these categories."[10]

The role of the family in the transmission of Irish identity and ethnicity is highlighted in the opening chapter of this book and its prominence has only been partially explored in studies about the group. Hasia Diner, Carole Groneman, Andrew Greeley, and Janet Nolan all write about the Irish-American family, and their interpretations stress negative features of domestic life, although Groneman testifies to the strength of immigrant families.[11] One reason for the negative quality of some of these studies may be the lack of reference to a broad spectrum of direct family accounts. Marjories Fallows, in her book *Irish-Americans: Identity and Assimilation*, uses some interview material, and Janet Nolan uses more, but the archives are not rich in direct family accounts and memoirs for this group. The most admirable use of such material is the immigrant correspondence in Kerby Miller's *Emigrants and Exiles: Ireland and the Irish Exodus to North America*, which shows the cultural damage inflicted by emigration and "exile." The picture drawn by Brian Mitchell in his *The Paddy Camps: The Irish of Lowell, 1821– 1861* affirms that Irish families did have a set of positive values that, although difficult to quantify, were a strong influence in controlling immigrant life. The exploration of how family memory has stimulated immigrant achievement is still in its early stages.[12] It is this memory that transmits much of the legacy emotionally and psychologically. The negative features of immigrant history are part of the group's heritage, but the positive features, including warm emotion, humor, admirable tenderness, personal sacrifice and family stability, are part of their heritage as well. The family stories used in this book include both.

The reinforcement and social extension of the ethnic consciousness imprinted in the family occurs through association that includes both formal and informal structures. These intermingle and express the energies of kinship, friendship, and communal and institutional affiliations.[13] That the Irish organized formal associations to meet ethnic needs was in no way exceptional. That they were able to adapt these groups over long time spans to align them with changing social conditions is most instructive. The struggles of dockworkers for over a century and the transfer of identity across class lines by the Brehon Society are two examples. The distinctive voluntary grouping characteristic of America was a matrix for immigrant affiliation, but the Irish networks afforded the framework for the construction of an entire lifestyle that not only accommodated waves of immigrants but served as attractions for them.[14] The influence of organizational bonds extended to the fourth and fifth generations of Irish-Americans in Philadelphia.

Communication in the view of John B. Newman consists of directed messages of primary and secondary information and the concentration and diffusion of the information plus a transmission of "consummatory" emotional messages. Ray L. Birdwhistell states that communication entails the employment of recognizable symbols needed for social organization, their utilization in relation to some social structure, and a concept of time for effective transmission.[15] In the urban situation in which the majority of the Irish found themselves in America, the range of communication was complex. Karl Deutsch notes that the modern city is "a huge engine of communications," and this was certainly true of Philadelphia with its publishing houses, radio stations, and constantly meeting organizations. The intensive communication network affecting the city's subcultures was ordained by the complexity of urban life. The way in which the Irish coming from a largely rural background joined and imitated this broader network was highly inventive. The historic position of the Irish as a subject people with respect to communications is clear in the adversary orientation of most of the Philadelphia Irish newspapers, as their editorials and news coverage reveal.[16] The romantic folk-bonding of the radio programs and the intellectual interest in Irish traditions on campuses reflects more positive features of the group's mentality.

The most recognizable symbol of the Irish subculture's organizational and communications infrastructure has been its leadership. Advocating, orating, agitating, educating, and at times exploiting and misleading, the Irish-American politicians, editors, and opinion leaders have widely contributed to this country's public life. They have helped to shape its discourse about minority rights, social problems and civic culture. Yet, the study of this leadership was for a long period prejudicial, and later was obscured by cults of publicity and inadequate biographies. Fortunately, more recent analytical studies of leadership probe more deeply the roles and significance of leaders of ethnic communities.[17]

The remarkable and interactive experience of the Irish revealed in all these citations is testimony to the fact noted by David Noel Doyle that the early Irish-Americans of the nineteenth century somehow saw in the growing urban experience of their group "the foreshadowing of a collective future at the heart of America's twentieth century modernity: the metropolis."[18]

Notes

Introduction

1. Dennis Clark, *Hibernia America: The Irish and Regional Cultures* (Westport, Conn.: Greenwood 1986), xiii-xiv.

2. These studies are listed in Seamus P. Metress, ed., *The Irish-American Experience: A Guide to the Literature* (Washington, D.C.: Univ. Press of America, 1981) 17-42, and in David Noel Doyle, "The Regional Bibliography of Irish America, 1800–1930," *Irish Historical Studies* 23, n. 91 (May 1983): 254-83.

3. David Noel Doyle, *Irish-Americans: Native Rights and National Empires* (New York: Arno, 1976), 86-95. Timothy J. Meagher, ed., *From Paddy To Studs: Irish-American Communities in the Turn of the Century Era, 1880–1920* Westport, Conn.: Greenwood, 1986), 6-9.

4. John Higham, "Intergrating America: The Problems of Assimilation in the Nineteenth Century," *Journal of American Ethnic History* 1, no. 1 (Fall 1981): 7-25.

5. For definitions of tradition, see S. Gopalan, *Tradition: A Social Analysis* (Madras, India: University of Madras Press, 1973), 21-33. Robert Anderson, *The Cultural Context* (Minneapolis, Minn.: Burgess, 1976), 39. David Kaplan and Robert Manner, *Culture Theory* (Englewood Cliffs, N.J.: Prentice-Hall, 1972), 87. Eric Hobsbawm and Terence Ranger, eds., *The Invention of Tradition* (New York: Cambridge Univ. Press, 1983), 2-3.

6. See, for instance, Theodore Hershberg, ed., *Philadelphia: Work, Space, Family and Group Experience in the Nineteenth Century* (New York: Oxford Univ. Press, 1981); Stephan Thernstrom, *The Other Bostonians* (Cambridge, Mass.: Harvard Univ. Press, 1973). Metress, *Irish-American Experience*, 17-42; Lawrence J. McCaffrey, *The Irish Diaspora in America* (Bloomington: Indiana Univ. Press, 1976); Andrew Greeley, *The Irish-Americans: The Rise to Power and Money* (New York: Harper and Row, 1981); Nathan Glazer and Daniel Patrick Moynihan, *Beyond the Melting Pot: The Negroes, Puerto Ricans, Jews, Italians and Irish of New York City* (Cambridge, Mass.: MIT Press, 1970).

7. Clark, *Hibernia America*, 175-96. Dennis Clark, *The Irish in Philadelphia: Ten Generations of Urban Experience* (Philadelphia, Pa.: Temple Univ. Press, 1973). Dennis Clark, *The Irish Relations: Trials of an Immigrant Tradition* (East Brunswick, N.J.: Associated Univ. Presses, 1982).

8. Milton M. Gordon, *Assimilation in American Life: The Role of Race, Religion and National Origin* (New York: Oxford Univ. Press, 1964), 242, notes the general process of ethnic retentivity.

9. Sam Bass Warner, Jr., *The Private City: Philadelphia in Three Periods of Its Growth* (Philadelphia: Univ. of Pennsylvania Press, 1968), vi.

10. Warren I. Susman, *Culture as History: The Transformation of American Society in the Twentieth Century* (New York: Pantheon, 1973), 288.

Identity: *Mind Yourself*

1. Nathan Glazer, "Beyond the Melting Pot: Twenty Years After," *Journal of American Ethnic History* 1, no. 1 (Fall 1981): 52.

2. John D. Buenker, "Assimilation and Acculturation: A Tiered Model," in David Claerbaut, ed., *New Directions in Ethnic Studies: Minorities in America* (Saratoga, Calif.: Century 21, 1981), 39-53. A.L. Epstein, *Ethos and Identity: Three Studies in Ethnicity* (London: Tavistock, 1978), 138-55, explains the development of

identity as it increases through influences in the immediate environment and the sociocultural context. He also notes the strong role of grandparents in the process.

3. Frederick Turner, "Performed Being: Word Art as Human Inheritance," *Oral Tradition* 1, no. 1 (Jan. 1984): 66-109. The process by which the personal identity is formed through family discourse is described in Michael Cole and Slyvia Scribner, *Culture and Thought: A Psychological Introduction* (New York: John Wiley and Sons, 1974), 138-39; Robert D. Hess and Gerald Handel, *Family Worlds: A Psychological Approach to Family Life* (Chicago: Quadrangle, 1959), 1-7; Richard J. Robbins, "Identity, Culture and Behavior," in John J. Honigmann, ed., *Handbook of Social and Cultural Anthropology* (Chicago: Rand McNally, 1973), 1199–1222; Pitirim Sorokin, *Society, Culture and Personality* (New York: Harper Brothers, 1947), 347-49.

4. Henry Glassie, *Passing the Time in Ballymenone* (Philadelphia: Univ. of Pennsylvania Press, 1982), 33-62. Sean MacReamoinn, "Words: Written, Spoken and Sung," in Sharon Gmelch, ed., *Irish Life and Traditions* (Syracuse, N.Y.: Syracuse Univ. Press, 1986), 209-21. Joseph J. Lee, "Continuity and Change in Ireland," in Joseph J. Lee, ed., *Ireland, 1945–1970* (Dublin: Gill and Macmillan, 1979), 168-69.

5. Vivian Mercier cites traditional storytellers who could each tell more than 350 stories. Vivian Mercier, ed., *Great Irish Short Stories* (New York: Dell, 1973), 9-11.

6. Oscar Handlin, *Boston's Immigrants, 1790–1880: A Study in Acculturation* (Cambridge: Harvard Univ. Press, 1979), 151-77. R. A. Burchell, *The San Francisco Irish, 1848–1880* (Berkeley: Univ. of California Press, 1980), 73-95. Hasia Diner, *Erin's Daughters in America: Irish Immigrant Women in the Nineteenth Century* (Baltimore, Md.: Johns Hopkins Univ. Press, 1983), 58-59. Andrew Greeley, *That Most Distressful Nation: The Taming of the American Irish* (Chicago: Quadrangle, 1972), 255-61.

7. Arnold Dashevsky, "Theoretical Frameworks in the Study of Ethnic Identity," *Ethnicity* 2, no. 1 (1975): 10-18. Susan Olzak, "A Competition Model of Ethnic Collective Action in American Cities," in Susan Olzak, ed., *Competitive Ethnic Relations* (Orlando: Univ. of Florida Press, 1983), 20. Maxine Seller, *To Seek America: A History of Ethnic Life in the United States* (Englewood Cliffs, N.J.: Jerome S. Ozer, 1977), 3-5.

8. Psychologist Jerome Bruner contends that the form of "life story" recollection and recitation affects the basic cultural outlook of the personality: Daniel Goleman, "In Memory People Re-create Their Lives," *New York Times*, C1, Oct. 21, 1987. Jean S. Phinney and Mary Jane Rotheram, eds., *Children's Ethnic Socialization: Pluralism and Development* (New York: Sage, 1987), 73-91, adds further interpretation, as does Charles T. Brown and Paul W. Keller, eds., *Monologue to Dialogue: An Exploration of Interpersonal Communication* (Englewood Cliffs, N.J.: Prentice-Hall, 1973), 9-10.

9. James Loughlin, *Gladstone, Home Rule and the Ulster Question* (Atlantic Highlands, N.J.: Humanities Press International, 1987), 16-17. For the persistence of the tradition, see James D. Delaney, "Three Midland Storytellers," *Béaloideas* 50 (1980): 44-53.

10. Interview of Owen B. Hunt by Dominick Quinn, 1976, (tape recording), Balch Institute for Ethnic Studies, Philadelphia (hereafter cited as Balch Institute). Maggie Jane McGinley, "The Greenhorn," *Irish Edition* (Philadelphia), June 1981. Nora Campbell, "The Donegal Society," Memorandum; Program of the 82nd Annual Ball, The Donegal Society, Nov. 28, 1970, Clark Collection, Balch Institute. Frank Devlin to Dennis Clark, family diary, June 2, 1945. Margaret O'Callaghan story recounted to Sean O'Callaghan, Dec. 24, 1986. Tom Hanson stories recounted by Geraldine Mulligan, July 9, 1987. The anecdotes of the following are taken from the

Irish Edition from the Greenhorn column by Maureen Benzing for the monthly editions noted: Peg Donnelly, Nov. 1981; Bill Drake, Oct. 1981; Una McAuley, July 1981; Tom Jordan, Sept. 1981; Vincent Gallagher, March 1984. Kate Collum Ferry stories collected by Nora Campbell in 1986 for the Donegal Society, Philadelphia, as were the stories of Edward Curran, John McGettigan, Mary O'Hagan Carr, James O'Brien, James McGoary, and Mickey Carr. "Mary Donovan's Boys," Introduction to bibliography of "The Irish," Balch Institute. Margaret Sheridan recollections in *A Heart in Camden for 100 Years* (Camden, N.J.: Sacred Heart Parish, 1986), 16. Margaret Lawless and Margaret McKinney recollections were in Mary Jane Shelley, "The Irish," *Chestnut Hill Local*, 7, (Dec. 16, 1976): 36. Sean Cronin, *The McGarrity Papers* (Tralee, Ireland: Anvil' 1972), 17. John Rossi, "Michael Francis Doyle," *Eire-Ireland*, 20, no. 2 (Summer 1985): 105-29. Dennis Clark, "Intrepid Men: Three Philadelphia Irish Leaders, 1880–1920," in Meagher, *From Paddy to Studs*, 95-97. Short stories of emigrant return are provided by George Moore, "Home Sickness," in Ben Forkner, ed., *Modern Irish Short Stories* (New York: Penguin, 1980), 45-59, and Edna O'Brien, "A Rose in the Heart of New York," in *A Fanatic Heart* (New York: Farrar, Straus and Giroux, 1984), 375-404. Tom Marron story from Donald Marron, interviewed by Dennis Clark, June 14, 1987. Robert V. Clarke story from an interview with Dennis Clark, Sept. 14, 1983. Maurice English story from an interview with Dennis Clark, Jan. 8, 1977. Hugh Breen story from an interview with Dennis Clark, Jan. 14, 1964. Dennis Clark, "Hugh Breen: A Tribute," *Irish Edition*, Aug. 1985. Patrick O'Callaghan, memorandum of a family story, Clark Collection, Balch Institute. Bernard Croke interviewed by Dennis Clark, Oct. 15, 1986. Joseph Coogan interviewed by Dennis Clark, Aug. 21, 1987. Anne Leahy story from an interview with Dennis Clark, Dec. 24, 1985. All the above interviews were conducted in Philadelphia.

11. Monica McGoldrick and John K. Pearce, "Family Therapy With Irish-Americans," *Family Process* 20, no. 1 (June 1981): 227. Hess and Handel, *Family Worlds*, 3.

12. Michael Aronowitz, "The Social and Emotional: A Review of the Literature," *International Migration Review* 18, no. 2 (Summer 1984): 240-41.

13. Helen Merrill Lynd, *On Shame and the Search for Identity* (New York: Harcourt, Brace, 1958), 210-11.

14. Harold R. Isaacs, "Basic Group Identity," in Nathan Glazer and Daniel P. Moynihan, eds., *Ethnicity: Theory and Experience* (Cambridge, Mass.: Harvard Univ. Press, 1975), 31. Heda Jason, "A Model For Narrative Structure in Oral Literature," in Heda Jason and Dmitri Segal, eds., *Patterns in Oral Literature* (The Hague: Mouton, 1977), 99-139.

15. Daniel Goleman, "In Memory People Re-Create Their Lives to Suit Their Present," C1, *New York Times*, June 23, 1987.

16. "Nothing does more to bind with cohesive sentiment than for people to have common experiences and to tell stylized stories—call them myths—about these experiences." Martin Marty, *New York Times Magazine*, April 2, 1988, 23.

17. David Noel Doyle, *Ireland, Irishmen and Revolutionary America, 1760–1820* (Cork, Ireland: Mercier, 1981), 39-49. John H. Campbell, *History of the Friendly Sons of St. Patrick and of the Hibernian Society for the Relief of Emigrants from Ireland in Philadelphia* (Philadelphia: Hibernian Society, 1892), 80.

18. Campbell, *History of the Friendly Sons*, 82.

19. Ibid., 75.

20. Dennis Clark, *A History of the Society of the Friendly Sons of St. Patrick for the Relief of Emigrants from Ireland in Philadelphia, 1951–1981* (Philadelphia: Society of the Friendly Sons of St. Patrick, 1982), 15 (hereafter cited as *Society of the Friendly Sons*). Campbell, *History of the Friendly Sons*, 179.

21. Richard Ned Lebow, *White Britain and Black Ireland: The Influence of Ste-reotypes on Colonial Policy* (Philadelphia: Institute for the Study of Human Issues, 1976), 40. Michael Feldberg, *The Philadelphia Riots of 1844: A Study of Ethnic Conflict* (Westport, Conn.: Greenwood, 1975), 81-83.

22. Campbell, *History of the Friendly Sons*, 183, 187. Clark, *Society of the Friendly Sons*, 15-17.

23. Mathew Carey, *Vindiciae Hiberniae: or, Ireland Vindicated* (Philadelphia: H.C. Carey and I. Lea, 1823), xi-xx. Richard B. Miller, *The Federalist City: A Study in Urban Politics, 1709–1801* (Port Washington, N.Y.: Kennikat, 1976), 97, 114-15. Maurice J. Bric, "Ireland, Irishmen, and the Broadening of the Late-Eighteenth Century Philadelphia Polity," (Ph.D. diss., Johns Hopkins University, 1990), 514-78.

24. Campbell, *History of the Friendly Sons*, 83, lists early members of various religious backgrounds. Clark, *Society of the Friendly Sons* vi-vii, reflects on this record.

25. Campbell, *History of the Friendly Sons*, 67, 168.

26. Ibid., 169, 197.

27. Samuel Eliot Morison, *The Oxford History of the American People* (New York: Oxford Univ. Press, 1965), 353. Ray Allen Billington, *The Protestant Crusade, 1800–1860: A Study of the Origins of American Nativism* (Chicago: Quadrangle, 1964), 322-38.

28. Campbell, *History of the Friendly Sons*, 205, lists political figures associated with the society such as mayor, aldermen, sheriff, judges, and city recorder.

29. Ibid., 224, 227, 243, 258-59, 290-313. The cult of organization membership is described by Arthur M. Schlesinger, "Biography of a Nation of Joiners," in Arthur M. Schlesinger, *Paths to the Present* (New York: Macmillan, 1949), 23-50.

30. Daniel Dougherty, *History of the Society of the Friendly Sons of St. Patrick for the Relief of Emigrants from Ireland of Philadelphia, 1892–1951* (Philadelphia: Friendly Sons of St. Patrick, 1952), 36, 61, 68.

31. Clark, *Irish Relations*, 103-25.

32. Campbell, *History of the Friendly Sons*, 203

33. Ibid., 44, 68, 102, 130, 184.

34. Cronin, *McGarrity Papers*, passim.

35. Dougherty, *History of the Friendly Sons*, 97-98, 136-39.

36. Clark, *Society of the Friendly Sons*, 17-18. There was for much of the twentieth century an extensive network of other kinds of organizations in the Irish community and a federation that linked them. See the "Irish in Philadelphia Project," Works Project Administration Writers Project, Federal Works Agency, Balch Institute.

37. Clark, *Society of the Friendly Sons*, 17-18.

38. Ibid., 19.

39. Clark, *Society of the Friendly Sons*, 19.

40. John F. Wilson, M.D., president of the Friendly Sons of St. Patrick, to Honorable Ronald Reagan, president of the United States, Sept. 17, 1981. Files of the Friendly Sons of St. Patrick.

41. These conclusions are drawn from a tabulation of biographical facts in each of the three volumes of the society's history cited above.

42. Lebow, *White Britain and Black Ireland*, 46. Maurice Bourgeois, *John Millington Synge and the Irish Theater* (New York: B. Blom, 1965), 109-10.

43. Thomas Wright, *A History of Caricature and Grotesque in Literature and Art* (New York: Frederick Unger, 1966), 4.

44. Dale Knobel, *Paddy and the Republic: Ethnicity and Nationality in Ante-Bellum America* (Middletown, Conn.: Wesleyan Univ. Press, 1968), 165-82.

45. Billington, *Protestant Crusade*, 166-92.

46. Meagher, *From Paddy to Studs*, 16.

47. Center for Irish Studies, "Images and Indignations: How Cartoons Shape Our Views," (teaching kit), Balch Institute, 1986.

48. John Apple, "From Shanties to Lace Curtains," *Comparative Studies in Society and History* 13 (Oct. 1971).

49. William Murrell, *A History of American Graphic Humor* (New York: Whitney Museum of American Art, 1933), 1: 9. Billington, *Protestant Crusade*, 337-38.

50. Rufus Shapley, pseudonym for Henry C. Lea, *Solid for Mulhooly: A Political Satire* (Philadelphia: Gebbie, 1889), 16, 20, 57, 71, 104.

51. Carey, *Vindiciae Hibernicae: or, Ireland Vindicated*, 2. Clark, *Irish in Philadelphia*, 14.

52. William D. Griffin, *A Portrait of the Irish in America* (New York: Charles Scribner's Sons, 1981), 209-16. Bob Callahan, ed., *The Big Book of American Irish Culture* (New York: Viking Penguin, 1987), 8-77, 250-65.

53. Daniel O'Connell, *The Enterprise Catholic Young Men's Association of Germantown, Philadelphia and Its Dramatic Club* (Philadelphia: Enterprise Catholic Young Men's Association, 1927), passim.

54. *Philadelphia Public Ledger*, 1, 3, March 29, 30; 3, April 1,; and May 14, 1903.

55. Peter Kavanaugh, *The Abbey Theater* (New York: Devin Adair, 1950), 95. Owen B. Hunt interviewed Dominick Quinn Balch Institute, 1976.

56. Mari Kathleen Fielder, "Wooing a Local Audience: The Irish-American Appeal of Philadelphia's Mae Desmond Players," *Theater History Studies* 1 (1981): 50-63. Fielder's heavily researched thesis, "Theater and Community in Early Twentieth Century Philadelphia: The Mae Desmond Players, 1917–1932" (Ph.D. thesis, University of California at Los Angeles, 1986) adds to this analysis.

57. Clark, *Hibernia America*, 154-58.

58. Randall M. Miller, ed., *The Kaleidoscopic Lens: How Hollwood Views Ethnic Groups*, (New York: Jerome Oxer, 1980), 98-113. See also Joseph M. Curran, *Hibernian Green on the Silver Screen: The Irish and American Movies* (Westport, Conn.: Greenwood, 1989).

59. Randall M. Miller, ed., *Ethnic Images in the American Film and Theater* (Philadelphia: Balch Institute, 1978), 88.

60. Dennis Clark, *Irish Blood: Northern Ireland and the American Conscience* (Port Washington, N.Y.: Kennikat, 1977), 34-40.

61. Ibid., 51-61.

62. Clark Collection, Balch Institute.

63. Archives of the Balch Institute.

64. Ibid.

65. F.S.L. Lyons, *Culture and Anarchy in Ireland: 1890–1939* (Oxford, England: Oxford Univ. Press, 1979), 57-84. Reflection of this cultural difficulty in modern drama is described by Benedict Nightingale, "Of Fathers and Mothers on the Irish Stage," *New York Times*, Oct. 9, 1983.

66. The continued volatility of this issue is evidenced by the articles and correspondence in *Irish-America Magazine*, published in New York, in its issues in 1988 and 1989 concerning portrayals of the Irish. For data on British propaganda, see Liz Curtis, *Nothing But The Same Old Story: The Roots of Anti-Irish Racism* (London: Information on Ireland, 1985), 66-97. Figures on the 1980 Irish population are cited in "Pennsylvania Irish," *Philadelphia Inquirer*, March 17, 1989.

2 Association: *Show Me Your Friends*

1. Michael Funchion, ed., *Irish-American Voluntary Organizations* (Westport, Conn.: Greenwood 1983).

2. Dale Light, "Class, Ethnicity and Urban Ecology in a Nineteenth Century City: Philadelphia's Irish, 1840–1890" (Ph.D. diss., University of Pennsylvania, 1979). Doyle, *Irish-Americans: Native Rights.*

3. Gordon, *Assimilation in American Life,* 33-40, explains these functions. Milton Barron, "Intermediacy: Conceptualization of the Irish Status in America," *Social Forces* 27, no. 3 (March 1949): 256, regards the Irish-Americans as a "culturally and demographically median group" and sees their role as social intermediaries as a highly important pluralist function.

4. The manifold ways that ethnic associations satisified these needs is made clear by Robert Ernst, "Consciousness of Kind," in John Lankford and David Reimers, eds., *Essays on American Social History* (New York: Holt, Rinehart and Winston, 1970), 152-62. Alice Kessler Harris and Virginia Yans McLaughlin, "European Immigrant Groups," in Thomas Sowell, ed., *American Ethnic Groups* (Washington, D.C.: Urban Institute, 1978), 107-31, note American conditions that reinforced Irish group consciousness. Arnold Rose, *The Power Structure: Political Process in American Life* (New York: Oxford Univ. Press, 1967), 247-49. Alfred Jacobs and Wilford Spradlin, *The Group as Agent of Change* (New York: Behavioral Publications, 1974), 100.

5. An ethnic organization of lawyers and judges is somewhat at variance with the popular assumption that "ethnic" signifies "peasant" or "blue collar worker." The retention of ethnic identity at sophisticated levels, however, is something that can overcome dissimilarities of status and vocational standing. See Frederick Barth, ed., *Ethnic Groups and Boundaries: The Social Organization of Cultural Difference* (Boston: Little, Brown, 1969), 15.

6. John Higham, *Send These to Me: Jews and Other Immigrants in Urban America* (New York: Atheneum, 1975), 12.

7. Anthony Marmion, *The Ancient and Modern History of the Maritime Ports of Ireland* (London: W. H. Cox, 1860), v-xxv.

8. H.A. Crone, et al., eds., *Essays in British and Irish History* (London: F. Muller Ltd., 1949), 209. E.P. Thompson, *The Making of the English Working Class* (New York: Random House, 1966), 222, 439. Lynn Lees, *Exiles of Erin* (Ithaca: Cornell Univ. Press, 1979), 240-41.

9. Committee of Seventy, *History of Governance in the Ports of Philadelphia* (Philadelphia: Committee of Seventy, 1980), 1.

10. *Pennsylvania Gazette,* April 2, 1767 and April 30, 1767; *Pennsylvania Evening Herald,* March 19, 1785.

11. Doyle, *Ireland, Irishmen and Revolutionary America,* 49.

12. Earl F. Niehaus, *The Irish in New Orleans, 1800–1860* (Baton Rouge: Louisiana State Univ. Press, 1965), 47.

13. A.B. Beck, "Catherine Fritsch, Visit to Philadelphia by a Moravian Sister," *Pennsylvania Magazine of History and Biography* 36 (1912): 346-61.

14. Bruce Laurie, *The Working People of Philadelphia, 1800–1850* (Philadelphia: Temple Univ. Press, 1980), 157.

15. Ibid., 148.

16. Ibid., 199.

17. David Brody, "Workers and Work in America," in James B. Gardner and George Rollie Adams, eds., *Ordinary People and Everyday Life: Perspectives on the New Social History* (Nashville, Tenn: American Association for State and Local History, 1983), 147. See also Dennis Clark, Commentary, in Mark Stolarik and Murray Friedman, eds., *Making It in America* (Lewisburg, Pa.: Bucknell Univ. Press, 1986), 116-19. Alan Dawley, *Class and Community: The Industrial Revolution in Lynn* (Cambridge, Mass.: Harvard Univ. Press, 1976), 239.

18. These and the following figures are drawn from the Philadelphia Social History Project, Manuscript Census Tabulations, First, Second and Fifth Wards (1850), and Hershberg, *Philadelphia: Work, Space, Family,* 110, 184-85, 246.

19. Reports of the Department of Markets, Wharves and Landings (1859–1864), Annual Reports of the Port Wardens (1873–1874), R.G. 60.1, Archives of the City of Philadelphia.

20. Admissions Book (1880), Pennsylvania Hospital, Philadelphia. Dr. Morris Vogel of Temple University has computerized these materials, and I thank him for sharing them with me.

21. Clark, *The Irish Relations*, 162-64.

22. William Seraile and Lester Rubin, *The Negro in the Longshore Industry in Philadelphia* (Philadelphia: Industrial Research Unit, Wharton School, University of Pennsylvania, Report No. 29, Univ. of Pennsylvania Press, 1974), 70-75. William Seraile, "Ben Fletcher: I.W.W. Organizer," *Pennsylvania History* 46, no. 3 (July 1979): 213-32. Philip S. Foner, *History of the Labor Movement in the United States* (New York: International Publishers, 1965), 4: 126.

23. This quotation and those that follow from longshoremen, unless otherwise noted, are drawn from the transcriptions of *Labor on the Delaware: The Longshoreman's Experience*, an oral history and film project of the Philadelphia Maritime Museum conducted in 1979–1980 under a grant from the Pennsylvania Humanities Council, coordinated by William Ward and Edward Kirlin.

24. John Donovan interviewed by Dennis Clark, Philadelphia, April 9, 1981.

25. *Philadelphia North American*, Feb. 27, 1913, and Sept. 5, 1913.

26. "Port Dispute," Philadelphia *Public Ledger*, May 28, 1913; "Port Work" *Philadelphia North American*, May 14, 29, 31, and Dec. 30, 1913.

27. *Public Ledger*, Dec. 5, 1914.

28. Foner, *History of the Labor Movement*, 126.

29. Seraile, "Ben Fletcher: I.W.W. Organizer," 232.

30. Ibid., 222.

31. Photographs and surveys of housing in the area are in the Collection of the Philadelphia Housing Association, Urban Archives, Paley Library, Temple University, Philadelphia.

32. Patrick Nolan interviewed by Dennis Clark, Philadelphia, Feb. 2, 1981.

33. Gerry Kelly interviewed by Dennis Clark, Philadelphia, Jan. 29, 1981.

34. E.J. Hobsbawm, *Labouring Men: Studies in the History of Labor* (New York: Basic Books, 1964), 207.

35. Reverend Dennis Comey interview, Jan. 29, 1979, Walter Phillips Collection, Urban Archives, Paley Library, Temple University, Philadelphia. *Evening Bulletin*, 16D, (Philadelphia), Jan. 30, 1981. "War on the Waterfront," *Philadelphia Magazine*, 53, no. 16. (Oct. 1962): 18. Dennis J. Comey, *The Waterfront Peacemaker.* (Philadelphia: St. Joseph's Univ. Press, 1983), 9-20.

36. "The Unfolding of a Scandal," *Philadelphia Inquirer*, Aug. 10, 1981.

37. Frank Eastman, *Courts and Lawyers of Pennsylvania: A History, 1623–1923*, 3 vols. (New York: American Historical Society, 1923), 579-83.

38. R.F. Williams, *The Members of the Philadelphia Bar, July 1776–July 1853* (Philadelphia: Decorative Printing House, 1855). Members listed by date of admission.

39. The Law Association of Philadelphia, *Addresses at the March 13, 1902 Centenniel Celebration of the Law Association of Philadelphia* (Philadelphia: Law Association, 1906), 385.

40. Philadelphia North American, *Philadelphia and Popular Philadelphians* (Philadelphia: North American, 1891), 41, 44, 58, 59, 279. Campbell, *History of the Friendly Sons*, 366.

41. Clipping Book of the Philadelphia Bar Association. Library of the Philadelphia Bar Association. Unnumbered pages.

42. Rossi, "Michael Francis Doyle," 105-29.

43. Nathaniel Burt, *The Perenniel Philadelphians* (Boston: Little, Brown, 1963), 114-40.

44. Edward Cuddy, "The Irish Question and the Revival of Anti-Catholicism in the 1920s," *Catholic Historical Review* 67, no. 2 (April 1981): 236-55.

45. Analysis of the firms dealt with by Burt, *Perenniel Philadelphians*, 114-40, compared with the year 1981 using *Martindale and Hubbell Law Directory* (Summit, N.J.: Martindale and Hubbell, 1981), 6 vols., 6: 961-1255, reveals representation of the Irish in most major law firms. See also E. Digby Baltzell, *Philadelphia Gentlemen: The Making of a National Upper Class* (New York: Free Press, 1958), 145-47.

46. Interviews by Dennis Clark with William A. Fitzpatrick, March 24, 1987, and Judge Isador Kranzel, April 30, 1987, Philadelphia.

47. Records of the Donegal Association of Philadelphia, Balch Institute.

48. Records of the Committee of Seventy, Philadelphia.

49. Minutes of the Brehon Society, May 13, 1977. Minutes in the possession of the society's president.

50. Brehon Society Executive Committee meeting, Aug. 3, 1977.

51. Ibid., Jan.1, 1979; Sept.8, 1978; Oct.15, 1979.

52. *Philadelphia Bar Association Directory* (Philadelphia: Philadelphia Bar Association, 1979), passim.

53. Peter McGrath, "Bi-Centenniel Philadelphia: The Quaking City," in Dennis Clark, ed., *Philadelphia: 1776–2076* (Port Washington, N.Y.: Kennikat, 1975), 69-100.

54. Membership List, Appendix to Minutes, Brehon Society records. n.d.

55. Minutes of the Brehon Society, Dec. 3, 1979.

56. Ibid.,

57. Minutes of the Brehon Society, Oct. 28, 1981.

58. Light, "Class, Ethnicity and Urban Ecology," passim.

59. "Judges Who Have Sold Out," *Philadelphia Inquirer,* Aug. 7 and 10, 1987. Adrian Lee, "Why the Judges Did It," *Philadelphia Daily News,* Aug. 25, 1987.

60. The Irish Catholics did support an extensive school and service network for blacks and Indians as a missionary work in the United States. John T. Gillard, *The Catholic Church and the American Negro* (Baltimore, Md.: St. Joseph's Society, 1929), 30, 38, 40-45, 58, 85, 126-28, 163, 187, 197, 205, 217. The Irish-American priests of the Josephite and Holy Ghost orders did heroic work, but this did not change the broader Irish racial antipathy toward blacks. Clark, *Irish Relations*, 143-59. Some data in this chapter is derived from the author's direct knowledge of Anna McGarry.

61. Letter of Daniel Kane to Dennis Clark, Dec. 18, 1981. Details of Anna McGarry's life are drawn from the recollections of her daughter, Mary McGarry Kane in Anna M. McGarry Papers, Archives, Marquette University, Milwaukee, Wis.

62. David J. O'Brien, *American Catholics and Social Reform: The New Deal Years* (New York: Oxford Univ. Press, 1968), 182-211.

63. Miriam Ershkowitz and Joseph Zikmund, eds., *Black Politics in Philadelphia* (New York: Basic Books, 1973), passim. Recollections of Anna McGarry, tape recording in possession of Raymond Schmandt, St. Joseph's University, Philadelphia.

64. Dennis Clark, *The Ghetto Game* (New York: Sheed and Ward, 1962), 30, 118-19.

65. Gary MacEoin, *All of Which I Saw, Part of Which I Was: The Autobiography of George K. Hunton* (Garden City, N.Y.: Doubleday, 1967), 195-99. Edwin Wolf II, *Philadelphia: Portrait of an American City* (Philadelphia: William Penn Foundation, 1975), 353.

66. RG. 148.3, Files of the Commission on Human Relations, Archives of the City of Philadelphia.

67. RG. 148.2, Files of the Commission on Human Relations.

68. "Schuylkill," *Sunday Bulletin* (Philadelphia), Nov. 23, 1969.

69. RG. 148.3, Files of the Commission on Human Relations.

70. Recollections of John Connors, interview with Dennis Clark, Jan. 10, 1982, Philadelphia, William Osborne, *The Segregated Covenant: Race Relations and American Catholics* (New York: Herder and Herder, 1967), 153-79.

71. RG. 148.4, Files of the Commission on Human Relations.

72. "Comeback Parish," *Interracial Review* 35 no. 10 (Nov. 1962): 250-52.

73. Raymond J. Schmandt, "The Origins of Casa del Carmen, Philadelphia's Catholic Hispanic Center," *Records of the American Catholic Historical Society of Philadelphia* 97, nos. 1-4 (March-Dec., 1986): 27-41.

74. In 1982, the Jesuit priests and neighbors of the Gesu parish dedicated a residence next to the church to the memory of Anna McGarry.

75. Osborne, *Segregated Covenant*, 233-47.

3 Communication: *Passing the Word*

1. Emile G. McAnany, Jorge Schnitman, and Noreene Janus, eds., *Communication and Social Structure* (New York: Praeger, 1981), 9.

2. L.G. Helles, *Communications Analysis and Methodology for Historians*, (New York: New York Univ. Press, 1972), 92-93.

3. Leo W. Feffres and Mildred Barnard, *Communication and the Persistence of Ethnicity* (Cleveland Ohio: Communications Research Center, Cleveland State University, 1982), 1-8.

4. Seymour Mandelbaum, *Community and Communications* (New York: W.W. Norton, 1972), 27. Young Yun Kim, *Interethnic Communication: Current Research* (Beverly Hills, Calif.: Sage, 1986), 225.

5. The utility of newspapers as historical records is explained by Louis Gottschalk, *Understanding History* (New York: Alfred A. Knopf, 1963), 96.

6. Examples of the use of newspapers to illuminate immigrant life are presented by Handlin, *Boston's Immigrants*, 172-75, and Donald B. Coyle, *Immigrant City: Lawrence, Massachusetts* (Chapel Hill: Univ. of North Carolina Press, 1963), passim.

7. L.M. Cullen, *The Emergence of Modern Ireland: 1600–1900* (Dublin: Gill and Macmillan, 1981), 236. Barbara Hayley and Enda McKay, *300 Years of Irish Periodicals* (Mullingar, Ireland: Irish Association of Learned Journals, 1987), 29-48. Luke Gibbons, "Commentary," *Irish Historical Studies* 20, no. 99 (May 1987): 335.

8. Frank Luther Mott, *American Journalism: A History, 1690–1960* (New York: Macmillan, 1962), 598-99. William Leonard Joyce, *Editors and Ethnicity: A History of the Irish-American Press* (New York: Arno, 1976), 155. See also Carl Wittke, *The Irish in America* (Baton Rouge: Louisiana State Univ. Press, 1956), 202-15; James P. Rodechko, *Patrick Ford and His Search for America: A Case Study of Irish-American Journalism, 1870–1913* (New York: Arno, 1976); Francis M. Carroll, *American Opinion and the Irish Question, 1910–1923* (New York: St. Martin's, 1978).

9. Thomas N. Brown, *Irish-American Nationalism*, (Philadelphia: Lippincott, 1966) 190.

10. A general view of the social history of Philadelphia is given by Warner, *Private City*. The course of Irish immigration to the city is described in Clark, *Irish in Philadelphia*, 3-23.

11. "Irish-American Weekly Honored on its Centenniel," *New York Times*, May 22, 1971.

12. Some of the Philadelphia Irish papers are listed in the *Checklist of Philadelphia Newspapers* (Philadelphia: Works Progress Administration, 1937). Those listed are Carey's *Pennsylvania Herald*, the *Clan na Gael*, the *Free Man and Irish-*

American Review, and *Griffin's Journal*. Wilfred Gregory, ed., *American Newspapers* (New York: H.W. Wilson, 1937), also lists some of the papers.

13. This paper ran from March 26, 1785, to Feb 14, 1788.

14. For data on Carey's publishing, see Earl L. Bradsher, *Mathew Carey: Editor, Author and Publisher* (New York: Columbia Univ. Press, 1912).

15. Dennis Clark, "The Writings of Philadelphia Irishmen," *Irish Edition*, Aug.–Sept. 1983.

16. Copies of this paper for 1823 are in the U.S. Library of Congress. Quotes and observations in this chapter are based on issues from Jan. through Sept. 1823.

17. Ibid., Jan. and Feb. 1823.

18. "Some Early Catholic Papers," *American Catholic Historical Researches* 19, 4 (Oct. 1902): 153, 18 (1911): 181.

19. The single issue is for Sept. 15, 1832. It is in the newspaper collection of the Logan Library of Philadelphia. George W. Pepper was a friend of "Young Ireland" leaders and had been imprisoned by the British before coming to America.

20. Thomas Ollive Mabbott, "Poe and the Philadelphia Irish Citizen," *Journal of the American Irish Historical Society* 29, (1930–1931): 127-31. There was apparently no counterpart in Philadelphia to *Irish Republic*, a Chicago paper from 1867 that supported nonsectarian Irish identity, the emancipation of slaves, a female role in the "Fenian Sisterhood," and promotion of the Irish language. The Philadelphia Fenians may have shared these views, but we have no printed evidence. Bound copies of the *Irish Republic* are in Falvey Library, Villanova University, Villanova, Pa.

21. Joseph George, "Philadelphia's Catholic Herald: The Civil War Years," *Pennsylvania Magazine of History and Biography* 103, no. 2 (April 1979): 196-221.

22. Mott, *American Journalism*, 450.

23. This paper is mentioned in the *Checklist of Philadelphia Newspapers*, 105. See also the biographical note on James O'Reilly in Campbell, *History of the Friendly Sons*, 493.

24. Kevin B. Nowlan, "The Origins of the Press in Ireland," in Brian Farrell, ed., *Communication and Community in Ireland* (Dublin: Mercier, 1984), 11-12.

25. Three issues of this paper exist, two in the Historical Society of Pennsylvania, Philadelphia, and one in the State Historical Society of Wisconsin, Madison. The dates of the issues are Feb. 12, Aug. 5 and 12, 1888.

26. References to these men are in Campbell, *History of the Friendly Sons*, 404, 519. For an account of the rise of newspaper enterprises, see Gunther Barth, "The Metropolitan Press," in Gunther Barth, ed., *City People: The Rise of Modern City Culture in Nineteenth Century America* (New York: Oxford Univ. Press, 1980), 48-109.

27. Some issues of this paper are in the Archives of the American Catholic Historical Society of Philadelphia, St. Charles Seminary, Philadelphia.

28. Ibid.

29. Campbell, *History of the Friendly Sons*, 454-55. Old-time Irish newsmen are recalled in the *Philadelphia Inquirer*, Feb. 18, 1981.

30. Campbell, *History of the Friendly Sons*, 454-88.

31. Issues in the Archives of the American Catholic Historical Society of Philadelphia, St. Charles Seminary, Philadelphia.

32. Ibid.

33. Morris Janowitz, *The Community Press in an Urban Setting* (Chicago: Univ. Chicago Press, 1967), 173.

34. Issues in the Archives of the American Catholic Historical Society of Philadelphia, St. Charles Seminary, Philadelphia.

35. Alice Macardle, *The Irish Republic* (London: Corgi, 1968), 287.

36. Library of the Balch Institute.

37. *Clan na Gael* (Philadelphia), Feb. 25, 1888, 1.

38. Issues of the *Irish Edition* are in the Balch Institute. For critique of Northern Ireland coverage, see John Elliott, *Ethnicity and the Media: An Analysis of Media Reporting in the United Kingdom, Canada and Ireland* (Paris: United Nations Educational, Scientific and Cultural Organization, 1977), passim. Liz Curtis, *Nothing But the Same Old Story* (London: Information on Ireland, 1985) 66-97. On readership, see Michael Schudson, *Discovering the News: A Social History of American Newspapers* (New York: Basic Books, 1978), 35-38, 43, 98, 131.

39. For the role of the press in affecting readers, see Schudson, *Discovering the News*, 35-38, 43, 98, 131.

40. Terence Brown, *Ireland: A Social and Cultural History, 1922–1979* (Glasgow: Fontana, 1981), 153.

41. Biographical details of Stanton's life are in the Papers of Patrick Stanton, Balch Institute, (hereafter cited as Stanton Papers), along with an extensive interview with Josephine Oristaglio, for many years Stanton's aide and business associate, Aug. 14, 1980, in Philadelphia, hereafter cited as Oristaglio Interview.

42. Stanton Papers.

43. Mrs. Joseph McGurk, interviewed by Dennis Clark, Philadelphia, Sept. 12, 1980.

44. Clark, *Irish Relations, 213-17.*

45. Remarks of Patrick Stanton, Irish Brigade Memorial Association, Dec. 2, 1961, Philadelphia, Stanton Papers.

46. Stanton Papers.

47. Oristaglio Interview.

48. Obituary, *Philadelphia Inquirer*, Dec. 10, 1981.

49. Samples of the music of Reavey and others are in the folk music collection of the Folklore Department, University of Pennsylvania.

50. Oristaglio Interview.

51. Prints of the films are in the Balch Institute.

52. Papers of Owen B. Hunt, Historical Society of Pennsylvania, Philadelphia.

53. Program Notes, March 7, 1946, Aug. 27, 1972, and Jan. 11, 1976, Stanton Papers.

54. Mrs. Margaret McGreal interviewed by Dennis Clark, Philadelphia, Jan. 20, 1981.

55. Oristaglio Interview.

56. Letter of Reverend Michael Jordan, SJ, to Dennis Clark, Sept. 22, 1981.

57. Oristaglio Interview.

58. Press clippings, Stanton Papers.

59. Clark, *Society of the Friendly Sons of St. Patrick*, 125-26.

60. Broadcast Script, March 14, 1976. Papers of Owen B. Hunt, Historical Society of Pennsylvania, Philadelphia.

61. Honorable James H.J. Tate interviewed by Dennis Clark, Philadelphia, Sept. 15, 1981.

62. By 1982, there were eighty-five Irish radio programs throughout the United States broadcasting weekly. *Irish American* (Chicago), July 1982, 1.

63. The role of churchmen promoting cultural cohesiveness of the Irish in the city according to Tridentine codes is explained by Dale Light, "The Role of Irish-American Organizations in Assimilation and Community Formation," in P.J. Drudy, ed., *The Irish in America: Emigration Assimilation and Impact* (Cambridge, England: Cambridge Univ. Press, 1985), 131-32. Kay Gavigan, "The Rise and Fall of Parish Cohesiveness in Philadelphia," in *Records of the American Catholic Historical Society*, 86, (1975): 107-31. Also, Dale Light, "Rome and the Republic: Francis

Patrick Kenrick and the Devotional Revolution in Philadelphia Catholicism, 1830–1851" (Paper presented to the Philadelphia Center for Early American Studies, Philadelphia, Sept. 12, 1986.)

64. Maureen Murphy, *A Guide to Irish Studies in the United States* (Hempstead, N.Y.: American Committee for Irish Studies, 1987).

65. Thomas G. Evans, "The American Motif in the Irish Literary Renaissance: The Old Lady's Lost Children," *Eire-Ireland* 22, no. 3 (Fall 1987): 4-14. Lawrence McCaffrey has argued that the narrowness of Irish-Catholic nationalist culture in Ireland after 1921 alienated the American Irish. David Noel Doyle and Owen Dudley Edwards, eds., *America and Ireland, 1776–1976: The American Identity and the Irish Connection* (Westport, Conn.: Greenwood, 1980) 81-92.

66. Glazer and Moynihan, *Beyond the Melting Pot*, 284-87. Michael Novak, *The Rise of the Unmeltable Ethnics: Politics and Culture in the Seventies* (New York: Macmillan, 1971), 135-66.

67 Lester Conner interviewed by Dennis Clark, Philadelphia, April 4, 1982.

68. Christine Kelly, "Beyond the Green," *Villanova Magazine* 6, no. 1 (Winter 1990): 2-5.

69. Joseph O'Grady, *How The Irish Became Americans* (New York: Twayne, 1973), 155-58.

70. Jack McCormick interviewed by Dennis Clark, Philadelphia, Sept. 22, 1987.

71. Mari Fielder Green, interviewed by Dennis Clark, Philadelphia, Jan. 1, 1989.

72. William Lynch interviewed by Dennis Clark, Philadelphia, June 26, 1982.

73. Michael Durkan interviewed by Dennis Clark, Philadelphia, Oct. 7, 1987. Michael Durkan and Ronald Ayling, *Sean O'Casey: A Bibliography* (London: Macmillan, 1978).

74. Robert Mulvihill interviewed by Dennis Clark, Philadelphia, June 4, 1974.

75. *Irish Edition* (Philadelphia), March 1981, 1; March 1982, 2.

76. Materials of the Center for Irish Studies, Balch Institute. Maurice Bric interviewed by Dennis Clark, Philadelphia, June 22, 1982.

77. Thomas Kinsella, trans. *The Tain* (Dublin: Dolmen, 1969), and Thomas Kinsella, *The Tain* (New York: Oxford Univ. Press, 1970).

78. Thomas Kinsella, *Poems, 1956–1973* (Winston-Salem, N.C.: Wake Forest Univ. Press, 1979).

79. Thomas Kinsella and Sean O'Tuama, eds., *An Duanaire: Poems of the Dispossessed* (Philadelphia: Univ. of Pennsylvania Press, 1981). Thomas Kinsella, ed., *The New Oxford Book of Irish Verse* (New York: Oxford Univ. Press, 1986). Patricia Craig, "Playing to Empty Pockets," *New York Review of Books* 29, no. 8 (May 13, 1982). Arthur B. McGuinness, "Bright Quidnunx Newly Risen: Thomas Kinsella's Inward 'I'," *Eire-Ireland* 15, no. 4 (Winter 1980): 106-25.

80. *Irish Edition*, March 1989, 1.

81. Daniel Patrick Moynihan, "The Irish of New York," in Lawrence H. Fuchs, ed., *American Ethnic Politics* (New York: Harper and Row, 1968), 89.

82. Richard Polenberg, *One Nation Divisible: Class, Race and Ethnicity in the United States since 1939* (New York: Viking, 1980), 247.

4 Leadership: *More Power to Them*

1. Meagher, *From Paddy to Studs*, 93-116.

2. Louis Schneider, "The Idea of Culture in the Social Sciences: Critical Questions," in Louis Schneider and Charles Bonjean, eds., *The Idea of Culture in the Social Sciences* (London: Cambridge Univ. Press, 1973) 120.

3. John Higham, "Leadership," in Stephan Thernstrom, eds., *The Harvard Encyclopedia of American Ethnic Groups*, (Cambridge, Mass., Harvard Univ. Press, 1980), 644-45.

4. Doob, *Personality, Power and Authority: A View from the Behavioral Sciences*, (Westport, Conn., Greenwood, 1983), 182. Robert D. Cross, "The Irish," in John Higham, ed., *Ethnic Leadership in America* (Baltimore, Md.: Johns Hopkins Univ. Press, 1978), 193.

5. Rose, *Power Structure*, 224.

6. Victor R. Greene, *American Immigrant Leaders, 1800–1910: Marginality and Identity* (Baltimore, Md.: Johns Hopkins Univ. Press, 1987), 1-40.

7. Brown, *Irish-American Nationalism*, 21. *Catholic Herald* (Philadelphia), March 17, 1866. Goldwyn Smith, "Why Send More Irish To America?" *Nineteenth Century* 13 (June 1883): 913. W.E. Lecky, *Leaders of Public Opinion in Ireland*, 2 vols. (New York: Longmans Green, 1912), 2:177.

8. Robert V. Clarke interviewed by Dennis Clark, Philadelphia, Jan. 5, 1980. Robert Clarke knew Mike McGinn for many years and is the source of the account of his youth.

9. W.J. O'Neill-Daunt, *Catechism of the History of Ireland: Ancient and Modern with an Account of the Land Agitation* (Dublin: James Duffy and Sons, 1884), passim.

10. Minutes of the Cavan Men's Catholic Social and Beneficial Association, Balch Institute.

11. K.R.M. Short, *The Dynamite War: Irish-American Bombers in Victorian Britain* (Dublin: Gill and Macmillan, 1979), 173-200. John T. Ennis, *The Clan na Gael and the Murder of Dr. Patrick Cronin* (Chicago: Published by the author, 1889).

12. Letterbook of Henri Le Caron (Thomas Beach), Balch Institute.

13. Minutes book, Irish-American Club, Balch Institute.

14. Clark, *Irish Relations*, 61-75.

15. W.E.B. Du Bois, *The Negro in Philadelphia* (Philadelphia: Univ. of Pennsylvania Press, 1899), passim.

16. Robert V. Clarke interviewed by Dennis Clark, Philadelphia, Jan. 5, 1980.

17. Information about McGinn's business and nationalist work is drawn from interviews by Dennis Clark with Michael Finn, Philadelphia, Feb. 26, 1978; John J. Reilly, Philadelphia, Jan. 18, 1982; Thomas Regan, Philadelphia, Feb. 2, 1982.

18. Cronin, *McGarrity Papers*, 28-35.

19. Clark, *Irish Relations*, 121-25.

20. Cronin, *McGarrity Papers*, 50-55.

21. Al McCann and Terry McCann interviewed by Dennis Clark, Philadelphia, Nov. 14, 1982. Al McCann is a nephew of Mike McGinn.

22. Cronin, *McGarrity Papers*, 57.

23. Owen B. Hunt interviewed by Dennis Clark, Philadelphia, May 12, 1976.

24. Mike McGinn's surviving papers were preserved and shared with me by Jack Kelly of the Irish Crossroads, Cinnaminson, New Jersey, who very kindly brought them to my attention and made it possible for me to study them. These papers contain details of nationalist activity in the early 1920s, including the telegram cited. The Clark Collection, Balch Institute.

25. Cronin, *McGarrity Papers*, 101-10.

26. Handbill, Patrick J. Stanton Papers, Balch Institute.

27. Padraic Colum and Edward J. O'Brien, eds., *Poems of the Irish Revolutionary Brotherhood* (Boston: Small, Maynard, 1916), 27.

28. Thomas Regan interviewed by Dennis Clark, Philadelphia, Feb. 2, 1982.

29. Joseph McGarrity, *Celtic Moods and Memories* (New York: Devi-Adair, 1942), 3.

30. "The tradition of nationality which meant not only the urge of the people to possess the soil and its products, but the free development of spiritual, cultural and imaginative qualities of the race, had been maintained not by the intellectuals, but by the people themselves who were the guardians of the remnants of culture." Ernie O'Malley, *On Another Man's Wound* (London: Rich and Cowan, 1936), i-ii.

31. Marc J. Swartz, ed., *Local-level Politics: Social and Cultural Perspectives* (Chicago: Aldine, 1968), 199. Daithi O'hÓgain, *The Hero in Irish Folk History* (Dublin: Gull and Macmillan, 1985), 192. For the process of transmission of traditional folk patterns to American urban settings, see Richard M. Dorson, "Is There a Folk in the City?" in Richard M. Dorson, *Folklore* (Bloomington: Indiana Univ. Press, 1972), 32-79, and Morton Leeds, "The Process of Cultural Stripping and Reintegration," in Americo Paredes and Ellen J. Stekert, eds., *The Urban Experience and Folk Tradition* (Austin: Univ. of Texas Press, 1971), 165-73.

32. Victor Walsh, " 'A Fanatic Heart': The Cause of Irish-American Nationalism in Pittsburgh during the Gilded Age," *Journal of Social History* 15, no. 2 (Winter 1982): 187-204. For a view of Ryan in another context, which contains some material used in this chapter, see Dennis Clark, "Intrepid Men: Three Philadelphia Irishmen, 1880–1920," in Meagher, *From Paddy to Studs*, 93-116.

33. Light, "Class, Ethnicity and Urban Ecology," passim.

34. *Philadelphia and Popular Philadelphians*, 58.

35. John J. Reilly interviewed by Dennis Clark, Philadelphia Jan. 18, 1982. Reilly knew Ryan well through his own long association with Irish affairs reflected in his papers in the Historical Society of Pennsylvania.

36. Clark, *Irish in Philadelphia*, 96, 121.

37. Light, "Class, Ethnicity and Ecology," 112. William O'Brien, *Recollections* (London: Macmillan, 1905), 411.

38. "Councils Meet," *Irish World* (New York), Oct. 18, 1890.

39. "1500 Welcome Dillon," *Irish World* (New York), Nov. 15, 1890.

40. F.S.L. Lyons, *Ireland since the Famine* (London: Weidenfeld and Nicholson, 1971), 177.

41. "UIL Report" *Irish World* (New York), Dec. 3, 1910.

42. Wittke, *Irish in America*, 168.

43. J.E. Kendle, "The Round Table Movement and 'Home Rule All Round,' " *Historical Journal* 11, no. 2 (1968): 332-53.

44. "Overseas Irish," *Irish World* (New York), Dec. 3, 1910.

45. "UIL Report," *Irish World* (New York), Nov. 3, 1910.

46. "Ryan Tells Why Dollars Aid," *Philadelphia Public Ledger* (Dec. 11, 1910).

47. "National Directory Meets," *Irish World* (New York), Feb. 4, 1911.

48. "Ryan Attacked," *Evening Bulletin* (Philadelphia), June 6, 1914.

49. "Ryan on Home Rule," *Evening Bulletin* (Philadelphia), Jan. 17, 1913. Carroll, *American Opinion and the Irish Question*, 33.

50. *Evening Bulletin* (Philadelphia), March 12, 1918. Carroll, *American Opinion and the Irish Question*, 27. Ryan's ties to the Clan na Gael are made clear in minutes of the Irish American Club, May 26, 1889, Balch Institute.

51. Carroll, *American Opinion and the Irish Question*, 38, 127. "Ryan Barred," *Evening Bulletin* (Philadelphia), May 12 and 13, 1919.

52. John B. Duff, "The Versailles Treaty and Irish-Americans," *Journal of American History* 4, no. 4 (Dec. 1968): 582-89.

53. "Ryan Leaves," *Evening Bulletin* (Philadelphia), March 31, 1919.

54. Duff, "The Versailles Treaty and Irish-Americans," 591-95.

55. Ibid., 599.

56. Alan Ward, *Ireland and Anglo-American Relations, 1899–1921* (Toronto: Univ. Of Toronto Press, 1969), 93, 181.

57. Joseph P. O'Grady, ed., *The Immigrants and Wilson's Peace Policies* (Lexington: Univ. of Kentucky Press, 1967), 84.

58. "League of Nations," *Evening Bulletin* (Philadelphia), March 14, 1919.

59. "Ryan Sees Secret Pact," *Evening Bulletin* (Philadelphia), June 9, 1919.

60. John J. Reilly interviewed by Dennis Clark, Philadelphia, Jan. 18, 1982. Reilly knew Ryan well and noted his personal vanity.

61. Ryan's attempt in 1910 to overcome factionalism in Irish circles by federation is one example of his mediating role. Carroll, *American Opinion and the Irish Question*, 15.

62. John J. Reilly interviewed by Dennis Clark, Philadelphia, Jan. 28, 1982.

63. Edward Levine, *The Irish and Irish Politicians* (Notre Dame, Ind.: Univ. of Notre Dame Press, 1966), 116-42. Harry Silcox, *Philadelphia Politics from the Bottom Up: The Life of Irishman William McMullen, 1824–1901* (Philadelphia: Balch Institute Press, 1989).

64. "Clark Dilworth," *Philadelphia Inquirer*, Oct. 13, and Nov. 2, 1951. "Reform," *Evening Bulletin* (Philadelphia), Jan. 14, 1974.

65. Irwin Frank Greenberg, "The Philadelphia Democratic Party, 1911–1934" (Ph.D. diss., Temple University, 1972). John L. Shover, "The Emergence of a Two-Party System in Republican Philadelphia, 1924–1936," *Journal of American History* 60, no. 4 (March 1974): 985-1002.

66. Joseph D. Crumlish, *A City Finds Itself: The Philadelphia Home Rule Charter Movement* (Detroit: Wayne State Univ. Press, 1959), passim. The Committee of Seventy, "History of the Committee of Seventy" (Files of the Committee of Seventy, Philadelphia, Mimeographed).

67. The interpretation of the reform of the 1950s as a socialite leadership effort is provided in James Reichley, *The Art of Government: Reform and Organization Politics in Philadelphia* (New York: Fund for the Republic, 1959), and Roger Butterfield, "Revolt in Philadelphia," *Saturday Evening Post*, November, 8, 15, and 22, 1954. Jeanne R. Lowe, *Cities in a Race with Time* (New York: Random, 1967), 320-29. An account of the reform is given by Joseph S. Clark and Dennis Clark, "Rally and Relapse," in Russell Weigley, ed., *Philadelphia: A 300 Year History* (New York: W.W. Norton, 1982), 649-703.

68. Biographical note on Michael J. Bradley, Files of the Friendly Sons of St. Patrick, Philadelphia. James H.J. Tate, "In Praise of Politicians" (Historical Society of Pennsylvania, typed manuscript), chapter 3, page 8.

69. "Reform," *Evening Bulletin* (Philadelphia), Jan. 14, 1974.

70. George Forde interviewed by Dennis Clark, Philadelphia, Jan. 24, 1982. Much of the following material is based on interviews in the Walter Phillips Collection, Urban Archives Temple University, hearafter cited as WPC. Interviews by Walter Phillips.

71. Herbert McGlinchey interviewed by Dennis Clark, Philadelphia, June 18, 1981.

72. Interviews of James Mahoney, July 30, 1979, and Joseph McLaughlin by Walter Phillips, Mar. 3, 1976, WPC.

73. Interview of Michael J. Byrne by Walter Phillips, June 6, 1978, WPC.

74. This estimate is based upon voting totals from wards 18, 19, 23, 25, 31, 33, 35, 36, 41, 42, 45, 46, and 51 in *Philadelphia Inquirer*, Nov. 7, 1951.

75. James H.J. Tate interviewed by Dennis Clark, Philadelphia, Sept. 15, 1981. Other key interviews by Walter Phillips in the WPC are those of William J. Green, Jr., William M. Lennox, Michael J. Bradley, and Joseph Burke.

76. Former Judge Herbert Levin interviewed by Dennis Clark, Philadelphia, Jan. 12, 1983.

77. Clark, *Society of the Friendly Sons*, 39.

78. "The Philadelphia Story: Citizens Clean Up Graft," *Newsweek*, June 14, 1948. Lowe, *Cities in a Race with Time*, 313-404.

79. Harold Libros, *Hard-Core Liberals: A Sociological Analysis of the Philadelphia Americans for Democratic Action* (Cambridge, Mass.: Schenkman, 1975), 44.

80. Tina Weintraub and Marjorie Apt, *An Outline of Philadelphia's Government, 1949* (Philadelphia: Philadelphia Bureau of Municipal Research and the Pennsylvania Economy League, 1956), 20, 44, 58-59.

81. Edward C. Banfield, *Big City Politics* (New York: Random, 1967), 110-111. Peter O. Muller, Kenneth C. Meyer, and Roman Cybriwsky, *Philadelphia: A Study of Conflicts and Social Cleavages* (Cambridge, Mass.: Ballinger, 1976), 14-33. Dennis Clark, "The Urban Ordeal: Reform and Policy in Philadelphia, 1947–1967" (Paper No. 1, Intergrative Paper Series, Philadelphia: Past, Present and Future Project, School of Urban and Public Policy, University of Pennsylvania, July 1982.

82. Joseph Gaffigan interviewed by Dennis Clark, Philadelphia, Jan. 10, 1979, WPC.

83. Interview of Leon Shull by Walter Phillips, May 4, 1976, WPC.

84. George Forde interviewed by Dennis Clark, Philadelphia, Dec. 13, 1977, WPC.

85. "Forde Dispute," *Evening Bulletin* (Philadelphia), Jan. 21, 1970.

86. Peter McGrath, "Bi-Centennial Philadelphia: A Quaking City," in Dennis Clark, ed., *Philadelphia: A Three Hundred Year View* (Port Washington, N.Y.: Kennikat, 1976), 79-80.

87. "Reform," *Evening Bulletin* (Philadelphia), Jan. 17, 1974. *Philadelphia Daily News*, Dec. 10, 1982. Banfield, *Big City Politics*, 111. The work of city lobbyist Patrick H. McLaughlin over eighteen years brought much of this federal funding to the city. *Philadelphia Inquirer*, June 16, 1982.

88. Steven P. Erie, *Rainbow's End: Irish-Americans and the Dilemmas of Urban Machine Politics, 1840–1985* (Berkeley: Univ. of California Press, 1988), 231.

89. For a retrospective view of the reform by various participants, see *Proceedings from Philadelphia's Political Reform Movement, 1946–1961 Symposium*, Feb. 27, 1988 (Philadelphia: Pennsylvania Historical Society, 1988). For an interpretation of the Irish role in urban affairs, see Dennis Clark, "The Milesians in the Metropolis: The Irish-Americans and the Problems of Urban Space" (paper delivered at the Mid-Atlantic Regional Conference, American Conference on Irish Studies, Feb. 5, 1988, Balch Institute.

Conclusion

1. Peter Marin, *Harper's* 277 no. 1658 (July 1988): 17.

2. Shalom Staub, *Yemenis in New York City: The Folklore of Ethnicity* (Philadelphia: Balch Institute Press, 1989), 31-32.

3. *Irish Edition*, 1 (Philadelphia), March 1989.

4. Ibid., Jan. through Dec., 1989.

5. Ibid., monthly columns of Donn Devine.

6. John Corr, "Fishtown," *Sunday Inquirer Magazine* (Philadelphia), Dec. 7, 1989. Articles in the Clark Collection and the papers of Patrick Lagan and James Hearl are in the Balch Institute. The memoirs of Mayor James H.J. Tate and books about movie actress Grace Kelly are in the Historical Society of Pennsylvania.

7. "Survey," *Irish Edition* (Philadelphia), Jan. 1990.

8. Clark Collection, Balch Institute.

9. Catalogs of the Irish American Cultural Institute and bookseller Thomas Ruane of Hammonton, New Jersey, Clark Collection, Balch Institute.

10. Biographical notes on these figures are in the Clark Collection, Balch Institute.

11. Hugh Dalziel Duncan, *Communication and Social Order* (New York: Bedminster, 1962), 165-76.

12. William M. Newman, *American Pluralism: A Study of Minority Groups and Social Theory* (New York: Harper and Row, 1973), 288-89.

13. Duncan, *Communication and Social Order*, 295-316.

14. Erie, *Rainbow's End*, passim.

15. David M. Emmons, *The Butte Irish: Class Ethnicity in an American Mining Town, 1875–1925* (Urbana: Univ. of Illinois Press, 1989), 94-132. Meagher, *From Paddy to Studs*, 986-87. Handlin, *Boston's Immigrants*, 207-29. Dennis P. Ryan, *Beyond the Ballot Box: A Social History of the Boston Irish, 1845–1917* (Rutherford, N.J.: Fairleigh Dickinson Univ. Press, 1983), 21-40. Lawrence J. McCaffrey, et al., eds., *The Irish in Chicago* (Urbana: Univ. of Illinois Press, 1987), 1-21. R.A. Burchell, *San Francisco Irish, 1848–1880*, 34-51. Jay Dolan, *The Immigrant Church: New York's Irish and German Catholics, 1815–1865* (Baltimore, Md.: (Johns Hopkins Univ. Press, 1975), 45-67. John Corry, *Golden Clan: The Murrays, The McDonnells and the Irish-American Aristocracy* (Boston: Houghton Mifflin, 1977), 22-36. An indication of the persistence of Irish identity nationally is furnished by the affirmations of it in forty-six biographies and memoirs of notable contemporary figures cited in "Lives of the Irish-Americans" in the Clark Collection, Balch Institute.

16. Emmons, *Butte Irish*, 94-132. Meagher, *From Paddy to Studs*, 86-87. Handlin, *Boston's Immigrants*, 207-29. Ryan, *Beyond the Ballot Box*, 21-40. Robert E. Sullivan and James M. O'Toole, eds., *Catholic Boston: Studies in Religion and Community, 1870–1970* (Boston: Roman Catholic Archbishop of Boston, 1985), 67-120. Dolan, *Immigrant Church*, 45-67. John T. Ridge, *Erin's Sons in America: The Ancient Order of Hibernians* (New York: Ancient Order of Hibernians, 1986), 46-50. John T. Ridge, *The St. Patrick's Day Parade in New York* (New York: St. Patrick's Day Parade Committee, 1988) 1-174.

17. Emmons, *Butte Irish*, 180-220, 292-339. Meagher, *From Paddy to Studs*, 90-91 citations: Brian Mitchell, *The Paddy Camps: The Irish of Lowell, 1821–1861* (Urbana: Univ. of Illinois Press, 1985), 64-78, 84, 151, cites similar sources. Ryan, *Beyond the Ballot Box*, 159-60. R. A. Harris, "Characteristics of Irish Immigrants in North America Derived from the Boston Pilot 'Missing Friends Data,' 1831–1850," *Working Papers in Irish Studies* no. 88-1, Northeastern University, Boston, Mass. Burchell, *San Francisco Irish* 189. Michael Funchion; *Chicago's Irish Nationalists, 1881–1890* (New York: Arno, 1976), passim. Charles Fanning, "The Literary Dimension," in McCaffrey, et al., *Irish in Chicago*, 98-145. Griffin, *Portrait of the Irish in America* (New York: Charles Scribner's Sons, 1981), 197-202.

18. Emmons, *Butte Irish*, 414. Meagher, *From Paddy to Studs*, 89-92. Ryan, *Beyond the Ballot Box*, 82-112. Sullivan and O'Toole, *Catholic Boston*, 171-200. James P. Walsh, *The San Francisco Irish, 1850–1976* (San Francisco: Irish Literary and Historical Society, 1978), 27-142. David Noel Doyle, "The Irish in Chicago," *Irish Historical Studies* 26, no. 103 (May 1989): 293-303. Glazer and Moynihan, *Beyond the Melting Pot*, 219-37. Corry, *Golden Clan*, 55-140.

19. Clark, *Hibernia America*, xi-xvii.

20. Rory Fitzpatrick, *God's Frontiersmen: The Scots-Irish Epic* (London: Weidenfeld and Nicolson, 1989), passim. Hasia Diner, *Erin's Daughters in America*. Janet A. Nolan, *Ourselves Alone: Women's Emigration from Ireland, 1885–1920* (Lexington: Univ. Press of Kentucky, 1989).

21. John Edwards, *Language, Society and Identity* (London: Basil Blackwell, 1985), 101-17.

22. Princess Grace Irish Library, *Irishness in a Changing Society* (Gerard's Cross, England: Colin Smith, 1988), 88-89.

Research Note

1. These studies are listed in Metress, *Irish-American Experience*, 17-42, and Doyle, "Regional Bibliography of Irish America," 254-83.
2. Glazer and Moynihan, *Beyond the Melting Pot*, 250-61.
3. Gordon, *Assimilation in American Life*, 242.
4. William Petersen, "Concepts in Ethnicity," in Stephan Thernstrom, et al., eds., *Harvard Encyclopedia of American Ethnic Groups* (Cambridge, Mass.: Harvard Univ. Press, 1980), 236-37; Wsevolod S. Isajiw, "Definitions of Ethnicity," *Ethnicity* 1, no. 2 (July 1974): 111-24. Newman in his *American Pluralism*, 109-79, summarizes various theories and presents his own view that ethnicity is developed and maintained because of social conflict. Barth in *Ethnic Groups and Boundaries*, 14, sees the boundary of group life as the determinant of ethnic traditions. Peter Kivisto, *The Ethnic Enigma: The Salience of Ethnicity for European Origin Groups* (Philadelphia: Balch Institute Press, 1989), 11-23. Jackson Lears, "Power, Culture and Memory," *Journal of American History* 75, no. 1 (June 1988): 137-40. Adaptive processes in ethnic life are described from an anthropological point of view in Jo Kibbee, "From Ethnic Groups to Ethnicity: Anthropologists and the Study of Ethnic Cultures in the U.S.," *Ethnic Forum* 8, no. 2 (1988): 52-61.
5. Alan Gailey, ed., *The Use of Tradition* (Cultra, Northern Ireland: Ulster Folk and Transport Museum, 1988), 61-67. Evans, *The Irishness of the Irish* (Belfast, Northern Ireland: Irish Association, 1967), passim. Hilary Tovey, Damian Hannan, and Hal Abramson, *Why Irish? Language and Identity in Ireland Today* (Dublin: Bord na Gaeilge, 1989), 1-34. Eugenia Shanklin, *Donegal's Changing Traditions: An Ethnographic Study* (New York: Gordon and Breach Science, 1985), 1-16.
6. Thomas Bender, *Community and Social Change in America* (Baltimore: Johns Hopkins Univ. Press, 1978), 7, 128-50.
7. Richard D. Alba, *Ethnic Identity: The Transformation of White America* (New Haven: Yale University Press, 1990), 20, 120, 313. Morton A. Kaplan, *Alienation and Identification* (New York: Free Press, 1976), 166. Thernstrom, et al. *The Harvard Encyclopedia of American Ethnic Groups*, vii. See also Abner Cohen, *Urban Ethnicity* (London: Tavistock, 1974), xxi.
8. Vytautas Kavolis, *Designs of Selfhood* (Rutherford, NJ: Associated University Presses, 1984), 22
9. Duncan, *Communications and Social Order*, 76.
10. "Belief Systems," in John J. Honigman, ed., *Handbook of Social and Cultural Anthropology*, (Chicago: Rand McNally, 1973), 534.
11. Diner, *Erin's Daughters in America*, 120-38. Carole Groneman, "The Bloody Ould Sixth: A Social Analysis of a Mid-Nineteenth Century New York City Working Class Community" (Ph.D. diss., University of Rochester, 1973). Greeley, *That Most Distressful Nation*, 95-116. Nolan, *Ourselves Alone*, 73-90. Elizabeth Stone, *Black Sheep and Kissing Cousins: How Our Family Stories Shape Us* (New York: Penguin, 1988), 15-96.
12. Marjorie Fallows, *Irish-Americans: Identity and Assimilation* (Englewood Cliffs, N.J.: Prentice-Hall, 1979), passim. Kerby Miller, *Emigrants and Exiles: Ireland and the Irish Exodus to North America* (New York: Oxford Univ. Press, 1985), 650-61. Brian Mitchell, *The Paddy Camps: The Irish of Lowell, 1821–1861* (Urbana: Univ. of Illinois Press, 1988), 154-55. David Thelen, "Memory and American History," *Journal of American History* 75, no. 4 (March 1989): 1117-29.

13. Michael Banton, ed., *The Social Anthropology of Complex Societies* (London: Tavistock, 1966), 1-14. Henry Glassie, *Irish Folk History* (Philadelphia: University of Pennsylvania Press, 1982), 1-17. M.A.G. O'Tuathaigh, ed., *Community, Culture and Conflict* (Galway, Ireland: Univ. of Galway Press, 1986), 64-81. Light, "Role of Irish-American Organizations," in Drudy, *Irish in America*, 113-42. Henry Glassie, *Irish Folk History* (Philadelphia: Univ. of Pennsylvania Press, 1982), passim.

14. Constance Smith and Anne Freedman, *Voluntary Associations: A Perspective on the Literature* (Cambridge, Mass.: Harvard Univ. Press, 1972), 1-11. Karl W. Deutsch, "On Social Communications and the Metropolis," in Larry S. Bourne, ed., *Internal Structure of the City: Readings on Space and Environment* (New York: Oxford Univ. Press, 1971), 22-30. Schlesinger, "Biography of a Nation of Joiners," 23-50.

15. John B. Newman, "A Rationale for a Definition of Communications," in Alfred B. Smith, ed., *Communications and Culture: Readings in Codes of Human Interaction* (New York: Holt, Rinehart and Winston, 1966), 55-63. Ray L. Birdwhistell, "Communications," in David Sills, ed., *International Encyclopedia of the Social Sciences* (New York: Macmillan, and Free Press, 1968), 24-33.

16. Herbert I. Schiller, *Communication and Cultural Domination* (White Plains, N.Y.: (Sharpe, 1976), 1-23. Hayley and McKay, *300 Years of Irish Periodicals*, 29-48. Hugh Oram, *The Newspaper Book: A History of Newspapers in Ireland, 1649–1983* (Dublin: M and O Books, 1983), 21-83.

17. James McGregor Burns, *Leadership* (New York: Harper and Row, 1978), passim. Doob, *Personality, Power and Authority*, 98, 125, 162-68, 183. Stephen Bochner, ed., *The Mediating Person: Bridges Between Cultures* (Boston: Hall, 1981), 12-73. Robin Williams, Jr., *Mutual Accommodation: Ethnic Conflict and Cooperations* (Minneapolis: Univ. of Minnesota Press, 1977), 295.

18. David Noel Doyle, "The Irish as Urban Pioneers in the United States, 1850–1870," in Ciaran Brady, ed., *The American City* (Dublin: Irish Association for American Studies, 1988), 9.

Bibliography

Archives

American Catholic Historical Society
Balch Institute for Ethnic Studies
Brehon Society of Philadelphia
Committee of Seventy of Philadelphia
Friendly Sons of St. Patrick of Philadelphia
Historical Society of Pennsylvania
Library of Congress
Marquette University
Pennsylvania Hospital
Philadelphia Bar Association
Philadelphia City Archives
Philadelphia Maritime Museum
Philadelphia Social History Project
State Historical Society of Wisconsin
Temple University Urban Archives
University of Pennsylvania Folklore Department

Newspapers and Magazines

Catholic Advocate and Irishman's Journal, (Philadelphia)
Catholic Herald, (Philadelphia)
Catholic Review of History and Politics, (Philadelphia)
Catholic Standard and Times, (Philadelphia)
Clan na Gael, (Philadelphia)
Chestnut Hill Local, (Philadelphia)
Erin, (Philadelphia)
Daily News, (Philadelphia)
Evening Bulletin, (Philadelphia)
Free Man and Irish American Review, (Philadelphia)
Irish American, (Chicago)
Irish American, (Philadelphia)
Irish American Herald, (Philadelphia)
Irish American Review, (Philadelphia)
Irish American Review and Celtic Literary Advocate, (Philadelphia)
Irish Edition, (Philadelphia)
Irish Press, (Philadelphia)
Irish Republican Shield and Literary Advocate, (Philadelphia)
Irish Standard, (Philadelphia)
Irishman and Weekly Review, (Philadelphia)
New York Times,

Pennsylvania Evening Herald, (Philadelphia)
Pennsylvania Gazette, (Philadelphia)
Philadelphia Hibernian,
Philadelphia Inquirer,
Philadelphia Item,
Philadelphia North American,
Philadelphia Public Ledger,
Philadelphia Times,
Press, (Philadelphia)
Shamrock, (Philadelphia)
Taggart's Sunday Times (Philadelphia)
Universe, (Philadelphia)

Journals and Magazines

American Catholic Historical Researches
Béaloideas
Catholic Historical Review
Comparative Studies in Society and History
Erie-Ireland
Ethnic Forum
Ethnic Groups
Ethnicity
Folklore
International Migration Review
Irish Historical Studies
Journal of American Ethnic History
Journal of American History
Journal of Social History
Newsweek
Nineteenth Century
Oral Tradition
Pennsylvania History
Pennsylvania Magazine of History and Biography
Philadelphia Magazine,
Records, Journal of the American Irish Historical Society
Records of the American Catholic Historical Society
Social Forces
Theater History Studies

Dissertations

Bric, Maurice J. "Ireland, Irishmen, and the Broadening of the Late-
   Eighteenth Century Philadelphia Polity." History. Johns Hopkins University, 1990.

Greenberg, Irwin Frank. "The Philadelphia Democratic Party, 1911–1934." History. Temple University, 1972.

Groneman, Carole. "The Bloody Ould Sixth: A Social Analysis of a Mid-Nineteenth Century New York City Working Class Community." History. University of Rochester, 1973.

Light, Dale E. "Class, Ethnicity and Urban Ecology in a Nineteenth Century City: Philadelphia's Irish, 1840–1890." History. University of Pennsylvania, 1979.

Morris, Stephanie. "From Northwest Ireland to America, 1864–1870: Tracing Migrants from Their Place of Origin to Their New Home in Philadelphia." History. Temple University, 1988.

Books

Baltzell, E. Digby. *Philadelphia Gentlemen: The Making of a National Upper Class.* New York: Free Press, 1958.

Banfield, Edward C. *Big City Politics.* New York: Random, 1967.

Banton, Michael, ed. *The Social Anthropology of Complex Societies.* London: Tavistock, 1966.

Barth, Frederick, ed., *Ethnic Groups and Boundaries: The Social Organization of Cultural Difference.* Boston: Little, Brown, 1969.

Barth, Gunther. *City People: The Rise of Modern City Culture in Nineteenth Century America.* New York: Oxford Univ. Press, 1980.

Bender, Thomas. *Community and Social Change in America.* Baltimore: John Hopkins Univ. Press, 1978.

Billington, Ray Allen. *The Protestant Crusade, 1800–1860: A Study of the Origins of American Nativism* Chicago: Quadrangle, 1964.

Blumin, Stuart M. *The Emergence of the Middle Class: Social Experience in the American City, 1760–1900.* New York: Cambridge Univ. Press, 1989.

Bochner, Stephen, ed. *The Mediating Person: Bridges between Cultures.* Boston: G.K. Hall, 1981.

Bourgeois, Maurice. *John Millington Synge and the Irish Theater.* New York: B. Blom, 1965.

Bourne, Larry S., ed. *The Internal Structure of the City: Readings on Space and Environment.* New York: Oxford Univ. Press, 1971.

Bradsher, Earl L. *Mathew Carey: Editor, Author and Publisher.* New York: Columbia Univ. Press, 1912.

Brady, Ciaran, ed. *The American City.* Dublin: Irish Association for American Studies, 1988.

Brown, Charles T., and Paul W. Keller, eds. *Monologue to Dialogue: An Exploration of Interpersonal Communication.* Englewood Cliffs, N.J.: Prentice-Hall, 1973.

Brown, Terence. *Ireland: A Social and Cultural History, 1922–1979.* Glasgow: Fontana, 1981.

Brown, Thomas N. *Irish-American Nationalism: 1870–1890.* Philadelphia: J.B. Lippincott, 1966.

Burchell, R.A. *The San Francisco Irish, 1848–1880.* Berkeley: Univ. of California Press, 1980.

Burns, James McGregor. *Leadership.* New York: Harper and Row. 1978.

Burt, Nathaniel. *The Perenniel Philadelphians.* Boston: Little, Brown, 1963.

Cahill, Kevin, *The American Irish Revival: A Decade of 'The Recorder,' 1974–1983.* Port Washington, N.Y.: Associated Faculty Press, 1985.

Campbell, John H. *History of the Friendly Sons of St. Patrick and of the Hibernian Society for the Relief of Emigrants from Ireland in Philadelphia.* Philadelphia: Hibernian Society, 1892.

Carey, Mathew. *Vindiciae Hibernicae: or, Ireland Vindicated.* Philadelphia: H.C. Carey and I. Lea, 1823.

Carroll, Francis M. *American Opinion and the Irish Question, 1910–1923.* New York: St. Martin's, 1978.

Checklist of Philadelphia Newspapers. Works Progress Administration. Philadelphia: Works Progress Administration, 1937.

Claerbaut, David, ed. *New Directions in Ethnic Studies: Minorities in America.* Saratoga, Calif.: Century 21, 1981.

Clark, Dennis. *The Ghetto Game.* New York: Sheed and Ward, 1962.

——— . *The Heart's Own People: A History of the Donegal Association of Philadelphia.* Philadelphia: Donegal Association of Philadelphia, 1988.

——— . *Hibernia America: The Irish and Regional Cultures.* Westport, Conn.: Greenwood, 1986.

——— . *A History of the Society of the Friendly Sons of St. Patrick for the Relief of Emigrants from Ireland in Philadelphia, 1951–1981.* Philadelphia: Society of the Friendly Sons of St. Patrick, 1982.

——— . *Irish Blood: Northern Ireland and the American Conscience.* Port Washington, N.Y.: Kennikat, 1977.

——— . *The Irish in Philadelphia: Ten Generations of Urban Experience.* Philadelphia: Temple Univ. Press, 1973.

——— . *The Irish Relations: Trials of an Immigrant Tradition.* East Brunswick, N.J.: Associated Univ. Presses, 1982.

——— . *Philadelphia, 1776–2076: A Three Hundred Year View.* Port Washington, N.Y.: Kennikat, 1975.

Cole, Michael, and Sylvia Scribner. *Culture and Thought: A Psychological Introduction.* New York: John Wiley and Sons, 1974.

Colum, Padraic, and Edward J. O'Brien, eds. *Poems of the Irish Revolutionary Brotherhood.* Boston: Small, Maynard, 1916.

Committee of Seventy. *History of Governance in the Ports of Philadelphia.* Philadelphia: Committee of Seventy, 1880.

Corry, John. *Golden Clan: The Murrays, McDonnells and the Irish-American Aristocracy.* Boston: Houghton Mifflin, 1977.

Coyle, Donald B. *Immigrant City: Lawrence, Massachusetts.* Chapel Hill: Univ. of North Carolina Press, 1963.

Cronin, Sean. *The McGarrity Papers.* Tralee, Ireland: Anvil, 1972.

Crumlish, Joseph D. *A City Finds Itself: The Philadelphia Home Rule Charter Movement.* Detroit: Wayne State Univ. Press, 1959.

Cullen, L.M. *The Emergence of Modern Ireland: 1600–1900.* Dublin: Gill and Macmillan, 1981.

Diner, Hasia. *Erin's Daughters in America: Irish Immigrant Women in the Nineteenth Century.* Baltimore, Md.: Johns Hopkins Univ. Press, 1983.

Dolan, Jay P. *The Immigrant Church: New York's Irish and German Catholics, 1815–1865.* Baltimore: Johns Hopkins Univ. Press, 1975.

Doob, Leonard. *Personality, Power and Authority: A View from the Behavioral Sciences.* Westport, Conn.: Greenwood, 1983.

Dougherty, Daniel. *History of the Society of the Friendly Sons of St. Patrick for Relief of Emigrants from Ireland of Philadelphia, 1892–1951.* Philadelphia: Friendly Sons of St. Patrick, 1952.

Doyle, David Noel. *Ireland, Irishmen and Revolutionary America: 1760–1820.* Cork, Ireland: Mercier, 1981.

———. *Irish-Americans: Native Rights and National Empires.* New York: Arno, 1976.

Doyle, David Noel, and Owen Dudley Edwards, eds.,. *America and Ireland, 1776–1976: The American Identity and the Irish Connection.* Westport, Conn.: Greenwood, 1980.

Drudy, P.J., ed. *The Irish in America: Emigration, Assimilation and Impact.* Cambridge, England: Cambridge Univ. Press, 1985.

Dubin, Robert. *Theory Building.* New York: Free Press, 1969.

Du Bois, W.E.B. *The Negro in Philadelphia.* Philadelphia: Univ. of Pennsylvania Press, 1899.

Durkan, Michael, and Ronald Ayling. *Sean O'Casey: A Bibliography.* London: Macmillan, 1978.

Edwards, John. *Language, Society and Identity.* London: Basil Blackwell, 1985.

Ehrlich, Richard L., ed. *Immigrants in Industrial America, 1850–1920.* Charlottesville: Univ. Press of Virginia, 1977.

Emmons, David M. *The Butte Irish: Class and Ethnicity in an American Mining Town, 1875–1925.* Urbana: Univ. of Illinois Press, 1989.

Ennis, John T. *The Clan na Gael and the Murder of Dr. Patrick Cronin.* Chicago: Published by the author, 1889.

Epstein, A.L. *Ethos and Identity: Three Studies of Ethnicity.* London: Tavistock, 1978.

Erie, Stephen P. *Rainbow's End: Irish-Americans and the Dilemmas of Urban Machine Politics, 1840–1985.* Berkeley: Univ. of California Press, 1988.

Ershkowitz, Miriam, and Joseph Zikmund, eds. *Black Politics in Philadelphia.* New York: Basic Books, 1973.

Evans, E. Estyn. *The Irishness of the Irish.* Belfast, Northern Ireland: Irish Association, 1967.

Fallows, Marjorie. *Irish-Americans: Identity and Assimilation.* Englewood Cliffs, N.J.: Prentice-Hall, 1978.

Farrell, Brian, ed. *Communication and Community in Ireland.* Dublin: Mercier, 1984.

Faules, Don. F., and Dennis C. Alexander, eds. *Communication and Social Behavior: A Symbolic Interaction Perspective.* Reading, Calif.: Addison-Wesley, 1978.

Feldberg, Michael. *The Philadelphia Riots of 1844: A Study of Ethnic Conflict.* Westport, Conn.: Greenwood, 1975.

Fitts, William H. et al. *The Self Concept and Self-Actualization.* Monograph 3. Nashville, Tenn.: Dade-Wallace Center, 1971.

Foner, Philip S. *History of the Labor Movement in the United States.* 4 vols. New York: International Publishers, 1965.

Forkner, Ben, ed. *Modern Irish Short Stories.* New York: Penguin, 1980.

Fuchs, Lawrence H., ed. *American Ethnic Politics.* New York: Harper and Row, 1968.

Funchion, Michael. *Chicago's Irish Nationalists, 1881–1890.* New York: Arno, 1976.

———, ed. *Irish-American Voluntary Organizations.* Westport, Conn.: Greenwood, 1983.

Gailey, Alan. *The Use of Tradition.* Cultra, Northern Ireland: Ulster Folk and Transport Museum, 1988.

Gardner, James B., and George Rollie Adams. *Ordinary People and Everyday Life: Perspectives on the New Social History.* Nashville, Tenn.: American Association for State and Local History, 1983.

Gillard, John T. *The Catholic Church and the American Negro.* Baltimore, Md.: St. Joseph's Society. 1929.

Glassie, Henry. *Passing the Time in Ballymenone.* Philadelphia: Univ. of Pennsylvania Press, 1982.

Glazer, Nathan, and Daniel Patrick Moynihan. *Beyond the Melting Pot: The Negroes, Puerto Ricans, Jews, Italians and Irish of New York City.* Cambridge, Mass.: MIT Press, 1970.

Gmelch, Sharon. *Irish Life and Traditions.* Syracuse, N.Y.: Syracuse Univ. Press, 1986.

Gopalan, S. *Tradition: A Social Analysis.* Madras: University of Madras, 1973.

Gordon, Milton. *Assimilation in American Life: The Role of Race, Religion and National Origin.* New York: Oxford Univ. Press, 1964.

Gottschalk, Louis. *Understanding History.* New York: Alfred A. Knopf, 1963.

Greeley, Andrew. *The Irish-Americans: The Rise to Power and Money.* New York: Harper and Row, 1981.

———. *That Most Distressful Nation: The Taming of the American Irish.* Chicago: Quadrangle, 1972.

Greene, Victor R. *American Immigrant Leaders, 1800–1910: Marginality and Identity.* Baltimore, Md.: Johns Hopkins Univ. Press, 1987.

Gregory, Wilfred, ed. *American Newspapers.* New York: H.W. Wilson, 1937.

Griffin, William D. *A Portrait of the Irish in America.* New York: Charles Scribner's Sons, 1981.

Handlin, Oscar. *Boston's Immigrants, 1790–1880: A Study in Acculturation.* Cambridge, Mass.: Harvard Univ. Press, 1979.

Hayley, Barbara, and Enda McKay. *300 Years of Irish Periodicals.* Mullingar, Ireland: Irish Association of Learned Journals, 1987.

Helles, L.G. *Communications Analysis and Methodology for Historians.* New York: New York Univ. Press, 1972.

Hershberg, Theodore, ed. *Philadelphia: Work, Space, Family and Group Experience in the Nineteenth Century.* New York: Oxford Univ. Press, 1981.

Hess, Robert D., and Gerald Handel. *Family Worlds: A Psychological Approach to Family Life.* Chicago: Quadrangle, 1959.

Higham, John, ed. *Ethnic Leadership in America.* Baltimore, Md.: Johns Hopkins Univ. Press, 1978.

Hobsbaum, Eric. *Studies in the History of Labor.* New York: Basic, 1964.

Honigmann, John J. *Handbook of Social and Cultural Anthropology.* Chicago: Rand McNally, 1973.

Irish in Philadelphia Project. Works Progress Administration Writers Project. Federal Works Agency. Philadelphia: National Archives Branch, 1937.

Jacobs, Alfred, and Wilford Spradlin. *The Group as Agent of Change.* New York: Behavioral Publications, 1974.

Janowitz, Morris. *The Community Press in an Urban Setting.* Chicago: Univ. of Chicago Press, 1967.

Jason, Heda, and Dmitri Segal, eds. *Patterns in Oral Literature.* The Hague: Mouton, 1977.

Jeffres, Leo W., and Mildred Barnard. *Communication and the Persistence of Ethnicity.* Cleveland, Oh.: Communication Research Center, 1982.

Joyce, William Leonard. *A History of the Irish-American Press, 1848–1883.* New York: Arno, 1976.

Kaplan, David, and Robert Manner. *Culture Theory.* Englewood Cliffs, N.J.: Prentice-Hall, 1972.

Kaplan, Morton. *Alienation and Identification.* New York: Free Press, 1976.

Kavolis, Vytautas. *Designs of Selfhood.* Rutherford, N.J.: Associated University Presses, 1984.

Kim, Young Yun. *Interethnic Communication: Current Research.* Beverly Hills, Calif.: Sage, 1986.

Kinsella, Thomas and Sean O'Tuama, eds. *An Duanaire: Poems of the Dispossessed.* Philadelphia: Univ. of Pennsylvania Press, 1981.

———, ed. *The New Oxford Book of Irish Verse.* New York: Oxford Univ. Press, 1986.

———. *Poems, 1956–1973.* Winston-Salem, N.C.: Wake Forest Univ. Press, 1979.

———, trans. *The Tain.* Dublin: Dolmen, 1969.

Kivisto, Peter. *The Ethnic Enigma: The Salience of Ethnicity for European Origin Groups.* Philadelphia: Balch Institute Press, 1987.

Klapp, Orrin E. *Symbolic Leaders: Public Dramas and Public Men.* Chicago: Aldine, 1964.

Knobel, Dale. *Paddy and the Republic: Ethnicity and Nationality in Ante-Bellum America.* Middletown, Conn.: Wesleyan Univ. Press, 1968.

Kobre, Sidney. *The Development of American Journalism.* Dubuque, Iowa: William C. Brown, 1969.

Lankford, John, and David Reimers, eds. *Essays on American Social History.* New York: Holt, Rinehart and Winston, 1976.

Laurie, Bruce. *The Working People of Philadelphia, 1800–1850.* Philadelphia: Temple Univ. Press, 1980.

The Law Association of Philadelphia, *Addresses at the March 13,1902 Centennial Celebration of the Law Association of Philadelphia.* Philadelphia: Law Association, 1906.

Lebow, Richard Ned. *White Britain and Black Ireland: The Influence of Stereotypes on Colonial Policy.* Philadelphia: Institute for the Study of Human Issues, 1976.

Lecky, W.E. *Leaders of Public Opinion in Ireland.* 2 vols. New York: Longmans Green, 1912.

Lee, Joseph J., ed., *Ireland, 1945–1970.* Dublin: Gill and Macmillan, 1979.

Libros, Harold. *Hard-Core Liberals: A Sociological Analysis of the Philadelphia Americans for Democratic Action.* Cambridge, Mass.: Schenkman, 1975.

Loughlin, James. *Gladstone, Home Rule and the Ulster Question.* Atlantic Highlands, N.J.: Humanities Press International, 1987.

Lowe, Jeanne R. *Cities in a Race with Time.* New York: Random, 1967.

Lynd, Helen Merrill. *On Shame and the Search for Identity.* New York: Harcourt Brace, 1958.

Lyons, F.S.L. *Culture and Anarchy in Ireland: 1890–1939.* Oxford, England: Oxford Univ. Press, 1979.

Macardle, Alice. *The Irish Republic.* London: Corgi, 1968.

MacEoin, Gary. *All of Which I Saw, Part of Which I Was: The Autobiography of George K. Hunton.* Garden City, N.Y.: Doubleday, 1967.

Mandelbaum, Seymour. *Community and Communications.* New York: W.W. Norton, 1972.

Marmion, Anthony. *The Ancient and Modern History of the Maritime Ports of Ireland.* London: W.H. Cox, 1860.

McAnany, Emile G., Jorge Schnitman, and Noreene James, eds. *Communication and Social Structure.* New York: Praeger, 1981.

McCaffrey, Lawrence, J., *The Irish Diaspora.* Bloomington: Indiana Univ. Press, 1976.

McCaffrey, Lawrence J. et al., eds. *The Irish in Chicago.* Urbana: Univ. of Illinois Press, 1987.

McGarrity, Joseph. *Celtic Moods amd Memories.* New York: Devin-Adair, 1942.

Meagher, Timothy, ed. *From Paddy to Studs: Irish-American Communities in the Turn of the Century Era, 1880–1920.* Westport, Conn.: Greenwood, 1986.

Mercier, Vivian, ed. *Great Irish Short Stories.* New York: Dell, 1973.

Metress, Seamus P., ed. *The Irish-American Experience: A Guide to the Literature.* Washington, D.C.: Univ. Press of America, 1981.

Meyer, Kenneth, and Roman Cybriwsky. *Philadelphia: A Study of Social Conflicts and Social Cleavages.* Cambridge, Mass.: Ballinger, 1976.

Miller, Kerby. *Emigrants and Exiles: Ireland and the Irish Exodus to North America.* New York: Oxford Univ. Press, 1985.

Miller, Randall M., ed. *The Kaleidoscopic Lens: How Hollywood Views Ethnic Groups.* New York: Jerome Ozer, 1980.

Miller, Richard B. *The Federalist City: A Study in Urban Politics, 1709–1801.* Port Washington, N.Y.: Kennikat, 1976.

Mitchell, Brian. *The Paddy Camps: The Irish of Lowell, 1821–1861.* Urbana: Univ. of Illinois Press, 1988.

Morison, Samuel Eliot. *The Oxford History of the American People.* New York: Oxford Univ. Press, 1965.

Mott, Frank Luther. *American Journalism: A History, 1690–1960.* New York: Macmillan, 1962.

Murphy, Maureen. *A Guide to Irish Studies in the United States.* Hempstead, N.Y.: American Committee for Irish Studies, 1987.

Murrell, William. *A History of American Graphic Humor,* 2 vols. New York: Whitney Museum of American Art, 1933.

Newman, William M. *American Pluralism: A Study of Minority Groups and Social Theory.* New York: Harper and Row, 1973.

Niehaus, Earl F. *The Irish in New Orleans: 1800–1860.* Baton Rouge: Louisiana State Univ. Press, 1965.

Novak, Michael. *The Rise of the Unmeltable Ethnics: Politics and Culture in the Seventies.* New York: Macmillan, 1971.

O'Brien, David J. *American Catholics and Social Reform: The New Deal Years.* New York: Oxford Univ. Press, 1968.

O'Brien, Edna. *A Fanatic Heart.* New York: Farrar, Straus and Giroux, 1984.

O'Brien, William. *Recollections.* London: Macmillan, 1905.

O'Connell, Daniel. *The Enterprise Catholic Young Men's Association of Germantown, Philadelphia and Its Dramatic Club.* Philadelphia: Enterprise Catholic Young Men's Association, 1927.

O'Grady, Joseph. *How the Irish Became Americans.* New York: Twayne, 1973.

———. *The Immigrants and Wilson's Peace Policies.* Lexington: Univ. of Kentucky Press, 1967.

Ó'hÓgain, Daithi. *The Hero in Irish Folk History.* Dublin: Gill and Macmillan, 1985.

Olzak, Susan, ed. *Competitive Ethnic Relations.* Orlando: Univ. Presses of Florida, 1983.

Osborne, William. *The Segregated Covenant: Race Relations and American Catholics.* New York: Herder and Herder, 1967.

O'Tuathaigh, M.A.G., ed. *Community Culture and Conflict.* Galway, Ireland: Galway Univ. Press, 1986.

Paredes, Americo, and Ellen J. Stekert, eds. *The Urban Experience and Folk Tradition.* Austin: Univ. of Texas Press, 1971.

Philadelphia and Popular Philadelphians. Philadelphia: North American, 1891.

Phinney, Jean S., and Mary Jane Rotheram, eds. *Children's Ethnic Socialization: Pluralism and Development.* New York: Sage, 1987

Polenberg, Richard. *One Nation Divisible: Class, Race and Ethnicity in the United States since 1936.* New York: Penguin, 1980.

Ridge, John T. *Erin's Sons in America: The Ancient Order of Hibernians.* New York: Ancient Order of Hibernians, 1986.

Rose, Arnold. *The Power Structure: Political Process in American Life.* New York: Oxford Univ. Press, 1967.

Ryan, Dennis P. *Beyond the Ballot Box: A Social History of the Boston Irish, 1845–1917.* Rutherford, N.J.: Fairleigh Dickinson Univ. Press, 1983.

Schlesinger, Arthur M. *Paths of the Present.* New York: Macmillan, 1949.

Schneider, Louis, and Charles Bonjean, eds. *The Idea of Culture in the Social Sciences.* London: Cambridge Univ. Press, 1973.

Schudson, Michael. *Discovering the News: A Social History of American Newspapers.* New York: Basic, 1978.

Seller, Maxine. *To Seek America: A History of Ethnic Life in the United States.* Englewood Cliffs, N.J.: Jerome S. Ozer, 1977.

Seraile, William, and Lester Rubin. *The Negro in the Longshore Industry in Philadelphia.* Philadelphia: Industrial Research Unit, Wharton School, Report No. 29, Univ. of Pennsylvania Press, 1974.

Shanklin, Eugenia. *Donegal's Changing Traditions: An Ethnographic Study.* New York: Gordon and Branch, 1985.

Shapley, Rufus (pseudonym for Henry C. Lea). *Solid for Mulhooly: A Political Satire.* Philadelphia: Gebbie, 1889.

Silcox, Harry. *Philadelphia Politics from the Bottom Up: The Life of Irishman William McMullen, 1824–1901.* Philadelphia: Balch Institute Press, 1989.

Sills, David, ed. *International Encyclopedia of the Social Sciences.* New York: Macmillan and Free Press, 1968.

Smith, Constance, and Anne Freedman. *Voluntary Associations: A Perspective on the Literature.* Cambridge, Mass.: Harvard Univ. Press, 1972.

Sorokin, Pitirim. *Society, Culture and Personality.* New York: Harper Brothers, 1947.

Sowell, Thomas, ed. *American Ethnic Groups.* Washington, D.C.: Urban Institute, 1978.

Stolarik, Mark, and Murray Friedman, eds. *Making It in America.* Lewisburg, Pa.: Bucknell Univ. Press, 1986.

Sullivan, Robert E., and James M. O'Toole, eds. *Catholic Boston: Studies in Religion and Community, 1870–1970.* Boston: Roman Catholic Archbishop of Boston, 1985.

Susman, Warren I. *Culture As History: The Transformation of American Society in the Twentieth Century.* New York: Pantheon, 1973.

Swartz, Marc J., ed. *Local-level Politics: Social and Cultural Perspectives.* Chicago: Aldine, 1968.

Thernstrom, Stephan, ed. *The Harvard Encyclopedia of American Ethnic Groups.* Cambridge, Mass.: Harvard Univ. Press, 1980.

———. *The Other Bostonians.* Cambridge, Mass.: Harvard Univ. Press, 1973.

Thompson, E.P. *The Making of the English Working Class.* New York: Random, 1966.

Tovey, Hilary, Damian Hannan, and Hal Abramson. *Why Irish? Language and Identity in Ireland Today.* Dublin: Bord na Gaeilge, 1989.

Walsh, James P. *The San Francisco Irish, 1850–1976.* San Francisco: Irish Literary and Historical Society, 1978.

Ward, Alan. *Ireland and Anglo-American Relations, 1899–1921.* Toronto: Univ. of Toronto Press, 1969.

Ward, David. *Poverty, Ethnicity and the American City, 1840–1925: Changing Conceptions of the Slum and the Ghetto.* New York: Cambridge Univ. Press, 1989.

Warner, Sam Bass, Jr., *The Private City: Philadelphia in Three Periods of Its Growth.* Philadelphia: Univ. of Pennsylvania Press, 1968.

Weigley, Russell. *Philadelphia: A Three Hundred Year View.* New York: W.W. Norton, 1982.

Williams, Robin M., Jr., *Mutual Accommodation: Ethnic Conflict and Cooperation.* Minneapolis: Univ. of Minnesota Press, 1977.

Wittke, Karl. *The Irish in America.* Baton Rouge: Louisiana State Univ. Press, 1956.

Wolf, Edwin II. *Philadelphia: Portrait of an American City.* Philadelphia: William Penn Foundation, 1975.

Wright, Thomas. *A History of Caricature and Grotesque in Literature and Art.* New York: Frederick Unger, 1966.

Oral Interviews

All interviews were conducted in Philadelphia, with the exception of Donald Marron, who was interviewed in New York City.

By Dennis Clark:
Hugh Breen, Jan. 14, 1964
Robert V. Clarke, Jan. 5, 1980 and Sept. 14, 1983
Lester Conner, Apr. 4, 1982
John Connors, Jan. 10, 1982
Joseph Coogan, Aug. 8, 1987
Bernard Croke, Oct. 15, 1986
Michael Durkan, Oct. 7, 1987
Maurice English, Jan. 8, 1977
Michael Finn, Feb. 26, 1978
William Fitzpatrick, Mar. 24, 1987
George S. Forde, Sr., Dec. 13, 1977

Joseph Gaffigan, Jan. 10, 1979
Mari Fielder Green, Jan. 1, 1989
Gerry Kelly, Jan. 29, 1981
Honorable Isador Kranzel, Apr. 30, 1987
Honorable Herbert Levin, Jan. 12, 1983
William Lynch, June 26, 1982
James Mahoney, July 30, 1979
Donald Marron, June 14, 1987
Al McCann and Terry McCann, Nov. 14, 1982
Jack McCormick, Sept. 22, 1987
Herbert McGlinchey, June 18, 1981
Margaret McGreal, Jan. 21, 1981
Mrs. Joseph McGurk, Sept. 12, 1980
Geraldine Clark Mulligan, July 9, 1987
Robert Mulvihill, June 4, 1974
Patrick Nolan, Feb. 24, 1981
Anne Leahy O'Callaghan, Dec. 24, 1986
Sean J. O'Callaghan, Dec. 24, 1986
Josephine Oristaglio, Aug. 14, 1980
Thomas Regan, Feb. 2, 1982
John J. Reilly, Jan. 18, 1982
Honorable James H.J. Tate, Sept. 15, 1981

By Nora Campbell in 1986, Donegal Association Memorandum, Nov. 28, 1970, Balch Institute, Philadelphia:
Mary O'Hagan Carr
Mickey Carr
Edward Curran
Kate Collum Ferry
John McGettigan
James McGroary
James O'Brien

By Maureen Benzing for her column "The Greenhorn" in the "Irish Edition," Philadelphia:
Peg Donnelly, Nov. 1981
Bill Drake, Oct. 1981
Vincent Gallagher, Mar. 1984
Tom Jordan, Sept. 1981
Una McAuley, July 1981
Maggie Jane McGinley, June 1981

By Dominick Quinn:
Owen B. Hunt, 1976, Tape recording, Balch Institute, Philadelphia.

By Walter Phillips:
Walter Phillips Collection, Urban Archives, Temple University, Philadelphia.

Index